AF184224

Perspectives on Punishment

PETER LANG
New York • Washington, D.C./Baltimore
Bern • Frankfurt am Main • Berlin • Vienna • Paris

Perspectives on Punishment

An Interdisciplinary Exploration

Edited by
Richard Mowery Andrews

PETER LANG
New York • Washington, D.C./Baltimore
Bern • Frankfurt am Main • Berlin • Vienna • Paris

Library of Congress Cataloging-in-Publication Data

Perspectives on punishment : an interdisciplinary exploration / edited by Richard M. Andrews.
p. cm.
Papers presented at a conference of the Society of Fellows in the Humanities, Columbia University, May 18–20, 1990.
Includes bibliographical references (p.) and index.
1. Punishment—Cross-cultural studies. I. Andrews, Richard Mowery.
HV9443.P85 1993 364.6—dc20 92-30407
ISBN 0-8204-1791-2 CIP

Die Deutsche Bibliothek-CIP-Einheitsaufnahme

Perspectives on Punishment: an interdisciplinary exploration / Richard M. Andrews (ed.). -
New York; Berlin; Bern; Frankfurt/M.; Paris; Wien: Lang, 1993
ISBN 0-8204-1791-2
NE: Andrews, Richard M. [Hrsg.]

The paper in this book meets the guidelines for permanence and durability of the Committee on Production Guidelines for Book Longevity of the Council on Library Resources.

© Peter Lang Publishing, Inc., New York 1997

All rights reserved.
Reprint or reproduction, even partially, in all forms such as microfilm, xerography, microfiche, microcard, offset strictly prohibited.

Printed in the United States of America.

TABLE OF CONTENTS

Part III. Issues in Contemporary Ethics and Jurisprudence

PREFACE

This book originated in a conference that was organized and hosted by the Columbia University Society of the Fellows in the Humanities, under the title of "Punishment: Meanings, Purposes, Practices. A critical interdisciplinary exploration." The conference, and this publication of its proceedings, were jointly subventioned by the Society of Fellows and the Heyman Center for the Humanities.

Twelve scholars from several disciplines came together in May, 1990 at the Kellogg Center of Columbia for two-and-a-half days of concentrated presentations and discussions on the subject of punishment. They were selected for their intellectual diversity and their expertise on crucial aspects of the subject. Ten of them contributed to this volume. That conference was a unique experience for the participants and the audience, an experience of communication, debate and accords across disciplinary boundaries. Their essays reflect those mutual influences and discoveries. They also express the purpose that has guided the Columbia Society of Fellows in the Humanities since its inception in 1977: collective, interdisciplinary examination of major issues in the humanities.

We wish especially to thank Loretta Nassar, former Director of the Society, for her devoted and superb organizational work in creating the conference. We also thank Richard Kuhns, former Chairman of the Society, as well as the members of the Governing Board of the Society of Fellows and the Heyman Center, for supporting the conference and publication of the essays.

Erik Ackerson, of Old Town Computer in Corvallis, Oregon, expertly prepared the manuscript for camera-ready reproduction by the publisher. As editor of this book, I wish to thank the National Endowment for the Humanities for a fellowship that facilitated the completion of my task.

Richard Mowery Andrews

INTRODUCTION

Punishment, both concept and realities, is larger and more protean than any legal philosophy or system. Like fear, shame, and awe, it is virtually a generic human experience. Comprehension of punishment requires collaborative exploration by jurists, philosophers, theologians, historians, literary scholars, and psychologists. This collection of interdisciplinary and cross-cultural studies is a contribution to that goal. From different methodological perspectives, the authors converge on some fundamental questions of punishment, theoretical and practical, past and present.

Part I examines doctrines and purposes of punishment as they developed historically within three great cultural traditions: classical China (Brian McKnight); medieval Islam (Bernard Weiss); Christian Europe of the Middle Ages and early modern era (Edward Peters.) The essays in Part II describe practices: the ideology, law, and enactment of the death penalty in Old Regime France (Richard Andrews); punishment, both legal and interpersonal, in Victorian England, as represented in the works of Charles Dickens (Steven Marcus); the dynamics of punishment in the formation of modern personality, according to clinical psychoanalysis (Robert Glick). Part III is concentrated on contemporary state punishment in the United States and Britain. It takes the form of a debate between Lois Forer, Jeffrie Murphy, Nigel Walker and Nicola Lacey over the efficacy of current penal methods and the validity of their justifications.

Representations of punishment are salient in the religious and secular thought of the Occident and other major cultures. Brian McKnight and Bernard Weiss describe the central positions occupied by ideas of punishment in the moral universe of, respectively, traditional China and the civilization of Islam. The essays by Edward Peters and Richard M. Andrews trace the impact of Christian doctrines—such as free will, confession, penitence, expiation, redemption, and mercy—on the formation of Western state penology, and the ways in which those doctrines historically bolstered an otherwise morally fragile state authority.

Students of modern literature are struck by the near-priestly roles assumed by nineteenth and twentieth-century European and American novelists, as definers, critics, or casuists of moral relations. Blaming, punishing and absolving are prominent actions in imaginative literature. They occur in ways that both parallel and rival those of the State and law (as in Melville's *Billy Budd*, Dostoievsky's *Crime and Punishment*, Camus' *The Stranger*, or Burrough's *The Western Lands*), but also in more intimate and pervasive domains of personal ambition, family, sexuality, gender conflict, and love. Steven Marcus, in his close analysis of *David Copperfield*, reveals Dickens as simultaneously witness, critic, and creature of the Victorian culture of punishment. In doing so, he suggests ways for new readings of other canonic novels of morality.

Steven Marcus, Robert Glick, and Jeffrie Murphy variously demonstrate how our modern moral consciousness—of self and others—is strongly conditioned, if not shaped, by the idea of punishment. That inner presence has deep roots and a long history. According to Jeffrie Murphy, punishment as retribution, or revenge, does satisfy a primal need, a primitive but vivid notion of justice shared by most of us. From the perspective of clinical psychoanalysis, Robert Glick explores the psychic mechanisms and consequences of morally educating infants, children, and adolescents by punishment, as well as gender differences in the formation of ethical personality. These authors echo Freud's grand metaphor of guilt and punishment within our civilization—"like a garrison in a conquered city" (*Civilization and Its Discontents*).

For the past two hundred years, Western state punishment has been centered on imprisonment accompanied by various forms of forced labor. That penal method has reached an apogee—in terms of the percentage of offenses punished by imprisonment, the size of the carceral population (and the numbers of recidivists), the economic and social costs of the system. Carceral penology is generally perceived to be failing in virtually all of its purposes (correction, deterence, even social prophyllaxis), with no alternatives on the horizon other than a dramatic return to the death penalty (especially in the United States), and experiments in psychotherapeutic treatment of offenders. Despite mandatory sentencing, bloated prisons, and reactivated electric chairs and gas chambers, the rates of violent crime, and particularly of homicide, increase exponentially. It seems that we are experiencing a "liminal" moment in the history of punishment, one that resembles the liminality of the eighteenth-century in Europe as described by Edward Peters: a long-regnant penal system has become obsolete, without yet being replaced.

The widely recognized present crisis of criminal justice in the United States and Western Europe has provoked considerable literature and public discussion on crimes and punishments. For the past two decades, each presidential administration in the United States has promised a new "war on crime." The core of those programs is always aggravated and mandatory punishment for certain crimes, by imprisonment or death. Much of that writing and of those programs is either technical or moralistic and highly political, and does not address basic issues of punishment in ways that are historically, legally, philosophically and psychologically informed.

The relations between punishment and positive law are, in reality, highly problematic. Legal punishments do not necessarily follow from the determination of criminal guilt. In many legal systems, both actual and historical, the guilty are sometimes absolved of responsibility for their actions or held responsible but pardoned or accorded mercy. In the United States today, "plea bargaining" and paroles serve as *de facto* clemency for offenders, and register the fact that the number of criminals far exceeds the capacity of the penal system. Conversely, certain legal and political systems intentionally punish those who are neither authors nor accomplices of criminal acts, but rather for ascribed characteristics—social class, race, ethnicity, religious or political identity. Such prejudical characteristics can also generate vulnerability to maximal punishments among those convicted of crimes in liberal constitutionalist regimes, as Lois Forer and Nicola Lacey argue in their examinations of contemporary American and British justice. At yet another extreme, there is often no direct relation between the incrimination of behavior and legal punishment for that behavior; certain types of criminal behavior are only randomly prosecuted or punished—for example, simple possession of narcotics, public drunkenness, slander and insult, sexual abuse, incest, family violence, injurious private disputes. The "space" between incrimination and punishment is one in which police and magistrates wield a discretionary power, the power not to prosecute and not to punish. How are such disjunctions between criminal law and punishment to be understood?

The exclusive power to incriminate, as well as the necessity and authority to punish wrong-doers, are assumptions embedded in most, if not all, modern political ideologies and legal systems. Since the sixteenth century, the authority of the state to punish, including the taking of life, has been defined as an essential attribute of sovereignty in Western thought, an attribute equal in importance to the monopoly of war. Those assumptions are rarely questioned by practitioners of law. They usually confront them only in "procedural" terms, on the further assumption that respect for the rights of defendants and for logic in ascertainment of criminal guilt and responsibility during trial and judgment do justify measured punishment of those found guilty. But does this suffice to justify the enterprise of state punishment? Punishment and its cognates—offense, blame, guilt—are normative conceptions and practices. They call for ethical and historical scrutiny. Can state punishment—the power relations between punisher and punished, and the infliction of stigma, suffering, or deprivation by the former on the latter—be justified rationally? What is the value, philosophical and practical, of the classic justifications: retribution; symbolic or material reparation of damages; obviation of private vengeance by the victim, and its possible disorders, through the formal punitive action of a "third" power; correction or removal of the offender; deterrence of potential offenders? Those justifications are examined, precisely and critically, by Lois Forer, Nigel Walker, Jeffrie Murphy, and Nicola Lacey. Is punishment, however incoherent and imperfect a form of discipline, a grim social and political necessity or can moral and public order exist without fear and actualities of punishment? Both Lois Forer and Nicola Lacey suggest ways for a public order and discipline that is not based on punishment, the former from her experience as a trial judge, the latter from the vantage of communitarian political theory.

What is required for a punishment to produce moral change in the offender, and not merely an experience of pain or aversion? The essays by Brian McKnight, Bernard Weiss, Edward Peters and Richard Andrews reveal that some of the most venerable cultural traditions have offered answers to that question. Within the classical Chinese, Islamic, and Christian traditions the efficacy of punishment depended on a common moral code, on spiritual values shared by the punishing agency and the punished. Penalty inflicted was an event of ethical pedagogy, and it was most often a public ritual. Punishment endured was an opportunity for contrition and repentance, purgation of guilt, and reintegration to a moral community. Those benefits, grounded in common moral consciousness, could make punishments simultaneously necesssary, just, and acceptable to the offender.

What then can be the moral efficacy of state punishment in contemporary societies that lack such cohesion? Can ideas and practices of deterence and retribution substitute for experiences of shame, contrition, expiation, and reintegration? Retribution is essentially revenge. Deterence is usually staged more for others than for the offender. If the modern offender does not believe in the values and authority from which his or her punishment derive, and therefore does not experience shame in wrong-doing, the punitive act cannot produce moral change. At best, it can produce aversion; at worst, resentment, contempt, and further alienation. In the racially and socially conflict-ridden societies of contemporary Europe, Britain, and the United States these problems are acute. Those who feel themselves excluded, by their race or economic condition, from any social contract or legitimate community of goods cannot be morally reformed, or even dissuaded from crime, by legal punishment; nor can those whose criminal acts result from addictions to alcohol and drugs. They are only punished, for the satisfaction of others.

In the concluding essay, Nicola Lacey confronts that modern dilemma. She employs critical utopian political theory to describe a democratic community—an egalitarian community of voices, rights and benefits—in which legal punishment would be restricted to enforcing only the most basic of shared values, in the least violent and deprivational of ways, for the reformation and reinclusion of offenders. In doing so, she recaptures, in secular language, the vision of spiritual community that we have lost, while exposing the extreme social inequalities, antagonisms, and contradictions that vitiate most current theories and practices of state punishment.

Through and beyond their heterogeneity, these essays form an experiment in dialogue, and a common exploration. Our goal has been to free a grand, even terrible, subject from parochial thinking, and thereby to provoke questioning and imagining among readers.

Richard Mowery Andrews

PART I

CULTURAL TRADITIONS

Punishments in Traditional China: from Family, to Group, to the State

Brian E. McKnight

All human communities create order out of disorder by a constant, and never wholly successful effort, of transmitting to newcomers sets of beliefs, attitudes, and values, which they have in turn received from others. Human groups are comprised of individuals each of whom is unique to his or her genetic endowment and by the particulars of time, place, and position in which he or she is enmeshed. Each individual must be taught the nature of his or her unique relationship with others in the social world. Indeed, to a traditional Chinese each individual was defined by these relationships and the roles they entailed. Becoming human is a matter of education. Each generation must seek to inculcate, indoctrinate, and train the succeeding generation with values if society is to continue. The traditional Chinese elite were acutely aware of the critical role played by socialization (education in the broadest sense) in creating human community. They frequently blamed serious, continuing deviance on failures in the educative process. Such failures in turn were seen as errors in communication.

The process of socialization never succeeds in making people identical. Discrepancies in communication and learning, the roots of what may be viewed as deviance, are inevitable.

All human societies must respond to attitudes and acts disruptive of the order they labor so hard to preserve. The spectrum of possible responses is limited. Societies can seek to change the behavior of the offender. They can alter the relationship of the offender to the group. They can remove the offender in some way from the group. Or they can change the group to conform to the position taken by the offender.

Punishments can be viewed as acts falling under the first three categories of responses to threatening behavior. The first type of response, transforming the behavior of the offender, corresponds in penal theory to the concept of rehabilitation, or changing the offender so that he or she voluntarily and with good will conforms with the desired norms. It can also mean transforming the overt behavior of the offender through control or deterrence, without any subjective change having occurred in the attitudes of the person restrained. The relationship of the deviant to the group can be altered. A deviant leader can be removed from power so that his or her deviance, even if it remains unchanged, is less threatening. A deviant can be put into a new social role which alerts future contacts to his or her deviant status and which often involves direct physical control by others. Deviants can be separated from the community: by execution; by isolation (as with imprisonment); by exile.

All cultures use two or more of these punitive approaches. Cultures differ in the ways in which the approaches are applied, the conditions under which they are applied, and the priority or importance assigned to the different practices. Traditional Chinese culture—the culture which arose with the political and, to a marked extent, intellectual unification of China in the third century B.C.—can illustrate these general patterns.

Members of the literate stratum in traditional China were well aware of the utility of penalties and the various goals for punishment. We can find discussions of rehabilitation, deterrence, and social defence in Chinese writings. The selection of means and the balancing of goals was partly, at least, a product of Chinese historical experience and of the most commonly shared view of human nature.

One important, but often overlooked, trait of early China influenced the way in which penalties were fitted into the social system in traditional China, Chinese perceptions of the political order, and by extension the proper ways to punish deviance. China was one of the few places in the world which witnessed the emergence of what anthropologists and historians have called the pristine state, that is to say a state which emerged directly out of the preceding non-state cultures. Pristine states do not arise in response to or in imitation of pre-existing states. They have been extremely rare. Almost all states were founded by people seeking either to resist attacks by already existing states or—in imitation of already existing states with which they were familiar—to take advantage of the increase in power made possible by state organization. A state—that is an organization capable of using violence to exercise sovereign control over disparate sets of people living in a given territory—emerged in China during the third millennium B.C. This state, called Xia, emerged coincidentally with the earliest Chinese development of writing and metallurgy. More importantly, the autonomous creation of a state made it possible for the Chinese to carry over into the new form of organization older sets of ideas and values which had dominated their lives in the preceding social conditions. Most importantly, they continued to think of the state in familial terms.

The character of this Xia state is intensely debated. But historians are agreed, on the importance of family and of the familial metaphor in the government of the first historic dynasty, the Shang (conventional dates 1766-1122 B.C.), and its successor, the Zhou (conventional dates 1122-256 B.C.). The kinship metaphor of association, which existed before formation of a state, continued to dominate politics throughout traditional Chinese history, and continues to influence political behavior today. The patriarchal, hierarchical, and authoritarian aspects of Chinese political culture can be traced back to the very origins of that culture. In the most widely accepted vision of the Chinese past among the traditional elite, the good things of life, including political society itself, were the special gifts to mankind of a succession of sage rulers. The consequences of this vision of the past (and its promise for the future) can be traced in many directions, including practices of punishment.

The Sages, who gave mankind so many cultural gifts, were also thought to be responsible for introducing penalties (although there is one passage in an early work which suggests that brutal punishments were to be blamed on foreigners).[1] The idea that the early Sage Kings created civil punishments, and that they did so in imitation of the processes of nature was stated unequivocally in the preface to the great Tang law code. The chief editor of that compilation quoted the early prognosticatory text called the *Book of Changes*. "In the heavens are suspended the heavenly bodies...The Sages imitated them."[2] The editor asserted that the Sages "observed the thunder and lightening, and so created awe-inspiring punishments; They saw the autumn frost and so had stern executions."[3] There was thus in Chinese minds an explicit connection between the enforced order among mankind and the order of nature.

Why did such order need to be enforced among men? This question goes to the root of the conception of human nature shared by the Chinese elite. That conception pictured mankind as one element in a triad: heaven, earth, and man were the three components of the world. Again, the *Book of Changes*, in describing the universe, stated that "the Way (*tao*) of Man is in it.[4] Each of the three constituent elements was thought to possess a distinctive and necessary trait which it contributed to the integrity of the whole. Man, in this vision, is distinguished by the fact that he alone possesses art. Only human beings can consciously make something more than what it is by nature through the application of craft. Only nature can make beautiful sunsets; only men and women can paint pictures of beautiful sunsets. The glory of men and women is that they alone are endowed with the capacity to make choices, to participate actively in the creation of the future.

However, there is a dark side to this ability. It makes serious deviance possible. In the simplistic views of the less thoughtful nineteenth-century European materialists, the universe (and men and women as parts of the universe) were seen as elements of a complex machine, like some sort of great celestial chronometer, each individual part doing what it had to do because of the way in which it was constructed. There was order without glory. The Chinese, by contrast, also clearly accepted the notion that the universe was an orderly place, and that men and women were parts of this order. But the Chinese vision of order was dramatic rather than mechanical. The universe, or more particularly the human universe, resembled a stage play. *Hamlet* , for example, is most definitely a ordered whole. Producers tamper with the order of its lines at their own peril, for they endanger the capacity of the work to achieve its goals. Actors, however, are human. An actor ought to perform a given role in a certain way. But he or she may not in fact do so. The failure may be the result of poor preparation or of ignorance. Or, the actor may deliberately sabotage the proper performance of the role. This, in the traditional Chinese view, was the case with men and women in general. They have roles to perform, but they may fail to perform them properly, because of ignorance, malice, greed, love, or other causes.

How were people to be prevented from failing to perform their assigned roles? Through reasoning from their experiences of life, members of the Chinese elite arrived at an intriguing vision of mankind. Most men and women, they believed, were basically inclined to act their roles properly. Given reasonable conditions, and a modicum of proper education, they would generally behave correctly. There were, however, two exceptional groups: the ethical elite, who would always and under any conceivable conditions do what was right no matter what the cost might be; the evil, those who would always act in a deviant way, no matter how promising the conditions and despite all attempts to educate them to right action. Men and women, we might say, were divided into the good, the bad, and the malleable.

From this vantage, we can examine the way in which traditional Chinese conceptions came together into an integrated whole. The conception of the place of mankind in nature, ideas of the nature of man, the familial vision of politics and society joined to produce a set of beliefs about penalties which was distinctive. It was distinctive not in having root concepts wholly absent elsewhere, but in blending those concepts in a unique fashion.

The traditional Chinese were aware of various goals which penalties might serve—to deter, to requite, to rehabilitate, and to defend society. Since generically there are only a handful of ways in which groups can respond to deviance, the Chinese spectrum of actual punishments was no more unusual than was their grasp of the possible uses of punishments. But when we examine actual practices, we find that basic Chinese beliefs molded a unique constellation of behaviors.

These beliefs affected actual Chinese responses in at least the following general ways. First, the vision of mankind as an integral part of an interrelated universe, in which mankind had the particular gift of art and needed to exercise that gift in order to fulfill its role, led the Chinese elite to see deviance as an ever present possibility, but a possibility which ought not to be answered by the imposition of rigid constraints, precisely because creative action was a part of being fully human. The emphasis was rather on trying to restore the fulfilling harmony which resulted when everyone played their roles correctly. One had to be very careful about responding appropriately to wrongdoing, since excessive harshness was at least as bad as excessive leniency. Second, this penchant for emphasizing carefulness and fittingness was strongly reinforced by the widely shared view of men and women as falling into the three groups of the moral elect, the irredeemably evil, and the malleable but fundamentally sound majority. The responses to the first two groups were relatively straightforward—the moral elect were really not the concern of those dealing with deviance, and the evil were to be suppressed using whatever means were needed. The great majority, however, required very careful handling. If their faults were dealt with appropriately they could ordinarily be rehabilitated. Third, the familial metaphor which underlay and colored Chinese thinking about state and society led the Chinese to emphasize the nested roles of a hierarchy of groups which ought to respond to deviance, beginning with the nuclear family, moving on to larger kin associations and to associations within which quasi-kin relationships were common, and ending with the formal mechanisms of state control. This led to a constant stress on the familial role of the emperor as supreme father and an emphasis on state support for the traditional family (with its own internal hierarchy) and for familial virtues, wherever they were to be found.

Given the general goal of restoring a harmonious ordering at the least cost and the emphasis on rehabilitating and reintegrating deviants (where that was possible), it was obviously important to respond early to the symptoms of wrongful behavior, to nip problems in the bud before they could evolve into major troubles. The answer of the Chinese was to have the primary group respond to the early signs of difficulties. Peers and relatives bore the original burden. In a newly rediscovered set of thirteenth-century Chinese judicial decisions it is striking how often the magistrates placed the responsibility for the deviant behavior of younger people on their elder relatives, who had clearly failed to teach their charges properly (often by failing to provide a proper example).[5] This sort of an emphasis on the role of primary level figures is of course true of all societies; its role in China was highlighted by the character of the traditional Chinese state.

The traditional Chinese state was an elaborate bureaucratic structure governed by a welter of legalistic rules. Because superficially it resembles a modern state in certain ways, there is a tendency to assume that it responded to deviance using methods which are common today. People who make this assumption are bemused by the decision of traditional Chinese regimes to allow non-official groups to deal with deviants and law-breakers. In fact, the traditional Chinese government, although elaborate and bureaucratic, had miniscule personnel in relation to the huge Chinese population. Furthermore, this government staff was able to gain control over only a small fraction of the national wealth. Therefore, it would have been quite impossible to enforce order using modern methods. The Chinese empire had no option but to allow much control to remain in the hands of unofficial agencies.

Necessity and ideology meshed. The unofficial agencies which had to be relied upon were exactly those agencies which could respond quickly to the initial symptoms of deviance. Emphasis on early response was associated with another trait of Chinese thinking which is traceable to core beliefs — the emphasis on fitting the response carefully to the initiating cause. Like the "Mikado" in Gilbert and Sullivan's operetta, the goal was to make the punishment fit the crime. If the response was insufficiently punitive it would neither encourage the reformation of the culprit nor deter observant others. On the other hand, if the response was excessively punitive, then again it would not encourage rehabilitation or deterrence, since it would produce a sense of grievance in the mind of the excessively punished culprit and of distrust of the authorities among others.

The result in theory, and to a remarkable degree in practice, was a system designed to respond to wrongdoing in a subtly graded way, which began with the minor sanctions usable by the primary group, passed to the minor but sometimes different sanctions available to intervening associations, and ended with the potential application of more severe penalties by the formal state authorities. One of the reasons for the strength and persistence of Chinese traditional values and institutions is this pattern of mirroring practices and attitudes at various levels from family, to peers, to judges.

Specific description of Chinese measures for controlling wrongful behavior commences with the role of primary associates, especially family members. The traditional family was supposed to be paternalistic, patriarchal, and hierarchical, thus the state in microcosm. Males were superior to females, elders to youngers, and higher generations to lower generations. Under these conditions, in practice, punishments were most commonly negative sanctions used by those with higher status and greater power to keep the family functioning on their terms and to suppress forms of behavior which seemed to threaten its continuance. The state upheld this pattern of family authority. Within families physical punishments, most commonly beatings, were not uncommon. Husbands beat wives. Fathers beat sons. It was the way of the world. For a family superior to beat a family inferior was not criminal, except in cases where the beating was "excessive," excessive being sometimes defined as resulting in serious physical injury. Even if the junior was beaten to death the person responsible might well be spared state punishment, if it was shown that the victim (1) had been habitually disobedient or otherwise seriously and continuously deviant, or (2) if the death was quite unintentional.

State law reinforced this situation, by excusing or meliorating violent acts against inferiors, and by punishing such acts by juniors against seniors with especial harshness. During the last traditional dynasty, the Quing (1644 - 1911), a case came up for review by the central authorities which revolved around the death of an old woman. The old woman had been berating her daughter-in-law, abusing her verbally, and even striking her. Finally, the younger woman, fearful of what might happen if the argument continued, turned and walked out of the house. The old woman, enraged because her daughter-in-law had turned her back, ran screaming out of the house, tripped over the door sill, fell, and broke her neck. At the time that this case came up for review, the younger woman had been sentenced to death by strangulation for having so acted as to cause the death of her mother-in-law. We may be quite sure that if the roles had been reversed and the daughter-in-law had died there would not even have been a trial of the older woman. Of course this is an extreme example, and the case was reviewed in part because the lower court judges were unhappy with what they saw as the need to sentence the young woman to death. The central authorities agreed, and reduced her sentence to life in exile.[6]

Little is known of the punitive activities of the intervening associations which stood between the family and the state in traditional

China. The roles of such agencies within the general structure of social control have been little studied, and indeed the sources for studying them are limited. In general, however, we can say that a large variety of groups, some of them based on kinship, some on geographical propinquity, and some on functional associations, could at times exercise punitive control over their members. Beatings might be used, perhaps especially in the kin-based groups, but other negative sanctions like fines, ostracism, or verbal reprimands were quite common. Guilds, neighborhood associations, religious brotherhoods, social clubs, benevolent societies, clans, lineage associations, the list of such groups is long, and all to one degree or another, were involved in controlling their members' misbehavior.

Let us turn to the punitive sphere of the traditional Chinese government. It might be useful to think of all state penalties as involving various forms of ostracism and deprivation. They were all intended to remove some valued good from those on whom they are inflicted, whether physical comfort, honor, social standing, power, or life. By withdrawing those goods, the state demonstrated its superior power. It also demonstrated this power when it forgave and reintegrated malefactors. Such actions were understood by the traditional Chinese elite to be messages. The traditional Chinese were profoundly concerned about the communicative underpinnings of social, political, and even natural order. The world only worked properly when the right persons sent the appropriate messages in the required fashion at the necessary time to the fitting recipients. Punishments were messages—to the sufferer, to witnesses, and also to those who inflicted them. As messages, they would only succeed in achieving their object when all the above conditions were fulfilled.

The history of state penalties in traditional China can be divided into two periods. From the origins of the Chinese state in the third millennium B.C. until the unification of the empire in the third century B.C. the primary punishments seem to have been corporeal: beatings; mutilations; and executions. From at least as early as the late years of the second millennium B.C., however, we already hear of penalties which were basically deprivations of liberty, and also of commutations of punishments. Although the evidence is fragmentary, it does seem at least possible that penalties entailing forced labor were becoming more common during the last few centuries before the unification of the empire by the Chin dynasty in 221 B.C.[7] In any event, it is clear the Chin made large scale use of forced labor as a form of punishment.[8] From the founding of the empire, the most commonly used penalties were beatings, forced labor, deprivations of liberty, fines (usually in the form of commutations), loss of rank or status, and execution.

This description can be refined by examining one element of the penal system during one dynasty. The penal system of the Song dynasty (A.D. 960-1279) was extraordinarily complicated, but one of its central practices reveals the principles which informed the whole. The standard forced labor penalty during the Song dynasty was called *p'ei*, a very interesting word which has a range of meanings clustering around the concept of matching, fitting, supplementing, or apportioning. For no very clear reason, this word began to be used in the tenth-century to mean a form of transportation with labor. We may simply call it penal registration.

As deployed during the Song, this penalty involved various elements. First, it was conceptualized, at least initially, as a reduction from a death penalty. Second, it involved the registration of the person so sentenced in certain special units of the Song armies. Third, it entailed labor for a limited term. Fourth, the place of registration might be distant from the place of conviction. Fifth, the labor penalty was preceded by a beating. Sixth, the convicts were often tattooed.

We may take these elements in order, and look at the ways in which they accorded with traditional Chinese ideology. First, it is important to note the origin of the punishment as a special act of grace, a reduction from the death penalty. This emphasized the patriarchal power of the emperor, who could extend his mercy, if he so wished. Mercy also had the effect of creating a condition of indebtedness toward the convicts' benefactor. By sparing the condemned, the emperor-father was providing them with an opportunity to reform themselves. He made it possible for them to fulfill their role as men.

Second, by registering these men in certain units of the army the Song authorities limited the interactions of the convicts with ordinary civil society without cutting them off entirely.[9] The special army convict units were stationed alongside regular garrison units. These regular garrison units served both to provide security against any trouble caused by the convicts, and to provide the convicts themselves with role models. Being in the army, albeit in specialized labor units, the convicts were placed in a structured environment with clear, fixed rules and an obvious hierarchy of authority. Song criminals, like criminals today, were predominantly young, unattached males with few life skills and short time horizons. The army, with its routinized schedules and clear-cut expectations, could serve them well.

Third, because the labor was for a limited term, the convicts were given hope. If a convict fulfilled his required term of labor without having committed new offenses, he could be returned to regular society. At this point, the registered labor system connected with another element of the

Song system of justice, a pattern of regular amnesties which either freed men entirely or ameliorated the conditions of their punishment. Major amnesties were issued on the average of once every eighteen months. They affected those sentenced to registered labor by either ending their term of labor, reducing its length, and/or allowing them to move their place of registration closer to their home region. The issuing of these amnesties, although frequent, was not perfectly regular. Thus, the convicts were rather like men who owned a great many tickets in an irregularly conducted sweepstakes game. At any moment they might find their conditions improved. This situation gave them a strong incentive to maintain good behavior, since the locally responsible officials could exclude those who had been troublemakers from the coverage of any amnesty. The very irregularity of the amnesties emphasized the effective power of the patriarchal emperor.

Fourth, the differing distances of the places for labor was a device to create subtlety in the grading of punishment. Song authorities, like those in other Chinese dynasties, believed that people felt increased distress the farther they were forced to live from their home region. Therefore, under the Song, the lightest penalty might involve serving a term in one's home prefecture. The next lightest could mean a neighboring prefecture. Beyond that point, the levels were measured in *li*, a unit of distance approximately equal to a kilometer. People might be sent to distances of 500, 1000, 1500 or even 2000 *li*. Worst of all, they might be sent to one of the dreaded sea islands near the coast.[10]

Fifth, the beating which preceded the move to the place of registered labor mirrored what was undoubtedly the most common form of punishment suffered by junior males within the Chinese family system. Family inferiors, including sons, and all too often wives, were subject to beatings. Therefore, this official punishment probably recapitulated the family experience of a great many convicts. The severity of the beating could be regulated so as to adjust the degree of suffering to the seriousness of the crime committed.

Sixth, and last, the tattooing of most of those sentenced to registered labor does not seem to accord with the idea of social reintegration, since the tattoos were permanently disfiguring. However, regular Song army troops were also tattooed with the names and locations of their units. The tattoos on most convicts were deliberately designed to mimic army tattoos. When a convict had completed his sentence, or when he had been released by amnesty, he would ordinarily be offered the option of joining another unit of the Song armies. If he chose to do so, his convict tattoo would be altered to allow him to play his new role properly. Thus, the Song government offered to these released convicts, most of whom were young men with few skills and few roots, a structured alternative life. After serving their sentences, they could continue to live within a world of clear, simple rules, surrounded by men like themselves, but with their living conditions much improved and the labor demands placed on them much reduced.

These devices embodied the Chinese concern to make punishments fit crimes. The importance attached to that symmetry derived from the idea that rulers, like fathers within families, ought to seek to reintegrate erring members, after doing them the least possible permanent damage.

The system mirrored the familial metaphor which underlay traditional Chinese social and political life. The family—patriarchal, paternalistic, hierarchical and authoritarian—was viewed as a natural unit, a part of the universe. The order enforced within the family was necessary for the order of the human community. The Song penal system was a magnification of that vision. It was centered on the power and moral responsibility of the emperor-patriarch. Responsible for the order of the group, he was also supposed to provide care to its members. Their misbehaviors reflected badly on his performance as teacher; clearly, he and the smaller order groups has failed as teachers of those miscreants. All who wielded authority had a vested interest in salvaging as many of the fallen as possible. The registered labor system gave convicts a structured and hierarchical environment which replicated aspects of the family.

This system did not work perfectly. Crime was endemic in traditional China. However, the elaboration of a punitive system in which the patterns in use on the primary, familial level were mirrored at higher levels probably contributed to the capacity of the traditional Chinese state to exercise a greater degree of influence over the lives of a greater number of people than any other traditional state was able to do over an extended period of time.

[1] In traditional China a section of the Book of Documents entitled the "Punishments of Lu" was believed to be a description of the penal system during the earliest stages of Chinese history. Brutal punishments were blamed on the non-Chinese Miao peoples. See Jame Legge (translator), *The Chinese Classics*, vol. III, *The Shoo King or Book of Documents* (Hong Kong: Hong Kong University Press, 1965), "The Prince of Leu on Punishments," p. 591.

[2] Richard Wilhelm, *The I Ching or Book of Changes* (Princeton: Princeton University Press, 1967), p. 320.

[3] Ch'ang-sun Wu-chi (ed.), *Tang-lü shu-i* (Taipei: Commercial Press, 1970), chapter 1; Wallace Johnson, *The Tang Code* (Princeton: Princeton University Press, 1979), p. 50.

[4] Wilhelm, *Book of Changes*, p. 351.

[5] See for example in the *Minggong shupan qingmind ji* (Beijing: Zhonghua shuzhu, 1987), pp. 201-03, 206-07.

[6] For illustrative examples of this type of judgment, see Ch'ü T'ung-tsu, *Law and Society in Traditional China* (The Hague: Mouton, 1965), chapter 1.

[7] Li Li, "Zhongguo gudai tuxing" ("On punishment by penal servitude in ancient China"), in *Zhongguo xuedao bao*, vol. 1, no. 1 (1987), pp. 37-38.

[8] A.F.P. Hulsewe, *Remnants of Ch'in Law* (Leiden: E.J. Brill, 1985).

[9] Here, I refer to such convicts as men, because in practice women were not subjected to this form of penal servitude.

[10] For further details on the Song penal system, see Brian E. McKnight, *Law and Order in Sung China* (Cambridge: Cambridge University Press, 1992).

Punishment, Retribution and Justice in Islamic Theology and Jurisprudence

Bernard Weiss

In Islam any discussion of punishment necessarily brings theology and jurisprudence together as a single enterprise, since the punishments of this life are closely bound up with the punishments of the hereafter and God is involved in both categories of punishment. In this essay, I shall not attempt to take into consideration modern discussions of punishment among Muslims but will confine myself to the world of medieval or traditional Islam. Within that world two very different ways of looking at punishment emerged, one rooted in a rationalist-intuitionist school of ethical thought, the other in a radically theocentric and voluntarist approach. The first was the way of the Mu'tazilites, the name given to a school of Muslin theologians which flourished in the ninth and tenth centuries; the second was the way of the orthodox Sunni theologians. As my use of the term "orthodox Sunni" implies, the point of view of the Mu'tazilites was ultimately defeated within Sunni Islam, although it was to become absorbed into the Shi'i tradition. Sunni Islam—which is the Islam of the vast majority of the world's Muslims—was to become incorrigibly voluntaristic.

The Mu'tazilites sought to find a place for punishment in a moral order that was independent of the divine will and could be discerned by the human intellect without the aid of divine revelation. My description of Mu'tazilite thought as rationalist-intuitionist is based on the work of the late Professor George Hourani on the writings of the great Mu'tazilite jurist and theologian, the Qadi Abd al-Jabbar.[1] Hourani showed that ethical truth was for the Mu'tazilites a system grounded in a body of intuited axioms. These axioms were in large part statements about what is good and what is evil.

For example, the statements "oppression (*zulm*) is evil" and "(Conferment of) benefit (*manfa'a*) is good" were among these axioms. So also was the statement "retribution is good," which translated into "deserved harm is good." The Arabic word here translated as "good," namely *hasan*, also, it should be noted, carries the sense of "appropriate, fitting." I shall in this discussion adhere to the more common rendering of the word as "good."

Thus, according to the Mu'tazilites, desert was a key factor in terms of which harm, that is to say punishment, was good or evil. We are here clearly in the company of a kind of retributivism. But the absence of desert did not necessarily make harm evil. The Mu'tazilites were well aware that in this life God allows or causes harm to fall upon the undeserving. This harm was, for many Mu'tazilites at least, good when an adequate indemnity or reward was provided. It was evil only in the absence of any indemnity or reward. Since God would always indemnify or reward innocent sufferers, his infliction of harm upon them was therefore not evil but good.

What was definitely evil—axiomatically evil, we should probably say—was the failure to inflict harm upon the deserving. Again, the Mu'tazilites were very much aware that in this life many offenders do not experience harm which they deserve. However, the punishments of the hereafter would take care of that and exonerate God of any charge of evil. So insistent were the Mu'tazilites that retribution must be visited upon offenders eventually, and that it must be visited upon them in full, that they were highly critical of the notion of the intercession of the Prophet Muhammad in the hereafter. For those who believed in this intercession, the Prophet could plead with God for the removal of believers from hell before they had endured the full punishment due to them. Only one offense barred human beings from this intercession, and that was unbelief. The unbeliever remained eternally in hell.

The Mu'tazilites did, it is true, affirm the idea of God's forgiveness (*ghufran*). This was a central Qur'anic idea which all Muslims were bound to affirm. The Mu'tazilites accommodated this idea to their retributivism by insisting that divine forgiveness was contingent upon the repentance of the offender. Repentance halted the process of retribution by rendering retribution inappropriate; that is to say, it eradicated desert. The retributivism of the Mu'tazilites thus remained intact: whenever desert was present, punishment was mandatory; repentance changed the situation by removing the desert. I should hasten to add that the Qur'an provides for expiation for certain offenses such that true repentance will, in the case of those offenses, necessarily be accompanied by the appropriate expiatory deeds. Where expiation was called for, it played a role in the eradication of desert. Otherwise, repentance alone was the eradicating factor, a kind of expiatory deed in and of itself. Once repentance occurred, divine forgiveness became *hasan*:, good or fitting.

Accordingly, the Mu'tazilites were generally opposed to the idea of divine forgiveness apart from repentance on the part of the offender. Given the divine rationality, God simply could not forgive where there was no repentance, and the Mu'tazilites insisted that the repentance must be in this life. Once the offender was in hell, repentance was ineffectual. The time for repentance came to an end at the moment when the time for punishment began: repentance amidst the torments of hell could hardly carry the same weight as repentance in this life when hell was a threat and not a reality. It was a cardinal Mu'tazilite conviction that God could not but act upon his threats. He could remove them in the face of repentance in this life; but a threat which remained in effect at the end of this life could not be removed in the Day of Judgment.

In short, God necessarily punishes the deserving because the punishing of the deserving is good and God does only what is good. Since this good is the good which is discernible to the human reason apart from revelation, God can be said to act in accordance with the norms of the natural conscience. This is not to say that the human reason stands over God, making God bow to its demands. Rather, God's own rationality necessitates his acting in accordance with the rationally discernible moral order, whence the necessity of his punishing of the deserving.

But how is desert linked to particular human acts? Or, to put the question differently, on what basis are certain acts classified as deserving of punishment. Retribution—the inflicting of punishment upon the deserving—comes into play only after desert has been established. How then is it established in regard to particular acts? Before we can really answer this question, we must take into account how the concept of desert enters into the definition of two important categories of Islamic ethics and jurisprudence: the obligatory act and the forbidden act. The former is defined by both Mu'tazilite and orthodox jurists as an act the non-doing of which makes one deserving of punishment, whereas the latter category, the forbidden act, is defined as an act the doing of which makes one deserving of punishment. This being the case, the question of how desert of punishment is linked to particular acts turns out to be a question of how or on what basis acts are classified as obligatory or forbidden.

The Mu'tazilite answer to this question again brings their rationalist-intuitionist bent into play. Just as the classification of acts as good or evil is for them the work of the reason operating with certain axioms, so also is the classification of acts as obligatory or forbidden. "Obligatory" and "forbidden" are, it should be noted, more specific categories than "good" and "evil." Not all good acts are obligatory: some fall into the category of recommended acts. And not all evil acts are forbidden: some fall into the category of disapproved acts. However, both at the more general level of "good" and "evil" and at the more specific level of "obligatory" and "forbidden" the reason worked with axiomatic principles to carry on its classification.

In attempting to spell out those principles that were operative in the classification of acts as "obligatory" or "forbidden," the Mu'tazilites generated a great variety of diverse opinions. Many Mu'tazilites gave a central place to the notion of welfare (*maslaha*), although there was disagreement as to whether this meant the welfare of the self only or the welfare of the self and of others, in other words, the welfare of the community. If one can take it as axiomatic that individuals have an obligation to act in a manner that promotes the welfare of the community, then one has a principle with which to judge whether or not particular acts are obligatory. If obligation is defined in terms of a deserving of punishment, then we can say that the non-doing of an act which promotes the welfare of the community makes one deserving of punishment. If forbiddenness is similarly defined, we can say that the doing of an act which militates against the welfare of the community makes one deserving of punishment.

The Mu'tazilite discussions of this subject were far more complex than this brief and somewhat superficial presentation would suggest. I am mainly interested to show how Mu'tazilite thought works, not to give a detailed account of the dialectic which developed among the Mu'tazilites. The essential point is that the deserving of punishment was linked to certain acts through a process of reasoning which proceeded from axiomatic foundations. If considerations of social utility were to have a place at all, they could have that place only at this level. That is to say, considerations of social utility could enter into the classification of an act (or non-doing of an act) as deserving of punishment. But once desert was established, punishment followed as a requirement of desert, not as an instrument of social welfare. Punishment as such was, for the Mu'tazilites, justified solely in terms of retribution. Their attitude toward retribution is shaped by the principle "retribution is good," which they believed to be axiomatic.

The Mu'tazilites regarded the concept of retribution as intimately bound up with the concept of justice. Their rationalism demanded this connection, for without it the concept of justice would be devoid of a specific content discernible to the human reason which would make it part of an objective moral order. So central was this rationalistic understanding of justice to the Mu'tazilite way of thinking that the Mu'tazilites called themselves, not Mu'tazilites (which carries the somewhat pejorative sense of "seceders"), but "the partisans of divine unity and justice" (*ahl al-tawhid wa'l-'adl*). Underlying this self-designation was a conviction that the orthodox theologians had seriously compromised the concept of justice and that they were calling the community back to a correct understanding of it.

Orthodox Sunni thinking developed around a number of important points of opposition to Mu'tazilite doctrine. To begin with, orthodox thinkers rejected the rationalist ethics of the Mu'tazilites. Good and evil proceeded solely from the divine command and prohibition and could not be discerned by the human reason apart from revelation. There were no restrictions which reason could bring to bear upon the content of divine commands and prohibitions. Contemplation of these commands and prohibitions did, it was true, lead to the realization that they were generally conducive to man's well-being; but this conduciveness was something to be discovered as a given fact, not to be posited in advance as a rational necessity. Furthermore, one could always take heart from God's frequent description of himself as compassionate.

Orthodox Sunni thought insisted upon God's justice but detached it from the notion of retribution. Should God fail to inflict injury upon the deserving or should he inflict injury upon the undeserving without indemnity, these acts would not constitute injustice or evil on God's part. To the contrary, they would constitute justice. The eponym of the major school of orthodox Sunni theology, Abu'l-Hasan al-Ash'ari, explained this position as follows:

> The proof that God is free to do whatever he does is that he is the supreme monarch, subject to no one, with no superior over him who can permit, or command, or chide, or forbid, or prescribe what he shall do and fix bounds for him. This being so, nothing can be evil (i.e., unjust) on the part of God. For a thing is evil on our part only because we transgress the limit and bound set for us and do what we have no right to do. But since the Creater is subject to no one and bound by no command, nothing can be evil on his part.[2]

Here we have the starkest imaginable affirmation of the absolute sovereignty of God over the moral life, and its starkness must be fully appreciated if we are to have an adequate understanding of orthodox Sunni thinking about punishment. The justification for God's punishment of men is to be found in the will of God and nowhere else. When God punishes, it is because he wills to punish, and the punishment is therefore ipso facto good and just. When he does not punish, it is similarly because he wills not to punish, and his failure to punish is thus likewise good and just. There is thus no necessary connection between divine punishment and desert which would restrict God's freedom.

This absolute sovereignty of God has its brighter side, for it entails not only the right of God to punish as he wills but also the right to forgive as he wills. It is this latter right which gives the intercessory role of the Prophet such importance in orthodox Sunni thought. Despite their deserving of punishment in hell for their acts of disobedience, believers may hope to be relieved of some or even all of the punishment of hell through the Prophet's intercession. In principle, unbelievers could also be spared of hell but for the fact that God has declared that they will not be. No such declaration pertains to believers: they are Muhammad's people, and they have Muhammad to look to as an intercessor.

In its emphasis on the sovereignty of divine forgiveness and its freedom from the constraints of retributive justice, orthodox Sunni thought stands in sharp contrast not only to Mu'tazilite thought but also to most Latin Christian thought. According to the common Latin view of the atonement, the one articulated in the writings of Anselm, Thomas Aquinas, Calvin and most Reformed theologians, God's forgiveness of sin is conditioned upon the satisfaction of divine justice, a justice which is clearly retributive. Christ's death upon the cross, whether viewed as a propitiatory or compensatory offering or as the vicarious bearing of a punishment deserved by man, is made necessary by the demands of retributive justice. Forgiveness apart from the cross is inconceivable.

Muslim thought, by contrast, was never able to make sense of the cross. It could hardly have wished to, considering that the Qur'an explicitly denies that Jesus was crucified. Quite apart from that, however, Muslim thought seems to have had an inherent logic which, intentionally or unintentionally, rendered the cross nonsensical. Mu'tazilite thought, which insisted that the demands of retributive justice must be satisfied, viewed repentance as a kind of satisfaction which made possible a divine forgiveness which was both compassionate and just. Desert could be cancelled by repentance, since God was not capable of loss such that satisfaction necessarily entailed compensation. Orthodox Sunni thought, by detaching justice from retribution, allowed God to cancel desert unilaterally or at least to set desert aside and to forgive without being bound by its demands. As sovereign, unbound by an constraints of rational thought, God could punish or forgive unconditionally. The very idea of a retributive justice whose demands must be satisfied was, as we have seen, called into question.

The radical theocentricity and voluntarism of orthodox Sunni thought determine not only how that tradition looks at punishment and forgiveness in the hereafter but also how it looks at punishment and forgiveness in this world. That is to say, they provide the intellectual underpinnings for the Islamic penal system, and it is to this subject that I would like to turn in the balance of this essay.[3]

The first thing that must be noted, before we proceed further, is that Islamic law is devoid of anything that may be regarded as a criminal law in the sense in which Western jurisprudence understands that term. This is because two important ingredients of criminal law are lacking: the very concept of crime and a distinct procedure to go with it. There is no such thing in Islamic law as an offense against the state or against society, since these have no status in the law. Only individuals are persons; the notion of the corporate person is non-existent. All offenses are therefore offenses against individuals. Among these individuals is God, and certain of the offenses which Western jurisprudence counts as crimes are treated as offenses against God. We may call them crimes if we wish, but then we will be departing from the common Western definition of crime. On the other hand, other offenses which in the West are counted as crimes are treated as injuries of man to man and as subject to what amounts to civil action.

God, like the human individual, is a bearer of certain rights. God's rights include, quite naturally, the right to be God, to receive obedience from man and to be the object of man's worship. God's rights are thus intimately bound up with the interests of organized religion. But they are also intimately bound up with the interests of the family and the social order. These are interests which transcend the interests of individuals *qua* individuals, and as such, given the non-recognition of the state or society as a legal entity or interested party, they can be maintained only with reference to divine rights. Thus fornication and false accusation of fornication, which undermine the marital bond and the legitimate propagation of the human race and thus militate against the health and stability of the social order over time, are both offenses against God. So also is theft, which undermines another pillar of the social order, namely security of property. And so also is the drinking of intoxicating beverages, which interferes with human rationality and thus with orderly social behavior and the proper disposition of the assets which God has bestowed upon his human creatures.

Homicide and bodily harm, on the other hand, are lumped together under the heading of offenses against human parties and thus seem to be treated more on the order of torts than on the order of what we would call crime. The injured party—in the case of a homicide victim this would usually be the nearest male relative acting on behalf of the victim's family or clan—is given a choice between three courses of action. He may demand retaliatory action, an eye for an eye, or life for a life, or whatever; or he may demand compensation; or, thirdly, he may forgive the offense altogether. When compensation is demanded, the offense clearly assumes a tort-like character. When retaliation is demanded, the offense resembles a crime in the sense that a kind of punishment is inflicted, but it falls short of actually constituting a crime in that the punishment is contingent upon the decision of the injured party. The punishment is a purely private affair.

Offenses against God are subject to textually fixed punishments, called in Arabic *hudud*.. Adulterous fornication is subject to stoning to death, whereas non-adulterous fornication, false accusation of fornication and drinking of alcoholic beverages are subject to flogging. Theft is subject to amputation of a hand. The justification of these punishments is, in orthodox Sunni thinking, the divine command, nothing more. The public authority must apply these punishments after the procedural requirements have been met simply because it is duty-bound under God to do so. No consideration of retributive justice or of social utility comes into the picture. As punishments stipulated by God they are, in effect, anticipations of punishment in the hereafter. That punishment may, as we have seen, be waived by God in favor of forgiveness. The *hudud* punishments may not be waived, since the command of God requires that they be applied without exception. Forgiveness is thus not an option for the public authority charged with applying these punishments, even though it is always in principle an option for God.

In the case of homicide and bodily harm, on the other hand, the option to forgive does belong to man. Punishment thus occurs by the will of the injured party. Islamic jurisprudence placed injury to the body, both fatal and non-fatal, in a category by itself distinct from other forms of injury, giving it a name of its own: *janaya*.. Such injury was in fact a privileged sort of injury in the sense that it and not the other forms of injury made the injured master of the situation. More specifically, it conferred upon the injured the right, as opposed to the duty, of retaliation or, in the event the injured chose not to exercise this right, the right to compensation. Even the right to compensation could be waived, as we have seen, in favor of complete forgiveness. However, the waiving of the right of retaliation was itself a kind of forgiveness and one which Islamic tradition encourages very strongly. We should view Islamic law as endeavoring to make a reluctant concession to the human impulse to seek vengeance without really absorbing the *lex talionis* into its ethos. Viewed from the standpoint of orthodox Sunni theology, retaliation has no intrinsic connection with justice, as we have seen. It is a private right, nothing more. And its status as a right is grounded in the divine will, nothing more. There is no room here for consideration of retributive justice as a justifying axiom.

The punishments considered thus far are all fixed by the law and may not be modified even slightly to suit a judge's own sense of the gravity of the offense. Their severity is obvious. On the other hand, they are all circumscribed by procedural constraints which are so rigorous as to make many of them virtually non-implementable. Herein lies a kind of anomaly. Fastidious adherence to procedural norms is one thing: we hallow this under the heading of due process. But procedure which comes near to obstructing application of penal sanctions is, it seems to me, quite another thing. The most commonly cited example pertains to fornication. In order for a conviction to be made, four witnesses must testify that they all simultaneously witnessed the actual penetration. Circumstantial evidence—which might consist, for example, of the couple's having been found together in bed—will not do. Considering that the Islamic law of evidence requires that witnesses be upright persons in good standing in the community, the scenario entailed in an acceptable witness to fornication becomes virtually unimaginable. But even if such a scenario were feasible, we would have to take into account the additional fact that some jurists consider it preferable for the witnesses to refrain from testifying so as to encourage the accused to settle the offense privately with God. What, then, are we to make of the prescribed punishment for fornication—stoning to death where adultery is involved, a hundred lashes where it is not? Is this a meaningful penal sanction, or is it more a statement about the moral heinousness of the offense, a way of expressing the divine attitude toward fornication in forceful language?

As is well known among historians of Islam, the textually fixed punishments have seldom—in fact, almost never—been implemented by Islamic states. Islamic law in fact realistically stipulates another category of punishments, the *ta'zir* or judicially determined punishments. These punishments apply to all offenses for which there is not textually fixed punishment, of which there are obviously many. But they also provide an alternative way of dealing with offenses which are subject to fixed punishments. For example, if one is unable to produce adequate testimony to fornication (which the Islamic rules of evidence make extremely difficult), one may bring forward a charge of illicit cohabitation, assuming that witnesses can be produced who will testify to a couple's having spent time in a private place together. Illicit cohabitation is distinct from fornication, but as it is ancillary to fornication action taken against it can amount to an action against fornication. Stoning to death or flogging will not occur, but at least some form of punishment will be applied.

Justification for judicially determined punishment is found, not in any abstract notion of retribution or social utility, but solely in the divine command. All punishments are grounded in the will of God; it makes no difference whether they be fixed by the letter of the law or left to the determinations of judges. It is not for the judge to decide whether to punish or not. Given that the offense has occurred, punishment must be meted out. The judge's task is to make the punishment commensurate with the offense. In performing this task, he is living out his obedience to God, nothing more.

In the case of punishments which are meted out by public authorities there is a clear connection between desert and punishment. This connection no doubt warrants our speaking of a retributive character of punishment in the public domain. But it is a retribution whose validity is not axiomatic, not grounded in a natural sense of justice. Rather than constituting a justifying principle in and of itself, retribution needs to be justified and this justification can be found in nothing other than the divine will. God wills that public authorities mete out punishment on the basis of desert, and for that reason alone retribution has a place in orthodox Sunni thinking about punishment. In the private sphere to which homicide and bodily harm belong, the connection between desert and punishment is not undergirded by a divine command, since it is the divine will that punishment be applied as a matter of right, not of duty. Desert may therefore occur without subsequent punishment. On the other hand, the right is connected with desert. No individual may call for retaliatory action against the undeserving. The freedom of the human individual in this regard is therefore not as great as the freedom of God.

On what basis is desert linked to particular human acts, according to the orthodox Sunni view? Like the Mu'tazilites, the orthodox jurists made the deserving of condemnation and hence of punishment a central factor in the definition both of obligation and of forbiddenness, so that the question, again, is tantamount to the question of the basis on which acts are classified as obligatory or forbidden. However, unlike the Mu'tazilites who insisted that this classification is the work of the reason operating independently of revelation, the orthodox Sunnis insisted that it occurs solely according to the dictates of the divine will. Thus whether an act is deserving of punishment or not is determined solely by the revealed will of God. This means that the will of God operates in two crucial ways: it determines whether an act is deserving of punishment; and it determines whether in a given case punishment will occur in consequence of desert.

Lest we think that orthodox Sunni thought makes of God an inscrutable and wholly capricious tyrant, we must continually keep in mind two elements: (1) the emphasis of Sunni orthodoxy upon God's frequent description of himself as compassionate and merciful, which was mentioned earlier, and (2) the great interest of orthodox Sunni jurisprudence in the benefits to human beings of the divine law. In regard to the first point, Sunni orthodoxy insists that the compassion and mercy of God are well grounded in his word and that his word is true and reliable. There is therefore much greater cause for rejoicing that in the austere and relentless moral rationalism of the Mu'tazilites. As for the second point, here is a dimension of orthodox Sunni jurisprudence that begs to be further explored. Orthodox thought insists that the welfare of human beings is something which God takes into account in ordaining all his laws, including those which relate to punishment. The great orthodox jurists were to see the divine law as concerned with the preservation of five things: the person, the faculty of reason, progeny, property and the worship of God. All of these were seen as ingredients of human happiness. The penal laws relate to these in specific ways. The person is protected by those laws which grant individuals the right to retaliation or compensation, thus giving them the capacity to deter aggression against their persons. The rational faculty, progeny and property are protected by the *hudud* penalties mentioned earlier. And the worship of God is protected in a variety of ways which are beyond the scope of this essay.

Do we not here have some sort of utilitarian outlook? Two points bear on this question. (1) The considerations of human welfare which I have mentioned are not something to which God is bound by any sort of rational necessity. In no way do these considerations infringe upon the voluntaristic spirit of orthodox Sunni thought. They are therefore not justifying principles in the final analysis. The sole justifying principle is always the will of God. (2) Orthodox Sunni jurisprudence does not allow jurists to treat these considerations of human welfare as abstract principles detached from sacred texts and freely develop law from them . Rather, it insists that these considerations may function only as guidelines in the interpretation of the sacred texts. Laws, including penal laws, must always have a demonstrable basis on those texts. If, within the context of this voluntarism and this centeredness on texts containing the revealed word of God it is possible to see some sort of utilitarianism at work, then so let it be.

[1]George F. Hourani, *Islamic Rationalism: the Ethics of 'Abd al-Jabbar* (Oxford: Claredon Press, 1971). My entire discussion of the Mu'tazilites in this essay is based primarily on this book.

[2]From the chapter entitled "Discussion of the Imputation of Justice and Injustice to God" in Richard J. McCarthy, S.J., *The Theology of al-Ash'ari* (Beirut: Imprimerie Catholique, 1953), p. 99.

[3]The best concise and most lucid account of the Islamic penal system is that of David F. Forte, "Comparative Criminal Law and Enforcement: Islam," in S. Kadish, ed., *The Encyclopedia of Crime and Justice* (New York: Free Press, 1983), pp. 193-200.

Juristic Theology? Medieval and Early Modern European Perspectives on Punishment

Edward Peters

Medieval and Early Modern European systems of criminal law and punishment are usually viewed by non-specialist readers from the perspective created by Enlightenment thinkers and publicists. In order to consider them in other terms, it is necessary first to consider that perspective and its reliability.

In few areas did Enlightenment thinkers assert their moral principles as dramatically as in their hostile characterization of the older criminal laws of western Europe, their repeated attempts to discredit them, and their insistence upon the obliteration and replacement of those laws by a more "rational and humane" system of criminal justice. With Cesare Beccaria's treatise *Dei delitti e delle pene* of 1764 as a centerpiece, one which circulated widely in French and English translations, and the famous individual cases that Voltaire made his own from the 1760s onward, many late eighteenth-century writers, whether jurists or not, capitalized upon reforms already underway in a number of European states—notably Lombardy and Austria—and upon internal changes within the older legal system, to which they paid little formal attention.[1] The result of this combination of theory and circumstance was not only the reform of criminal legal systems throughout Europe and the Americas, but new rationales for punishment, and indeed the erection into law and state policy of a new conception of human beings and their relation to the state.

The received wisdom generated by these criticisms and their apparent results is that the criminal justice of the Ancien Regime was capricious, inconsistent, unprofessional, and spectacularly brutal. It served a social and political elite by publicly inflicting exemplary punishments upon the bodies of its victims. It was replaced during the late eighteenth and early nineteenth centuries by a reformed system that was socially and politically more broadly based, that aimed for consistency, and that substituted reforming punishments—e.g., the prison—for the physical torment that had once characterized criminal discipline. Although some scholars, notably Michel Foucault, argued that the new system was more vicious than the old (because it manipulated the mind and spirit of the condemned in invidious ways), most historians accept the general improvement in criminal justice with little criticism of its nature or causes.

Despite significant modifications over time, the system put into place at the end of the eighteenth century is still in place. It is now coming under heavy criticism from as wide a variety of sources as had its predecessor. Moreover, historians have begun to re-examine the premises and methods of the original eighteenth-century critics of the older system and have found some of them, at least, either inaccurate or unfounded. The present criticisms of the reformed system and the critical undercutting of other bases of its original attack on the older system raise a number of questions, not least concerning the stability of any system of criminal justice over any length of time, as well as the relationship between criminal legal systems and the larger legal systems and societies of which they are a part.

The basis for much of Enlightenment critique of the criminal legal system of Old Europe may be suggested by the opening paragraph of Beccaria's Preface to *On Crimes and Punishments*:

> Certain residues of the laws of a race of conquerors in times long past, compiled by order of an emperor who ruled in Constantinople twelve centuries ago, later intermingled with Lombard usages, and eventually gathered into ill digested tomes by obscure commentators who spoke only for themselves—such go to form the body of traditional opinion which passes for law in the greater part of Europe today. It is as pernicious as it is prevalent that a view put forward by Carpzov, or an ancient custom to which Caro happened to allude, or some torture proposed with irate satisfaction by Farinacci, should now be laws blandly accepted by those who ought to be abashed by the responsibility of governing the lives and fortunes of human beings. These laws—this debris of barbarous times, are examined in this book in so far as they have a bearing on criminal procedure.[2]

Richard Andrews has criticized several of Beccaria's discrediting strategies in this and similar passages: not individual "obscure commentators," but urban, royal and imperial authorities had created the system attacked by Beccaria; they had been advised by magistrates and other judicial officials; their law had been taught in law schools and commented upon extensively by legal scholars.[3] In addition, Beccaria's reading of Roman history was, in the best tradition of Enlightenment polemic, highly selective. Roman law had served as the basis of European legal systems, neither because of the authority of Justinian nor the power of conquering armies, but because of its appeal as a coherent system of jurisprudence.[4] In any case, although many eighteenth-century thinkers shared Beccaria's distaste for the validity of Roman criminal law in eighteenth-century Europe—Gibbon himself had called it "an oppressive and irregular system"—the line of criticism upon which Beccaria had drawn in this instance had begun in the sixteenth century, and from within the very system which Beccaria had criticized.[5]

But even beyond the calculus of rationalism, utility, and rhetoric that characterized Beccaria's criticisms there lay yet other criticisms of the criminal law of the "ancien regime," some of them internalist and illustrated by a number of near contemporary works, including the *Osservazione sulla tortura* by Beccaria's friend Pietro Verri, and the comments of the Netherlands jurist Goswin de Fierlant, writing in the 1770s and 1780s.[6] Fierlant claimed that judges did not know the law, either because they were not well educated or because the law did not circulate as it should. Tribunals were filled with unqualified or incompetent officials. Lower officials depended upon superior officials who commanded high justice and followed their own private interests, denying costly justice to the poor and mechanically applying harsh laws to a people which did not know its rights of appeal and could not perceive the injustice of the magistrates. Judges were not often jurisconsults and did not know the fullness of the law; they based their opinions upon their own natural judgement guided only by a superficial notion of the rules, or by the opinions of others which they followed blindly, without reflection or consideration. There were too few qualified officials, and those who did function held too many jobs concurrently. Prosecutors were privileged members of the counsels of judges. The very pomp and rigidity of legal procedure not only condemned the innocent, but permitted the guilty to escape. Cost and poverty determined the course of the law.

Modern scholarship (especially the work of Michel Foucault, Pieter Spierenburg, Lionello Puppi, and Richard van Dulmen) has supplemented late-eighteenth century criticism by studies of the detailed operations of courts and the mechanisms of punishment they dealt out, the importance of ideas of purification, satisfaction, and retribution in setting punishments, and the aims of political intimidation and spectacular exemplary punishment in sustaining the legitimacy of authority.[7]

Such diverse and comprehensive criticism of the system of justice in the "ancien regime" contrasts sharply with another, related, historical circumstance—the role of jurisprudence in the movement of intellectual, political, and social renewal that is sometimes termed the "Renaissance of the Twelfth Century."[8] Since the system so roundly condemned in the late eighteenth century was created in the twelfth, how are we to comprehend what presumably went wrong? Where did the first system of criminal justice in European history fail? Does its sad history offer any answers for assessing the problem of criminal justice in the late twentieth century?

A number of historians have attempted to account for the shift from promising beginning to later disaster. Perhaps the most characteristic summary of this attitude is that of Walter Ullmann:

> The progressive decline of legal studies at the universities in later centuries [the fifteenth and sixteenth] brought forth a lower standard of the lawyers who were called to serve the cause of law. The authority of the scholars diminished likewise, and their influence upon the practical administration of the law gradually faded away. The law itself was no longer regarded with that respect which was characteristic of previous centuries: lawlessness in social life and a laxity in the application of the law went hand in hand. The standard of public administration, like that of public and private morality, deteriorated considerably. The public administrators were no longer imbued with that spirit of responsibility, that sense of loyalty towards the law, and that respect for the individual which distinguished the judges of previous centuries. Instead of regarding themselves as restricted in their discretionary powers by the law, the judges largely ignored it in the transition from medieval days to modern times. The law had lost its sacrosanct character. Mainly on account of the deterioration of moral standards in social and public life, the protection and interests of the individual counted far less than in the heyday of medieval culture. The low standard of legal training, the loss of the humanizing influence of the universities on the lawyers, the disregard of moral principles and the resulting lack of respect for the interests of the accused, largely explain the lamentable over-severity and brutality with which torture came to be used in the sixteenth and seventeenth centuries. The recourse to a *sindicatus* process was of no avail any more, since universities and scholars had ceased speaking with

> authority...The brutality with which torture was employed was but a concomitant feature of the cultural crisis which resulted from the disintegration of medieval civilization and society.[9]

I have cited Ullmann at such length not because he is exceptional but because he echoes a number of other historians, some of whom are far better known and more influential. The first chapter of Huizinga's *Waning of the Middle Ages* presents a similar, but more horrifying because more richly detailed, picture: "the decline of the middle ages was the great period of the flowering of cruel justice and of judicial cruelty," opposed to all subsequent ideas of justice:

> the idea of mitigated responsibility, that of the fallibility of judges, the notion that society is in some measure responsible for the actions of some of its members, the argument that it is preferable and possible to correct the criminal, rather than to punish him...[10]

According to Huizinga, late medieval justice knew only extremes—the entire spectrum of brutal punishments, or outright pardon, gratuitous (and hence irrational) mercy.

Huizinga cites three reasons for this condition. First, the formalism of the law which considered each case in the abstract without considering individual circumstances. Second, what he calls the egoist mentality of the magistrates: choleric, sensual, and passionate men, they punished in their victims faults that they wished to scourge from themselves. Third, the late medieval magistrate answered to no one and nothing outside himself. These three aspects, taken with Ullman's mixed argument about the decline of learning and morality, make our understanding of the late medieval and early modern criminal justice system derive from a particular view of the cultural climate of the fifteenth, sixteenth, and seventeenth centuries.

Was there, indeed, such a collapse of the legal system between the fourteenth and the late eighteenth centuries? Such a collapse would have to include a very large inventory: the decline of universities (or at least of law schools), the corresponding decline of academic legal authority and influence, a growing social disrespect for law, a growth of lawlessness, laxity in law enforcement, a deterioration of standards of public morality, irresponsible public administrators, including magistrates, less respect for the individual, and the contamination of judicial discretion by private interests, all of these along with the lists provided by Beccaria, Fierlant, and other eighteenth-century critics. Answering this question requires some discussion of the system of criminal justice that emerged in the twelfth century and operated until the end of the eighteenth, and a reappraisal of the various models of its history that were produced between the late eighteenth century and the present.

A comprehensive answer is impossible in a single essay. But examination of some of the most important aspects of the old system of European criminal law can suggest the directions for a reappraisal of the entire issue.

II

The system of criminal justice that lasted from the twelfth to the end of the eighteenth century depended upon state authority (real or asserted) and the state's reliance upon legal science as represented in a magistracy/judiciary, legislation, and an academicized legal profession. Studies of the place of punishment within this system have differed considerably. Given the general independence from Roman law of the societies of western Europe between the sixth and the twelfth centuries, the prevalence of private violence (revenge, feud, vendetta), the practice of voluntarily arbitrated composition of disputes, the accusatorial procedure and the narrowness of the functions of public authority, a few scholars have argued nevertheless that publicly established and enforced punishment did on occasion exist as early as the sixth and seventh centuries.[11] Others have argued that as territorial rulers, particularly kings, asserted their superior relationship to all other free men, they were able to impose punishment in place of private settlement of wrongs.[12] Yet others have argued that the system of punishment sprang up suddenly in the twelfth-century, when moral disapproval on the part of an impersonal magistrate or ruler transformed the private injury into a public crime.[13]

The most recent and coherent argument, that of Pieter Spierenburg, focuses upon the twelfth-century, although he correctly warns against any argument assuming a sudden transformation. Private senses of personal injury survived for centuries after the twelfth. The actual power of a central authority, whether king or town, needed time to build up and articulate itself so as to create a system of criminal law. The inquisitorial procedure (the procedural basis of the law of the Old Regime) also needed time to be articulated, understood, and established.[14] With judicial torture as an incident of inquisitorial procedure, the features of system of the ancien regime became clearer, and not until the middle of the sixteenth century had "a more or less stable repression...been established in most of western Europe."[15]

None of these views seems entirely satisfactory. Few of them deal at all with the parallel problem of religious influence upon temporal institutions, particularly regarding the question of crime and sin, ecclesiastical discipline (even when applied to layfolk), or the reciprocal influence of ecclesiastical and secular laws. Few deal with the rule of the revived study and application of Roman law during the twelfth century and the subsequent impact of a learned jurisprudence over the entire course of the period between the twelfth and the eighteenth centuries.[16]

Although it is very likely that a theory of punishment (partly derived from memories of Roman law, partly from ecclesiastical sources) existed among the early Germanic inhabitants of western Europe, and that (with ecclesiastical discipline) an ambitious, but short-lived attempt was made under the Carolingians to assert crown authority over wrongdoing, so many of the elements that need to be considered for the actual development of a criminal justice *system* did not meet until the twelfth century that the system must be considered to have begun then.

As R.C. Van Caenegem has pointed out, the twelfth-century witnessed, foremost, the increasing assertion on the part of royal, papal, and territorial principalities of their judicial authority and their development of institutions to make that authority determine procedure and instance—the royal writ in England, the papal judges delegate and rescripts of justice, and parallel institutions in *Francia* and Flanders.[17] Secondly, there was the twelfth-century specialization of judicial activity, its separation from other functions and its consequent creation of a legal discipline in *ordines judiciarii* and the creation of judges. Thirdly, Van Caenegem considers the considerable increase of writing in the service of the law, including the new importance of written evidence, contracts, notarial instruments, written agreements, and charters. Finally, Van Caenegem notes the importance of the revived study of logic to the intricacies of legal exchange and the definition of legal relationships, including those of crime and punishment.

It is in this context—which in itself widens the scope of the earlier discussions of the birth of punishment—that Van Caenegem places the revived study of Roman law, but with some shrewd contextual advice: "[T]he point was not that Roman concepts became victorious over Germanic ones, but that society shed a good deal of its more primitive characteristics, many but not all of which happened to be Germanic, and developed into a more advanced society with characteristics, some but not all of which were Roman."[18]

One of the virtues of Van Caenegem's approach is that it takes legal change in general as its context for change in specific legal aspects of society. Similarly, recent studies by Stephan Kuttner and Knut Wolfgang Nörr describe the sources and institutions of twelfth century jurisprudence, without consideration of which the problem of criminal punishment and criminal law in general tends to become abstract and detached from the larger systems of thought and practice in which it was imbedded.[19] Kuttner, for instance, considers the rediscovery and circulation of Justinian's *Digest* within the particular context of the twelfth century intellectual culture in which its circulation (including its teaching, learning, and application) took place; Nörr too considers the larger institutions of the twelfth century: universities and their schools of law, institutions and their specialized personnel, the Roman Curia, delegated jurisdiction, the establishment of a judicial hierarchy, and the appearance of prosecuting officials in ecclesiastical and secular court systems.

Criminal justice can only in a specialized sense be studied in isolation. If the criminal justice system of Old Europe began in the twelfth century, it responded to twelfth-century contexts and circumstances. And one of these circumstances was a new answer to the question: what is crime? And what is to be done with the person who commits a crime?

III

The earliest element in the twelfth century creation of a criminal justice system was the body of criminal regulations found in Justinian's *Digest* and *Code*.[20] The pertinent texts, which had originated among jurists of the second and third centuries and imperial constitutions from the fourth, fifth, and sixth, had replaced or assimilated earlier laws governing the *quaestiones perpetuae*, the public crimes of *perduellio* and the malfeasance of provincial governors, and the requirement of a private accuser. They were supplanted by a series of rules that, however, contained no specific definition of crime and an extremely rudimentary definition of the criminal.

In spite of references to the function of law as making men fearful of punishment, Roman law actually says little about the nature of crime. Every reader of that segment of Ulpian's *Institutes* that constitutes the first text in Justinian's *Digest* will have learned that jurists then, as now, professed to "cultivate the virtue of justice and claim awareness of what is good and fair, discriminating between fair and unfair, distinguished lawful from unlawful, aiming to make men good *not only through fear of penalties* but also indeed under allurement of rewards, and affecting a philosophy which, if I am not deceived, is genuine, not a sham."[21] *Metus Poenarum* may not be the most important, but it is the first lesson that the law teaches, at least rhetorically for Ulpian. Elsewhere, in *Digest* 2. 1. 3, Ulpian defines simple *imperium* as the power to punish the wicked, and in Papinian's discussion of delegated jurisdiction (*Dig*. 21.1) the problem of delegation is illustrated by examples from the criminal law. The assumption behind these views derives from only a rudimentary criminal psychology: some people have a *voluntas perniciosae libidinis* "a proclivity for base desires" (Paulus, *Dig*. 47.11.1)—that is the *dolus malus*, the evil intent, that creates the *mens rea*, the criminal mind. Although jurists also insisted that those accused of a particular crime must be examined as to their state of mind (*Dig*. 48.19.5.2), Roman criminal law was concerned chiefly with prohibited actions rather than with any more elaborate theory of crime or criminals. Slender as this elementary criminal psychology was, it sufficed for the writers of the texts in the *Digest* and the *Code*. In addition, the elaborate system of punishments fell much more heavily upon members of the lower social orders. The difference in the application of criminal sanctions has been called the best evidence of the difference between the social ranks of *honestiores* and *humiliores*.[22] The growing use of the procedure known as *cognitio extraordinaria*, the earliest form of the *inquisitio* procedure, tended to make the application of the law even more mechanical, and during the fourth and fifth centuries the most severe sanctions began to be applied with greater regularity to higher ranks of society, first for particularly heinous offenses, and later for more routine ones. This feature, the upward mobility of punishments originally designated for the lowest orders of Roman society, accounts for the growing use of torture, for example, and its inclusion as an incident of criminal legal procedure.[23]

The relatively spare Roman criminal jurisprudence and its elementary criminal psychology tended to blur earlier distinctions among *crimen*, *peccatum*, *delictum*, and *maleficium*. Moreover, *peccatum* entered the Latin Christian vocabulary, heavily influenced by the Jewish understanding of sin, the concept of sin as a violation of religious and of moral responsibility, and by the linguistic identification of crime and sin in the Latin version of Scripture (*Amos* 5: 11-25). These ideas came into Latin Christianity via Paul and James, in the Latin versions of whose writings *peccatum* became the violation of the natural law inscribed in the hearts of all men (*Romans* 2:15), a product of disordered will, and the individual responsibility of those who committed it.

Although the Fathers of the Church rejected much of the apparatus of Roman criminal law—some of them having been its victims, or having known those who had—the Roman state extended the application of its criminal law to a number of aspects of ecclesiology, including, for example, the extension of doctrines of *infamia* and *perduellio/majestas* to heretics and schismatics. The dilemma that this extension posed for Christians is reflected in the ambivalent attitude of St. Augustine toward coercion.[24] From the fifth century on, the problem of crime and punishment was complicated by the often competing rationales of spiritual and temporal authorities in regard to the problem of ecclesiastical discipline. As Richard Fraher has recently argued,

> The fathers of the Latin Church had decidedly rejected the preoccupation of fifth-century Roman law with maintaining social control through harsh penal sanctions. Although Ambrose, Augustine, Jerome, and Gregory the Great filled their letters and sermons with the vocabulary of the Roman

> law, so that sin, *peccatum*, became synonymous with *crimen*, *delictum*, and *maleficium*, the Latin fathers employed these terms without accepting the conceptual framework from which the vocabulary was drawn.[25]

The language of Ulpian and other jurists was thus made compatible with the vocabulary of the Latin fathers, although the apparatus of punishment and coercion advocated by Ulpian was not endorsed by them. From Gregory the Great until the late eleventh century churchmen preferred penitential reconciliation to penal sanctions, and in cases that were hidden they were reluctant to judge at all.[26]

During the same period, of course, the general privatization of law, the accusatory procedure, the resolution of conflict by arbitration, purgatory oaths, or ordeals—as well as the emergency of what has often wrongly been termed a mechanized system of tariff penances—suggest that neither Roman criminal law nor the penitential psychology of the Church fathers stood much chance of survival—or revival.[27] But they did not disappear, nor did the insistence of theologians upon the role of reason and will in human responsibility, and in the course of the eleventh and twelfth centuries they re-emerged as major elements in a changing world that insisted urgently upon the establishment of public order. It is in this context that the new system of criminal justice was worked out by public authorities, jurists, and theologians in the course of the twelfth century.

IV

The emergence of a system of criminal justice depended, of course, upon a society organized so as to require and be capable of sustaining one. The economic and social changes of the eleventh and twelfth centuries are well known: the rise of towns, the increasingly sensed *public* character of the authority of lords and kings, the academic concern with intellectual as well as public order and precision, the theological rehearsal of the distinctions between sin and crime. All of these were the necessary components for the creation of legal systems that satisfactorily addressed contemporary needs. The rediscovered text of Justinian's *Digest* offered less the authority of an emperor and the revered name of Rome than a mine of legal science that had only to be explained in order to be made applicable to twelfth-century conditions. In canon law, a vast mass of conflicting authorities had to be ordered and interpreted in such a way that it, too, offered the logic, authority, and coherence already thought to be present in Roman law. Whether or not Roman law was considered legally binding on any people in western Europe, it was certainly recognized as a supplementary law in Italy and southern France, and its intellectual elegance gave it considerable influence even in areas in which Rome had never ruled.[28]

The same principles that led twelfth-century students of Roman law to hunt throughout the entire text for applicable principles, perhaps led on by Justinian's assertion that his law contained no contradictions, led to a new systematization. Contract law, the law of corporate entities, procedure, and criminal law were erected into more coherent structures than they had been in the original materials.

At the same time, older Germanic compilations—for example, the Lombard law—were glossed, commented upon, and taught from a Romanist perspective. Where the older laws failed (and they failed increasingly as the character of the societies that used them changed), learned law could now step in, either to reform or to supplement older laws. The new powers of the twelfth century saw it in their interest to support legal change, since law in both the Roman and Germanic worlds had been associated with kings and other rulers. As kings, lords, and towns embraced legal reform, the social status of jurists rose, and they became *domini* (lords), or the *militia legum*, the "knighthood of jurists." Their schools attracted larger numbers of students, many from areas in which Roman law did not exist, and in themselves became economic assets (and social troubles) to the towns in which they were located, initially Bologna.[29]

From the publication of Gratian's *Concordia discordantium canonum* around 1140 and its subsequent revisions and additions, ecclesiastical law, too, became as compact, systematic, and scientific as the Roman law. Many jurists became experts in both. Students in canon law attended the same schools, were trained as rigorously, and exhibited the same degree of legal science as their counterparts in civil law.[30] By the 1160s, a combination of social, political and intellectual change had established the "two laws"—canon and civil—as the pinnacle and standard of learned law.

V

Historians of criminology have tended to neglect the elements of learned law and the religious circumstances surrounding the making and application of law. It is worth remembering at the outset that all of the lawmakers, professors, judges, lawyers, and magistrates in the system of early European criminal justice were believing (and practicing) Christians, as was the vast majority of those accused and convicted of criminal activity. Both belief and practice have differed among Christians according to difference in places and times, but far more of individual and civil life in pre-1800 Europe was lived within a public Christian context than ever afterwards. All jurists and criminals were dealt with in terms of their relation to God and in terms of the relation between this life and the next.

These concerns were expressed in many ways; here suffice it to observe that the execution of insane persons was generally forbidden, even in civil courts, largely on the grounds that insane persons could not understand their punishment, could not repent their sins, and therefore could not be saved.[31]

In addressing this aspect of legal history at the time of the Reformation of the sixteenth century, Gerald Strauss made a point that applies to the twelfth century as readily as to the sixteenth:

> At the time of the Reformation, the lavishly orchestrated religious consonances surrounding the concept of law significantly affected the ways people understood and experienced their legal order and the institutions upholding it. Their perceptions of legal constraints, and of the ways in which these constraints bound them to their political and social world, were governed at least as much by religious expectations as by political awareness. The religious side of consciousness was in any case more highly developed, and much more pervasive, than the political side. Public responses to law and to the whole legal situation were therefore significantly more complex, ambivalent, and unstable in the Age of Reformation than the judicial context alone suggests.[32]

So pervasive were the religious dimensions of life and society, that a number of historians have termed much of early European law "juristic theology," and one has recently characterized the entire western legal tradition as a "secular theology."[33] The figure of God as judge, Christ *Pantocrator*, images of the Final Judgement, the judicial proceedings against Christ himself, joined a rich and popular literature that conceived the gaining or losing of salvation, or the amount of repentance to be spent in the newly imagined Purgatory. In terms of offenses against divine law, the new eleventh and twelfth century emphasis on the internal character of sin and penance, and the ethical emphasis on the internal spiritual condition of both judge and defendant not only illuminates the religious framework of judicial reform and innovation, but also brought the vast and formidable weight of moral theology to bear on the concept of the criminal offender and helped create the first practical theories of criminal psychology.[34]

The sharp distinction between clerical and lay status and proper spheres of competence that had been given great impetus by the reform movement of the eleventh and twelfth centuries created a new sphere of competence over sin—the confessional and the ecclesiastical court—and permitted temporal authorities to take cognizance only of worldly offenses and to punish only these worldly offenses or "crimes"—legitimately. Thus, a crime might also be a sin, but the two terms were no longer synonymous, and their separation in twelfth century theology and law had considerable consequences for the ensuing development of criminal jurisprudence. Certain classes of criminal offenses that were also sinful or that required a temporal punishment that the Church could not inflict led to a certain degree of shared jurisdiction, or to a collaborative jurisdiction/execution system. Heresy and other similarly severe offenses sustained this collaborative system as long as Church courts were recognized in European states. For the most part, however, sins were separated from crimes and treated as matters of individual penitence and absolution in the "forum of conscience," the confessional or, if they were severe or had given rise to *scandalum*, in the "external forum," of an ecclesiastical court. Crimes, on the other hand, while often being sins as well (and bringing to bear on the idea of the criminal the idea of the sinner), were to be defined and dealt with in this world by the duly constituted powers of this world, emulating in earthly justice the model of divine justice.[35]

During the later twelfth and thirteenth centuries, then, western Europe began to know two systems of law, that of the Church and that of temporal courts. Although much attention has been paid to the differences between these—as in, e.g., Thomas Becket's resistance to Henry II's attempt to punish criminous clerks—both systems derived from an increasingly learned law. Within the world of clerical malefactors the experience of canon lawyers offered much of interest to temporal judges.

Not only had the Latin fathers rejected the apparatus of Roman criminal law, but they had also built into the structure of ecclesiastical discipline a number of safeguards for clerical defendants. First, they had restricted the ways by which laypeople might accuse prelates of crimes by applying the Roman doctrine of *infamia* as a restriction of accusatory status; second, they had insisted upon either confession or the testimony of two eyewitnesses (Matt 26.60), and they had left many routes of appeal for the convicted cleric to follow. In the age of ecclesiastical reform associated with the name and pontificate of Gregory VII, and its aim for a purified distinct, and elite body of Christian clergy, a number of earlier clerical offenses began to loom large in the minds and eyes of reformers.[36] Among these were clerical concubinage and simony, and several reformers well into the twelfth century expressed willingness to disregard earlier procedural safeguards in the name of reform and clerical purity. As Richard Fraher has recently pointed out, a number of twelfth and early thirteenth century changes within the canon law of clergy may be understood with these needs in mind, particularly Pope Alexander III's insistence upon the fact that clerical offenses against the Church be tried in the external forum, that every *crimen* in this sense is an offense against the Church and hence a public crime, and Innocent II's urging the laity to avoid sacraments performed by sinful clergy.[37] These enthusiastic changes were then themselves regulated, as Fraher points out, by Pope Innocent III (1198-1216), who formulated the doctrine that the accusatory procedure should be replaced by the *inquisitio* procedure. In addition, with the institution of summary procedure for "enormous crimes"—such as homicide, simony, heresy, and usury—appeal was restricted, and an elaborate development of the idea of *fama* and *notorium* supported these changes. Innocent III also proclaimed that public utility required "that crimes not go unpunished," which Fraher regards as the first enunciation of a doctrinal theory of deterrence.[38] Both the concepts of public interest and deterrence are to be found in the literature of Roman law, but the steps taken by Innocent III represent the first applications of these to European legal practice.

With the new emphasis upon character, reputation, and public knowledge of crimes and criminals, the emerging idea of deterrence, and the application of a judicial procedure that had solid grounding in learned law, the growth of a clerical criminal law could also be extended to those areas of shared jurisdiction—for example in such offenses as heresy, homicide, incest, and perjury—in which similar procedures could appeal to temporal courts as well as to courts Christian. In the *Speculum Juris* of Guillelmus Durantis, written around 1270, this development in canon law was summed up and made available to other courts.

VI

That procedures developed to combat clerical crime were adopted in other courts is well known, and that the development of particular procedures within special ecclesiastical courts—those of the inquisitors—extended Innocent III's innovations well beyond the norms of the new criminal jurisprudence is well known. But the ecclesiastical character of these changes should not obscure the contemporary concerns of secular jurists during the twelfth and thirteenth centuries, for they offered the other system of laws and courts a number of appealing solutions to problems that were also of public interest and public utility. They appealed to a strong sense that crimes not go unpunished.

The ecclesiastical law of clerical crimes and criminals applied, we should remember, to a class of free individuals subject by will and law to ecclesiastical jurisdiction. In addition, punishments applied in canon law to criminous clergy were, in the eyes of laypeople, relatively light: removal from office, degradation, incapacity to be appointed to higher office, and public *purgatio* or public penance were the chief punishments that could be inflicted. Therefore, the refinement of judicial procedure and the changes in rules of evidence by late twelfth-century popes and councils led within the clerical order to punishments that, while satisfying the high conception of clerical status produced by the Gregorian reformers, were not in themselves physically severe enough to retard the rationalizing of judicial procedure that led to their application. The growth of learned Roman law beside the extension of canon law, however, offered to temporal courts both a rational procedure and a greater degree of certainty in criminal justice that entailed, upon conviction, much stiffer punishments as well as elements of procedure that had not existed in the clerical world in which these principles had been first formulated.

Unlike ecclesiastical courts, temporal courts possessed "blood justice," and they administered a range of sanctions that, while not identical to those of Roman criminal law, were far more physically severe than those available to courts which punished clerics. Roman criminal law recognized exile (with or without confiscation of property), condemnation to labor or gladiatorial combat, decapitation, and the aggravated sentence of death: crucifixion, burning, or condemnation to the beasts in the circus, along with the archaic punishments of the *cullens* and the walling up alive of ruined Vestal Virgins. Several of these punishments ceased to exist—labor, combat, and the circus—and also crucifixion, which was regarded differently by medieval jurists.

Decapitation and burnings, however, survived from Roman law. Other forms of criminal sanction appeared to have derived from customary punishments of slaves or from local custom. Hanging, the wheel, drowning, and quartering, became the punishments for various capital crimes. Aggravated sentences of death included dragging the criminal publicly to the scene of execution, exposure of the corpse on the wheel, tearing with hot pincers, and death on the wheel with the death blow reserved for the end of the procedure. Whipping might be inflicted alone or as an aggravated death penalty, and exile also survived from Roman law. Amputation and branding might also be separate sanctions or parts of an aggravated sentence of death.

With the adoption of the inquisitorial procedure, of course, the requirement of two eyewitnesses or a confession when *indicia* (including *fama*) indicated guilt introduced torture as a legal device to solicit confession, and, after conviction, as a device for identifying accomplices or other crimes.

In the twelfth century, those areas of lay government that were directed by strong central authorities and applied to a spatially compact population addressed the problem of criminality and criminal justice with much of the freedom enjoyed by ecclesiastical tribunals and few of the restrictions that limited those courts.[39] In the towns of northern Italy and southern France, in Flanders, and in compact territorial states, criminal justice responded to increased perceptions of the danger of crime by utilizing state power to install a new criminal procedure, whose results upon the conviction of the defendants were far more severe than they were upon convicted criminous clergy.

In few places did the new procedures and rules of evidence instantly replace the old. Northern Italian communes may have had a freer hand in instituting laws and procedures, but even here, and certainly in the more northern parts of western Europe, accusatory and inquisitorial systems overlapped for a long time: dispute settlement survived alongside a stricter world of *lex* and *judicium*; feud continued to exist along with state-directed peace making. But the very existence of a formal system of state-controlled and applied criminal jurisprudence tended to dominate the surviving elements of earlier systems. Even in northern Italy, and certainly in northern Europe, certain groups were exempted from the most severe and humiliating forms of criminal punishment and were made relatively invulnerable to certain kinds of testimony and the character of certain kinds of witnesses. Thus, as temporal courts on the continent adopted learned procedure—backed by centralized state authority and a direct state contact with citizen bodies—they were able to deploy the new procedure and attach to its consequences the severity of older forms of punishment, first to those of the lowest social status, and only later, well into the thirteenth century, upon all convicted criminals without regard to social standing.

Judges who had to undertake the management of the new criminal procedure were political appointees, but they also had a substantial reference literature available to them by the end of the twelfth-century. Treatises on crime and criminal law began to appear throughout Europe, first in southern France by 1155, and in greater numbers and complexity in northern Italy and the rest of Europe during the thirteenth century.[40] The publication of Albertus Gandinus' *Tractatus de maleficiis*, at about the same time as Durantis' *Speculum judiciale* constituted a civil law counterpart to Durantis' canonist work. At the same time, treatises on procedure, the *ordines judiciarii*, appeared in greater numbers.[41] Finally, several of the greatest jurists in both laws—Azo, Tancred, Hostiensis—wrote extensively on both topics. Between 1150 and 1300 the learned law of the schools had produced a formidable practical, working literature of criminal jurisprudence.

In some parts of Europe, notably England, the Low Countries, and Scandinavia, the public prosecution of crime, although it too grew more regular and was tied more closely to centralized authorities with a sense of public interest, took other forms—the jury (grand and petit) of England, the *seventuig* of Frisia, the *verité des eschevins* of Flanders, and the *namnden* of Scandinavia.[42] Elsewhere, notably in northern Italy and France by 1154, the inquest/*inquisito* procedure rapidly gained ground. It was supported by a growing learned literature, and the support of both communal and princely governments. In some areas, the inquest was further developed by state authority into the secret inquest:

> that is, the hearing of witnesses in secret, the refusal to communicate to the accused the deposition or names of his accusers, etc. In consequence the legal procedure that emerged put the suspect at great disadvantage, taking away the means of defending himself freely and from that time tending to give extraordinary weight to the suspicions of the judge based on hearsay, insinuations, and reports of informers.[43]

Although jurists argued long and learnedly about the reliability of proofs derived from such procedures, including torture and the energy and excessive zeal of judges and state prosecutors, the spread of inquest procedure entailed the acceptance of other standards of proof as well as the incidence of judicial torture.

The definition of crime expanded to include many disputes that had heretofore been considered private, and the powers of judges expanded with it to try cases by *inquisitio* procedure that had once been settled as private litigation. The research of Sarah Blanshei and others on the criminalization of homicide in thirteenth and fourteenth century Bologna and elsewhere offers an example of this process of expanded criminalization.[44] In some parts of northern Italy, especially in cities in which the "popular party," the *popolo*, assumed governmental power, privileged noble status also fell before enthusiasm for civic peace, and the once exempt higher orders of society fell under the same system of criminal justice as had the lower. Often, the punishments of nobles were more spectacular and better publicized than those of the lower social orders.[45]

By 1500 the new system of criminal justice was in place throughout most of Europe. Even in those northern areas in which the *inquisitio* procedure did not take root similar principles of criminal justice were acknowledged. A wide range of criminal behavior was identified, as public authorities claimed and successfully defended their legitimacy as definers of crime and prosecutors of criminals. Older limitations on both the definition of crime and the status of the accused were largely gone by 1500, and a learned jurisprudence had been produced that the advent of print only increased and circulated more widely. Finally, most of the principles that emerged between the twelfth and the sixteenth century were embodied in legislative codes, beginning with the *Carolina* of 1532.[46] This is the system that operated into the eighteenth century and brought down upon itself the critical assaults of Enlightenment thinkers.

VII

The revolutions in theories and definitions of crime, the learned jurisprudence of criminology, the attachment of archaic forms of punishment to new criminal procedures, and the training of a new judiciary may be traced in both academic literature and the study of statistical data culled from actual runs of court records.[47] Yet another aspect of the creation of the system considered here is the problem of marginal society. From the thirteenth century onward, many of the new procedures were accompanied by cautionary statements regarding those social groups to which elements of the new procedures would not apply, or at least would not apply in certain instances. Louis IX of France, for instance, in instituting the *inquisitio* procedure for criminal cases, stated that torture should not be used on honest citizens, even if they happened to be poor. But in the course of the fourteenth and fifteenth centuries, a number of groups in late medieval society came to be considered marginal, and with this division, part of society became particularly vulnerable to the effects of the new criminal jurisprudence.

One of the most influential studies of this phenomenon, Bronislaw Geremek's *The Margins of Society in Late Medieval Paris*, deals with the emergence of the legal recognition of superior and inferior levels of Parisian society in the fourteenth century, the latter comprised of people located by others, locating themselves, excluded or excluding themselves—from the contemporary process of production, and living a life incompatible with the norms of contemporary social comportment.[48] In urban societies of estates, marginal people belonged to no estate; they defined themselves negatively in terms of those elements that constituted the essence of membership in any of the estates: dignity, honor, and respect. They had no permanent function in economic or social life. Geremek's marginal people—criminals generally, bohemians, beggars, lepers, actors, and prostitutes—were framed largely by French vernacular criminal law. What characterizes Geremek's marginal people is the fact that they are the component of society "that is struck by the seal or stamp of infamy," and they are seen by their contemporaries as "useless to the world."

In a work that was strongly influenced by that of Geremek, Jacques Chiffoleau's *Les Justices du Pape* of 1984, the place of marginalization is spelled out in more detail in regard to the criminal law.[49] Chiffoleau points out that violent and sanguinary punishments declined in Avignon between the late thirteenth and the mid-fifteenth centuries. Punishments were dealt out according to a scale of shame, and this scale influenced the pronouncement of aggravated sentences of death. Some punishments aimed at inflicting suffering in a shameful manner as a means of correcting behavior. Others were applied to enormous crimes and consisted of aggravated capital punishment. Justices in Avignon increasingly believed in the existence of a criminal underworld—of what would later be called *classes dangereuses*—and that membership in such a group could be determined by *vagabondage* (having no fixed dwelling), by the lack of a *metier* (*ars vivendi*) or the possession of one but the failure to practice it, and by habitual association with dishonest people and places, notably taverns, brothels, and games of chance. Yet Chiffoleau also argues that the justices themselves neither created nor systematically hunted out such marginal people.

Rather,

> The essential impact of the work of the magistrates is... in their capacity, not to marginalize, but to group together (*encadrer*), to oversee (*surveillier*), to make an important part of the population pass before them every year, even for acts of little importance, and, in doing this, to give to the body social a certain image of its proper kind of cohesion, in spite of the civil and military crisis. Thus there imposed itself upon those subject to local justice the idea of the omnipotence of justice itself, and an awareness, properly political, of participating in a civil society from which it became easier and easier to exclude dangerous and uncontrollable elements.[50]

In the work of Geremek and Chiffoleau it is possible to see the process of marginalization taking place within a larger and remarkable set of changes in social attitudes, particularly toward crime and the nature of criminals. A society of estates was taking shape, especially rapidly in urban space. Dignity, honor, and respect had to be accorded to each estate. A *metier* and its practice were presumptively honorable (thus making respectable a number of occupations that had earlier been considered *metiers vils*, dishonorable trades), as was stability and continuity of habitation. Respectable people associated only with other respectable people. The function of justice, particularly criminal justice, was to teach these truths to both the good citizen and the bad. Finally, public shame and publicly witnessed punishment were effective instruments in this process. This last component, social in its identification of a likely criminal society and social also in its insistence upon the pedagogic value of public punishment—Spierenburg's "spectacle of suffering"—is the last but one of the topics I address here. The last is the magistrates themselves.

VIII

Between learned academic/professional jurisprudence and the legislative powers of states and rulers lay the legal profession itself. Judges and magistrates mediated the law and its rationale to those accused of crimes, and, not surprisingly, judges and magistrates bore much of the brunt of the heaviest criticism of the criminal legal system from the thirteenth to the nineteenth centuries.[51] For a group that played such a central role, however, judges (and the magistracy generally) have received far less study than the criminal defendants who have occupied and dominated the work of recent social historians. Out of the general undifferentiated groups of *scabini*, *schofen*, and *boni homines* of Carolingian and post-Carolingian Europe, *judices* and *jurisperiti* appeared in European sources in the twelfth century, and in very different functions from those of their earlier Roman counterparts. They were the targets of much of Huizinga's criticism, and only infrequently has that criticism been assessed and answered by more recent scholars.

In the most articulate response to Huizinga's criticism of the judges, Louis Theo Maes addressed both Huizinga's reading of eighteenth century polemic and his reliance upon literary and chronicle sources.[52] While admitting particular, and even general instances of judicial corruptibility, sensuality, and insensibility, Maes also warns against using exceptional conditions as a norm of assessment and against the unilateral depiction of a class without differentiating among its members in different places over time and without considering the legal literature concerning the figure of the judge. In the latter, for example (and his points are echoed in the burgeoning criminal legal literature of the sixteenth and seventeenth centuries), the old idea of the judge as a "priest of the law" is continued in assertions that judges should lead better moral lives than mendicants or other religious personnel, that the judicial oaths insist upon the impartial duty of judges and specifically forbid family relationship, friendship, or remuneration from influencing a judge's decision. Cruel or self-interested judges are routinely condemned in the legal literature of the sixteenth and seventeenth centuries. Moreover, judges had to be willing to be frequently uprooted and transferred; trials had to be accurately and minutely recorded, especially if they were to be reviewed later by higher authorities. Judges were urged to consider the poverty or otherwise mitigating circumstances of the accused; they had to hold steadfast in the face of popular resistance; they depended upon strict formality because it removed them from face-to-face relationships in small, emotionally intense societies. They had to remain aloof from the details of torture and the "vulgar" work done by other officials. Judges were, particularly from the sixteenth century on, spiritually responsible for the accused and the condemned; they had to inspect prisons. Even the much debated issue of attitudes toward judicial discretion centered upon both the dangers of interested judges and the ideal of responsive and flexible administration and application of the law.

Parallel work by Alfred Soman on archival records in sixteenth and seventeenth century France suggests that Maes's reading of the jurisprudential literature was consistent with the actual practice of law as recorded in the archives: a broadening right of appeal in capital cases; a relative decline in the harshness of punishments; the differences between *cas enormes*, *crimina excepta*, and other offenses; the introduction of extraordinary punishments for particularly perceived rashes of crime; the reduction of visible mutilations and banishments in favor of the condemnation to the galleys; the emergence of alternate punishments and the increased weight of partial proofs reduced the necessity of confessions, and hence torture.[53] As Soman remarks,

> As confessions lost their central importance, torture became less necessary and the way was paved for its eventual abolition. That, however, did not disappear until 1780. In the interim what happened was only natural; as the need for torture diminished, its violence could be correspondingly reduced.[54]

In turn, the literature of jurisprudence and the records of actual applications of the law are not so very different. If the literature held up an ideal for the judges that often failed in practice, institutions might correct judicial failure in an increasing number of instances, and internal changes in the area of punishment worked to mitigate the formal severity of the naked law.

The complaints of Beccaria, Goswin de Fierlant, and others, as inconsistent with both legal literature and archival records as they were, were nevertheless heeded, and they were followed by the French Revolution and its dramatic, if short-lived, penal reforms, by the criminal code of Napoleonic France, and by proposals and active efforts to reform the criminal jurisprudence of nearly all of western Europe. Judicial torture was abolished by the end of the eighteenth century; the concept and category of exceptional crimes was greatly reduced, as was the number of capital crimes; the formal role of infamy disappeared, as did, except in countries that retained a prominent place for case-law, the discretion of the judge. Finally, punitive imprisonment expanded on a very large scale, and the law began to confine the criminal's body in order to correct and adjust the failed mechanism of his soul. Public interest, deterrence, rehabilitation, and appropriate punishment now assumed new forms from those they had acquired in their first prominence during the twelfth and thirteenth centuries.

Criminal justice history requires that past practice and theory be assessed in terms of the whole legal systems of which they form a part, as well as from the perspective of the present. The results of much recent research have substantially undercut the most severe assessments made by Enlightenment critics and by those historians who have accepted their polemic too literally. Yet public interest, deterrence, and appropriateness of punishment are still central concerns of both history and present public policy, the first because the definition of crime is a public matter, the second because it is in the public interest to reduce the incidence of crime, and the third because punishment is the most readily adjustable component of criminal justice systems. That is, its revision requires fewer changes in the entire structure of the law than does the revision of the definition of crime or the rules of criminal procedure.

On the other hand, the history of both the first and second systems of criminal justice in European history suggests another aspect of punishment and crime that is worth considering; that criminal justice is a component of larger legal systems that lacks the capacity to satisfy its critics for any considerable length of time in the ways by which contract law, for example, or other areas of civil law may very well do. Beccaria, we must remember, although he condemned all contemporary law on the same grounds that he condemned criminal law, only argued for a revision of criminal law. Criminal justice systems, characterized by a sense of urgency and public safety, may come under heavy criticism because they appear to fail to respond to that sense of urgency, and the appearance of a criminal justice system is a substantial part of its legitimacy.

In a recent study of execution rituals in fifteenth century Paris, Esther Cohen addressed the same problem that had drawn such different conclusions from Huizinga and Maes.[55] The chronicles indeed, Cohen observes, were filled with depictions of grim executions, but:

> It is only when one digs below the level of the spectacular, reaching the mundane daily routine of justice, that one discovers how small a proportion of the offenders actually ascended the gallows...[56]

But the chroniclers were not entirely wrong, "lax or unobservant":

> Like any magician's audience, they saw exactly what they were meant to see and only that; the majesty of the law in its full efficacy. What they recorded for us was not how the law worked, but how people saw it working.

Criminal justice is the most perceivable aspect of any legal order, and how people perceive it to work—whether their perceptions are engineered by public authority or individually acquired—may very well be more important to them than its actual operation. The consequences of their perception may then generate yet another system, one that also depends for its public legitimacy on perception and which may itself fail when the new law is seen to have lost its majesty.

---

[1]The best modern English translation of Beccaria's work is that of Jane Grigson in *Allesandro Manzoni, The column of Infamy Prefaced by Cesare Beccaria's Of Crimes and Punishments*, trans. Kenelm Foster, O.P. and Jane Grigson, with an Introduction by A.P. d'Entreves (London: Oxford University Press, 1964). See also Cesare Beccaria, *On Crimes and Punishments*, trans. with intro. by Henry Paolucci (Indianapolis: Bobbs-Merill, 1963). The standard account is that of M.T. Maestro, *Voltaire and Beccaria as Reformers of Criminal Law* (New York: 1942). The introductory essays by d'Entreves and Paolucci offer extensive bibliographical references. See also Bernard Schnapper, "Les Peines arbitraires du XXIIe au XVIIIe siècle (doctrines savantes et usages français)," *Tijdschrift voor Rechtsgeschiedinis/Revue d'histoire du droit* 41 (1973), 237-277, and 42 (1974), 81-112, esp. pp. 103-106. Marcello Maestro, *Cesare Beccaria and the Origins of Penal Reform* (Philadelphia: Temple University Press, 1973).

On Beccaria's (non-) reception in Rome and Naples, as well as a valuable portrait of a complex late eighteenth-century criminal jurisdiction, see Hanns Gross, *Rome in the Age of Enlightenment* (Cambridge: Cambridge University Press, 1990), Ch. 9, pp. 214-231. For south Italy, see now Vittorio Sciuti Russi, "La contrastata modernizzazione del sistema penale in Sicilia," *La Leopoldina* 11 (1990), *Le politiche criminali nel XVIII secolo* (Milan: Giuffre, 1990), 143-174. I am grateful to Professor Sciuti Russi for this reference.

I am grateful to my fellow-members of the Conference on *Punishment: Meanings, Purposes, Practices* held by the Columbia University Society of Fellows in the Humanities for their conversation and helpful comments. I am also grateful to James B. Given for his advice upon an earlier draft of this paper.

[2]Grigson trans., p. 6.

[3]Richard Andrews, "The Cunning of Imagery: Rhetoric and Ideology in Cesare Beccaria's Treatise *On Crimes and Punishments*," in Mary B. Campbell and Mark Rollins, eds., *Begetting Images: Studies in the Art and Science of Symbol Production* (New York-Bern: Peter Lang Inc., 1989), 113-132. Beccaria's attack focused upon the Roman origins of contemporary late eighteenth-century law, the antiquity (and hence contemporary unsuitability) of the laws, the intrusion of Lombard law, the allegedly purely private authority of earlier jurists, and the general character of eighteenth-century law as part of "the debris of barbarous times."

[4]Donald R. Kelley, *The Human Measure: Social Thought in the Western Legal Tradition* (Cambridge: Harvard University Press, 1990). A number of recent studies have reconsidered the fortunes of Roman Law in the period between the late fifteenth and the nineteenth centuries. Particularly important are those of Alan Watson, *Sources of Law, Legal Change and Ambiguity* (Philadelphia: University of Pennsylvania Press, 1984); Gerald Strauss, *Law, Resistance, and the State: The Opposition to Roman Law in Reformation Germany* (Princeton: Princeton University Press, 1986); James Q. Whitman, *The Legacy of Roman Law in the German Romantic Era* (Princeton: Princeton University Press, 1990).

[5]Edward Gibbon, *The Decline and Fall of the Roman Empire* (many editions), Ch. 45. See the studies of Donald Kelley, *The Foundations of Modern Historical Scholarship* (New York: Columbia University Press, 1970), and *History, Law and the Human Sciences* (London: Variorum, 1984).

[6]J.W. Bosch, "Le jugement de Goswin de Fierlant sur la magistrature en Belgique à la fin du XVIIIe siècle selon les deux manuscrits du *Premieres Idées sur la Reformation des Loix Criminelles*," in*Tijdschrift voor Rechtsgeschiedenis/Revue d'Histoire du Droit* 24 (1956), 48-60.

[7]Michel Foucault, *Discipline and Punish: The Birth of the Prison* (New York: Pantheon, 1977); Pieter Spierenburg, *The Spectacle of Suffering* (New York, Cambridge University Press,1985); Richard van Dülmen, *Theater des Schreckens: Gerichtspraxis und Strafrituale in der frühen Neuzeit* (Munich: Beck, 1985) Eng. trans.. *Theatre of Horror: Crime and Punishment in Early Modern Germany*, trans. Elizabeth Neu (Cambridge: Polity Press, 1990); Lionello Puppi, *Torment in Art: Pain, Violence and Martyrdom*, trans. Jeremy Scott (New York: Rizzoli, 1992). Of these works, Foucault's is the most dramatic, but least convincing. That of Spierenburg is the most reliable.

[8]See the studies of Stephan Kuttner and Knut Wolfgang Nörr in Robert L. Benson and Giles Constable, with Carol Lanham, eds., *Renaissance and Renewal in the Twelfth Century* (Cambridge, Massachusetts: Harvard University Press, 1982). See below, n. 19.

[9]Walter Ullmann, "Reflections on Medieval Torture," *The Juridical Review* 56 (1944), 123-137 and 136-137. Cf. Walter Ullmann, *The Medieval Idea of Law as Represented by Lucas de Penna* (London: Methuen, 1946), 142-162.

[10]Johann Huizinga *The Waning of the Middle Ages*, trans. F. Hopman (rpt. New York: Anchor, n.d.), p. 25. See also below, n. 52.

[11]Julius Goebel, Jr., *Felony and Misdemeanor: A Study in the History of Criminal Law* (rpt. Philadelphia: University of Pennsylvania Press, 1976); Ekkehard Kaufmann, *Die Erfolgshaftung, Untersuchungen über die strafrechtliche Zurechnung im Rechtsdenken des frühen Mittelalters* (Frankfurt: Vittorio Klostenhann, 1958).

[12]P.W.A. Immink, *La liberté et la peine. étude sur la transformation de la liberté et sur le developpement du droit pénal public en Occident avant le XIIe siècle*, ed., P. Sarolea (Assen: Van Gorcum, 1973).

[13]Viktor Achter, *Geburt der Strafe* (Frankfurt: 1951).

[14]Patricia O'Brien, "Crime and Punishment as an Historical Problem," *Journal of Social History* 11 (1978), 508-520. The last two of these views are discussed in the first chapter of Pieter Spierenburg, *The Spectacle of Suffering* (above, n. 7). Another recent discussion is that of Philippe Robert and René Lévy, "Histoire et question pénal," *Revue d'histoire moderne et contemporaine* 32 (1985), 481-526, with an extensive, but, for medieval Europe, incomplete, bibliography.

[15]Spierenburg, *The Spectacle of Suffering*, p. 12.

[16]The best general survey is now that of O.F. Robinson, T.D. Fergus, and W.M. Gordon, *An Introduction to European Legal History* (Abingdon: Professional Books, 1985).

[17]R.C. Van Caenegem, "The Law of Evidence in the Twelfth Century: European Perspective and Intellectual Background."

[18]Van Caenegem, "The Law of Evidence," p. 305.

[19]Stephan Kuttner, "The Revival of Jurisprudence," and Knut Wolfgang Nôrr, "Institutional Foundations of the New Jurisprudence," both in Benson and Constable, *Renaissance and Renewal* (above n, 8), 299-323 and 324-338.

[20]All references to the *Digest* and *Code* below will be internal.

[21]*Dig.* 1.1.1. The fundamental work on Roman criminal law is still that of Theodor Mommsen, *Romisches Strafrecht* (Leipzig, 1899). There is a summary in Israel Drapkin, M.D., *Crime and Punishment in the Ancient World* (Lexington-Toronto: Lexington Books, 1989), pp. 45-83. On Roman and other ancient forms of punishment, see the volume *Du chatiment dans la cité antique: Supplices corporels et peine de mort dans le monde antique*, *Collection de l'Ecole Francaise de Rome* 79 (Rome, 1984) and *La Peine*, Premiere partie, *Antiquité*, Vol. 55, t.1 of the *Recueils de la Societé Jean Bodin pour l'histoire comparative des institutions* (Brussels: De Boeck Université, 1992). The best analytical study of both ancient and modern concepts of crime and punishment is that of Mary Margaret MacKenzie, *Plato on Punishment* (Berkeley-Los Angeles: University of California Press, 1981), a work that ranges far more widely than its title suggests. More recently, see Trevor J. Saunders, *Plato's Penal Code: Tradition, Controversy and Reform in Greek Penology* (Oxford: Clarendon Press, 1991).

[22]J.A. Crook, *Law and Life of Rome, 90 B.C.—A.D. 212* (Ithaca: Cornell University Press, 1967), p.274.

[23]See the history in Edward Peters, *Torture* (New York: Blackwell, 1985), with the reservations of Richard Fraher, below, nn. 25, 35.

[24]See R.A. Markus, *Saeculum: History and Society in the Theology of St. Augustine* (Cambridge: Cambridge University Press, 1970), pp.133-153.

[25]Richard M. Fraher, "Preventing Crime in the High Middle Ages: The Medieval Lawyers' Search for Deterrence." in James Ross Sweeney and Stanley Chodrow, eds., *Popes, Teachers, and Canon Law in the Middle Ages* (Ithaca: Cornell University Press, 1989), pp. 212-233, and 214. See also Jean Gaudemet, "Le problème de la responsabilité pénale dans l'antiquité," *Studi in Honore de Enrico Betti*, Vol. II (Milan, 1962) 481-508, rpt. in Gaudemet, *L'Eglise dans l'empire romain (Ive-Ve siecles)*, Vol. III of G. Le Bras, ed., *Histoire du droit et des institutions de l'Eglise en Occident* (Paris: Sirey, 1958).

[26]Stephan Kuttner, "Ecclesia de occultis non judicat: Problemata ex doctrina poenali decretistarum et decretalistarum a Gratiano usque ad Gregorium PP. IX," *Actus Congressus Iuridicis Internationalis* (Rome, 1936), Vol. III, 225-246.

[27]William Ian Miller, *Bloodtaking and Peacemaking: Feud, Law, and Society in Saga Iceland* (Chicago: The University of Chicago Press, 1990). See the extensive literature on disputes and settlements in John Bossy, ed., *Disputes and settlements: Law and Human Relations in the West* (Cambridge: Cambridge University Press, 1983); Wendy Davies and Paul Fouracre, eds., *The Settlement of Disputes in Early Medieval Europe* (Cambridge: Cambridge University Press, 1986); Stephen D. White, "Feuding and Peace-Making in the Touraine Around the Year 1100," *Traditio* 42 (1986), 195-263; Edward Peters, "The Death of the Subdean: Ecclesiastical Order and Disorder in Eleventh-Century Francia," in Bernard S. Bachrach and David Nicholas, eds., *Law, Custom and the Social Fabric in Medieval Europe: Essays in Honor of Bryce Lyon* (Kalamazoo: Medieval Institute, 1990), 51-72.

[28]As early as the late eleventh century the applicability of Roman law as a *lex generalis* is discussed in the *Expositio* to the *Liber Papiensis*. See Giovanni Diurni, *L'Expositio ad Librum Papiensem e la scienza giuridica preirneriana* (Rome: 1976).

[29]Ernst H. Kantorowicz, "Kingship under the Impact of Scientific Jurisprudence," in Marshall Clagett, Gaines Post, and Robert L. Reynolds, eds., *Twelfth-Century Europe and the Foundations of Modern Society* (Madison: University of Wisconsin Press, 1966), 89-111 (rpt. in Ernst H. Kantorowicz, *Selected Studies* (Locust Valley, N.Y.: J.J. Augustin, 1965), 151-166); Johannes Fried, *Die Entstehung des Juristenstandes im 12. Jahrhundert* (Cologne: Bohlan, 1974); James A. Brundage, "The Medieval Advocate's Profession," *Law and History Review* 6 (1988), 439-464.

[30]For the personnel, see J.A. Clarence Smith, *Medieval Law Teachers and Writers Civilian and Canonist* (Ottawa: University of Ottawa Press, 1975).

[31]On the relationship between criminal law and theology, see Stephan Kuttner, *Kanonistische Schuldlehre von Gratian bis auf die Dekretalen Gregors IX* (Vatican City: Biblio Varicana, 1935). In English, see the discussion in Harold J. Berman, *Law and Revolution: The Formation of the Western Legal Tradition* (Cambridge, Massachusetts: Harvard University Press, 1983), 165-198. See also the discussion in Peter Landau, "Neuere Forschungen zu Quellen und Institutionen des klassischen kanonischen Rechts bis zum Liber Sextus. Ergenbnisse und Zukunftsperspektiven," *Proceedings of the Seventh International Congress of Medieval Canon Law, Monumenta Iuris Canonici*, Series C: Subsidia, Vol. 8 (1988), pp. 27-47, esp. 35.

[32]Gerald Strauss, *Law, Resistance, and the State*, p. 199.

[33]Berman, *Law and Revolution*, p. 165.

[34]For a graphic illustration of the relations between these elements in literature, see Alison Morgan, *Dante and the Medieval Other World* (Cambridge: Cambridge University Press, 1990), 118-174.

[35]See the superb discussion in Fraher, "Preventing Crime," cited above, n. 25, and Richard M. Fraher, "Conviction According to Conscience: The Medieval Jurists' Debate Concerning Judicial Discretion and the Law of Proof." *Law and History Review* 7 (1989), 23-88. These essays substantially revise the conclusions of most earlier studies of historical criminal justice. On *Infamia*, see my study, "Wounded

Names: The Medieval Doctrine of Infamy," in Edward B. King and Susan J. Ridyard, eds., *Law in Medieval Life and Thought, Sewanee Medieval Studies* 5 (1990), 43-89. The most recent general survey is the volume *La Peine, Recueils de la Societé Jean Bodin pour l'histoire comparative des institutions*, Vol. 55, partie 2, *Europe avant le XVIIIe siècle* (Brussels: De Boeck Universite, 1992). The best recent survey of the age of reform is that of Uta-Renate Blumenthal, *The Investiture Controversy: Church and Monarchy from the Ninth to the Twelfth Century* (Philadelphia: University of Pennsylvania Press, 1988).

[36]Fraher, "Preventing Crime."

[37]Richard M. Fraher, "The Theoretical Justification for the New Criminal Law of the High Middle Ages: *Rei publicae interest, ne crimina remaneant impunita," Illinois Law Review* (1984), 577-595, and Fraher, "Preventing Crime." On the persecution of heretics, see Lothar Kolmer, *Ad capiendas vulpes. Die Ketzerbekampfung in Sudfrankreich in der ersten Halfte des 13. Jahrhunderts und die Ausbildung des Inquisitionsverfahrens* (Cologne: Ludwig Rohrscheid Verlag, 1982), and Edward Peters, *Inquisition* (New York: The Free Press, 1988). On one kind of medieval punishment, prisons, see Edward Peters, "Prisons and Criminal Legal Systems in Mediterranean Antiquity and Early European History," Ch. 1 of Norval Morris and David Rothman, eds., *The Oxford History of Prisons* (New York: Oxford University Press, forthcoming).

[38]In addition to the studies of Fraher and myself cited above, see also Francesco Migliorino, *Fama e infamia: problemi della societa medievale nel pensiero giuridico nei secoli XII e XIII* (Catania: Gianota, 1985).

[39]On the genre *tractatus criminum*, see Andre Gouron, "Zu den Ursprungen des Strafrechts: die ersten Strafrechtstraktate," in Karl Kroeschell, ed., *Festchrift für Hans Thieme zu seinem 80. Geburtstag* (Sigmaringen: Jan Thorbeck, 1986), 43-57, rpt. in Gouron, *études sur la diffusion des doctrines juridiques médivales* (London: Variorum, 1987), IX.

[40]Hermann Kantorowicz, *Albertus Gandinus und das Strafrecht der Scholastik*, 2 vols. (Berlin-Leipzig: Walter de Gruyter, 1926), and the discussion in Fraher, "Conviction according to Conscience."

[41]Linda Fowler-Magerl, *Ordo iudiciorum vel ordo iudiciarius; Begriff und Litteraturgattung* (Frankfurt: Virtorio Klostermann, 1984).

[42]There is an extensive discussion in R.C. Van Caenegem, "Methods of Proof in Western Medieval Law," *Mededelingen van de Koninklijke Academie voor Wetenschappen, Letteren en Schone Kunsten van Belgie*, Klasse der Letteren, 45 (1983), 83-127, and *idem*, "The Public Prosecution of Crime in Twelfth-Century England."

[43]Van Caenegem, "Methods of Proof," 112-113.

[44]See the studies cited and discussed in Sarah R. Blanshei, "Criminal Justice in Medieval Perugia and Bologna," *Law and History Review*, I (1983), 251-275; Laura Ikins Stern, "Inquisition Procedure and Crime in Early Fifteenth-Century Florence,"

Law and History Review 8 (1990), 297-308; Samuel Kline Cohen, Jr., "Criminality and the State in Renaissance Florence, 1344-1466," *Journal of Social History* 14 (1981), 211-233; Andrea Zorzi, *L'amministrazione della giustizia penale nella Reppublica fiorentina: Aspetti e problemi* (Florence: Leo S. Olschki, 1988).

[45]The point is made in Samuel Y. Edgerton, Jr., *Pictures and Punishment: Art and Criminal Prosecution during the Florentine Renaissance* (Ithaca: Cornell University Press, 1985).

[46]See the discussion in John Langbein, *Prosecuting Crime in the Renaissance: England, Germany, France* (Cambridge, Massachusetts: Harvard University Press, 1974).

[47]See James B. Given, *Society and Homicide in Thirteenth-Century England* (Stanford: Stanford University Press, 1977); Barbara Hanawalt, *Crime and Conflict in English Communities, 1300-1348* (Cambridge, Massachusetts: Harvard University Press, 1979); Alfred Soman, "Deviance and Criminal Justice in Western Europe, 1300-1800: An Essay in Structure," *Criminal Justice History: An International Annual* 1 (1980), 1-28, and idem, "Criminal Jurisprudence in Ancien-Regime France: The Parliament of Paris in the Sixteenth and Seventeenth Centuries," in Louis A. Knafla, ed., *Crime and Criminal Justice in Europe and Canada* (Atlantic Highlands, N.J.: Humanities Press, 1985), 43-76.

[48]Bronislaw Geremek, *The Margins of Society of Late Medieval Paris*, trans. Jean Birrell (Cambridge: Cambridge University Press, 1987)..

[49]Jacques Chiffoleau, *Les Justices du Pape: Delinquance et criminalité dans la région d'Avignon au quatorzieme siecle* (Paris: Publications de la Sorbonne, 1985). Yvonne Lanhers, "Crimes et criminels au XIVe siecle," *Revue historique* 240 (1968), 325-338; Francoise Gasparry, *Proces criminel au temps du roi René (procedure criminelle au xv siecle)* (1988).

[50] Chiffoleau, *Les justices du Pape*, p. 260.

[51]See especially the work of Johannes Fried, cited above, n. 29; Françoise Autrand, *Naissance d'un grand corps de l'état. Les gens du Parlement de Paris, 1345-1454* (Paris: Université de Paris 1 Panthéon Sorbonne, 1981). On judges, see John P. Dawson, *Oracles of the Law* (Ann Arbor: University of Michigan Law School, 1968).

[52]Louis Theo Maes, "L'Humanité de la magistrature du declin du Moyen Age," *Tijdschrift voor Rechtsgeschiedenis/Revue d'Histoire du droit* 19 (1951), 158-193. This is the most thorough critique of Huizinga's position before that of Ester Cohen, cited below, n. 55.

[53]John H. Langbein, *Torture and the Law of Proof* (Chicago: University of Chicago Press, 1977).

[54]Soman, "Criminal Jurisprudence," cited above, n. 47, p. 54.

[55]Esther Cohen, "To Die a Criminal for the Public Good: The Execution Ritual in Late Medieval Paris," in Bernard S. Bachrach and David Nicholas, eds., *Law, Custom, and the Social Fabric in Medieval Europe: Essays in Honor of Bryce Lyon* (Kalamazoo: Medieval Institute, 1990), 285-304, at 299. Cf, James Ross Sweeney, "High Justice in

Fifteenth-Century Normandy: The Prosecution of Sandrin Bourel," *Journal of Medieval History* 10 (1984), 295-313.

[56]Cohen, "'To Die a Criminal'," p. 300. Cf. Esther Cohen, "Symbols of Culpability and the Universal Language of Justice: The Ritual of Public Executions in Late Medieval Europe," *History of European Ideas* 11 (1989), 407-416.

PART II

PRACTICES

THE DEATH PENALTY IN OLD REGIME FRANCE

Richard Mowery Andrews

On 3 August 1751 the Criminal Appeals Chamber of the Parlement of Paris sentenced Jean Masson to death by hanging on the Place de Grève for robbery of his employer and murder of a tavern girl at Versailles. That was the statutory penalty for intentional homicide. In the late afternoon of the 4th, and in the shadow of the gallows, he confessed to both crimes before the priest-confessor and the two judges presiding at his execution. The priest intoned the final blessing for the condemned and the ritual prayers for Masson's soul were then sung by the assembly. The executioner led Masson up the gallows ladder, tightened the noose, and thrust him into the air. The rope broke and he fell to the ground. The executioner retied the rope, manhandled Masson back up the ladder, and thrust him out again. The rope parted a second time. To complete execution of sentence, the judges ordered the executioner to strangle Masson to death on the ground with the noose. As he was doing so, the front ranks of the large crowed surged forward shouting "Pardon him! Pardon him! Have mercy!" They halted only when the encircling guard force turned about-face, closed ranks, and levelled its bayonets. The executioner and his assistants retied the rope, then hoisted and held Masson's corpse high up the gallows, to demonstrate that he had indeed been hanged "until death ensues" by judgment of the Parlement.[1]

Such accidents were rare in eighteenth century Parisian executions, but they did sometimes occur. Masson's judges had no authority to retract their sentence or to suspend its execution. The criminal law dictated that they carry through the sentence of their court.[2] In the words of François Serpillon, one of the most authoritative of eighteenth century jurists:

> It is not from cruelty that judges have the criminal who has evaded the instrument of execution brought back to that instrument; justice has no desire to sate itself on his blood; it proportions the scale of punishments to the enormity of crimes only to inspire horror of crimes, and that is why executions are performed in public and on days when there will be a maximum of spectators; it is necessary, for the preservation of social order, that death sentences be executed no matter what accident occurs. If judges subscribed to the beliefs of the people, who are constantly ready to perceive the marvellous and supernatural and usually describe as miracles events that are merely extraordinary, then one would often find marvellous reasons to spare the guilty. That would accord impunity to crimes... Besides, judges do not have authority to pardon; their power over a defendant is consummated when they have judged him, and they cannot revoke their judgments. They are obliged to ensure that those judgments are executed.[3]

The Parlement of Paris followed the same logic in the case of Louis Martin. In December, 1737, the rural constabulary of Orléans arrested and jailed him on charges of theft. He hanged himself in his cell while awaiting trial by the presidial court of Orléans. Suicide, a mortal sin, was also a capital offense in law. The Provost of Constabulary, on his own initiative, cancelled the theft charge against Martin and had him buried. The presidial judges vigorously protested the illegality of the Provost's action. They asserted, in an appeal to the Parlement, that the jail and Martin's corpse were under the jurisdiction of their court, not the Provost, and that Martin's apparent suicide was a new crime that required trial and judgment. The cadaver should have been preserved until the conclusion of that trial. The Parlement ruled in favor of the presidial, and ordered it to try the "memory" of Louis Martin on the charge of suicide, with a court-appointed trustee, or "curateur," standing for him during the trial:

> It is no longer a question of punishing the prisoner; it is the cadaver and the memory of the prisoner—over which the first Judge [the Provost] had no authority—that must be stigmatized; this is a fresh crime that cannot be regarded as a sequel to the first, alleged crimes, because liability for those crimes was annulled by death... The principle of law is clear in this case; conviction of the accused [on the charge of suicide] is equivalent to a death sentence.[4]

The law prescribed that if Martin were found guilty of suicide, either his corpse or a pictorial effigy of him was to be dragged face-down on a frame through the streets of Orléans, hanged from the gallows on a main public square, and then thrown on the town refuse dump.[5]

What were the sources and incidence of that seeming judicial implacability? How was it mitigated, even redeemed, in Old Regime practice? By Old Regime, I mean the period from 1670, year of the last great royal ordinance on criminal procedure, to late 1789 and the beginnings of systemic changes in criminal justice.

The history of incrimination in France has not been written. There is a common misconception that most of traditional French criminal law was slowly created by independent case rulings of Parlements, the original thirteen superior courts of France, rulings dually informed by Roman law and canon law and then explicated by jurists. That was so during the Middle Ages and into the sixteenth-century. But during about two hundred years, from the 1530s to the 1730s, the kings and chancellors of France developed a comprehensive statutory criminal law: definitions and penalties for serious and capital offenses; mandatory codes for trial procedure; the jurisdictional powers of various royal and seigneurial courts; a magistracy invested and regulated by the monarchy . Royal statutes defined and penalized most forms of treason, rebellion and sedition, slander and libel, private violence, fraud, theft and depredation on properties, offenses to religion, public morals, marriage and the family. Their prehension expressed the ideology of monarchical sovereignty, as well as the enlarged conception of social order and discipline that issued from the seventeenth-century Counter-Reformation. The statutory legacy was very powerful: most crimes defined in the Revolutionary Penal Code of 1791 had been defined originally by royal legislation during 1530 - 1730, although the authors of the Penal Code concealed their inheritance.

Law courts, both superior and subaltern, were bound to apply, interpret or, when necessary, reason from analogy with royal statutes. Parlements and other superior appeals courts were obliged to enforce that adherence in lower courts, and chancellors to enforce it over Parlements. Royal law was binding on jurisdictions in every province of the realm unless exceptions were specified (which was rarely done from the mid-sixteenth century to the Revolution.) It encompassed all subjects of the Crown—clerics and laymen, Peers of the Realm and plebeians. It was exclusive of all other laws: "The judgments rendered and contracts or obligations agreed in foreign realms and sovereignties, for whatever cause, will have no authority or execution in France."[6] Its language was exclusively French: "... we wish that all decrees and all procedures, whether of sovereign or subaltern and inferior courts, whether in registers, inquests, contracts, commissions, sentences, testaments and all other actions and writs of justice, be henceforth pronounced, registered and delivered to all parties involved in the maternal French language, and in no other."[7] Royal criminal law was one of the most important instruments for the political and social unification of France. It laid foundations for a "nation."

Old Regime legal punishment combined heritages of Roman law and Church doctrine with monarchical ideology and pragmatic goals. It was at once religious and secular in nature, like the French State, as well as retributive and deterrent in purpose.

Royal justice punished malefactors in the names and on behalf of their victims, and virtually all penal sentences included monetary reparations to victims: those levies against the convicted were for "the actual harm caused the victim by the crime," at least symbolically.[8] There was also public monetary reparation, paid to the king and court, as both indemnity for trial costs and a form of punishment. But royal justice punished foremost in the nomenclature of a sovereign moral and public order: a crime was a wound or "lesion" of that order and not only of the victim's being, a wound remediable only by punishment. "The issue is always the same: public order has been disrupted, and the general interest requires punishment [of the offender] for that disruption and the reestablishment of order."[9] Punishments—whether defaming, corporal, or capital—were themselves essential retribution, at once action, experience and symbol. This was expressed most dramatically in the public *amende honorable in figuris* that accompanied most death sentences for violent capital offenses. It was a secular paraphrase of the sacraments of confession and penitence. Bareheaded, barefooted, clothed only in the long woolen shirt of the condemned, wearing a placard around his or her neck that proclaimed the crime, and carrying a large burning candle, the condemned person was led in broad daylight to the main portal of a church. There, he was obliged to kneel, loudly relate his crime and its victims, and then beg forgiveness of "God, the King, and Justice."[10] Retribution of those three entities and the order that they encompassed was, ideologically, generic to virtually all punishments in criminal law.

Penal doctrine was consequentialist. Punishments alone gave force to the law and its commands; without them, there could be no empire of the law over crimes, criminals and the generality of civil society. As stated by the eighteenth century criminal jurist, Muyart de Vouglans:

> ...however intrinsically wise the Law may be, it would soon become useless to society, for whose welfare it has been established, if he who made the law did not have the power to command respect for its authority by the punishment of those who wish to defy that authority. Therefore, the power to inflict penalties is the most essential element of Legislation, because that power alone can give strength to the Law & assure, by

> such means, peace and tranquillity within a State. That power, known as the power of Life and Death,because it encompasses the lives of men, can only belong to the supreme authority that Divine Providence confers on Sovereigns. Sovereigns cannot always exercize that power themselves, because of the great extent of their States, and are obliged to confide its exercize to Judges whom they appoint, while reservingfor themselves only the right of pardon as befits Royal Majesty.[11]

This echoed the preamble to the 1670 Criminal Ordinance of Louis XIV:

> The great benefits that our subjects have received from the care that we have devoted to reforming civil procedure by our Ordinances of April, 1667 and August, 1669 have persuaded us to give similar attention to criminal procedure, which is all the more important because not only does it conserve individuals in the peaceful enjoyment of their properties, as with civil justice, but it also secures public order, and restrains by the fear of punishments those who are not restrained by their duty.[12]

The hierarchy in punishments, from the most benign to the most devastating, also served to proclaim for the public the official moral hierarchy of crimes and, by inversion of those crimes, the hierarchy of officially cherished and protected values. Acquittal for the innocent, attenuation of penalty for those with mitigating circumstances, royal pardon or commutation of penalty for some of the guilty, even justice itself had meaning only in their dialectical relations to punishment.

Kings, jurists and magistrates believed that "moral order" and "public order" did not and could not exist without the criminal law—despite the authority wielded by the patriarchal family, the Church, schools and "collèges," village and town councils, craft and commercial guilds, seigneurial landlords, and the multiplicity of other institutions in French society, despite the fact that most of those entities had powers of chastisement over their members—censures, fines, suspensions, ostracisms, rituals of shaming. In the themistocratic mind, those institutions contributed to public order but remained dependents of royal criminal law. That law encompassed and subsumed all of them within its simultaneously protective and punitive jurisdiction. The jurisdiction was a monopoly: "victims of crime are never allowed to take justice into their own hands, except in cases of legitimate self-defense against aggression."[13]

The imperative of punishment derived from a venerable construction of human nature, one stated by the magistrate and jurist Daniel Jousse:

> If men were not disturbed by passions and by delusions, shame alone would be a force sufficient to prevent them from unjust

> actions; but those passions are so strong in some persons, and dominate them so completely, that it is absolutely necessary to employ means more rigorous than shame, such as the fear of chastisements, in order to prevent them from commiting crimes that are urged by their passions. All crimes that supervene in society have their source in the frivolity and inconstancy of the human mind, in lack of education, in corrupted desire, and even in contempt for Religion and the Laws, from which are born greed, idleness, debauchery, vengefulness, ambition and all the rest of life's disorders; & those passions often have a dominion so powerful over certain persons that even the fear of chastisements and torments is not sufficient to restrain them.[14]

And, with greater pessimism and hyperbole, by Guillaume Le Trosne:

> Insatiable appetite for gain, cruel vengeance, implacable hatred, murderous envy, jealous love, frantic debauchery: all passions, in a thousand different forms, combine against public security; they would burst forth and make of society a dreadful theatre of treachery, horror and carnage if justice did not present a salutary bulwark against such a torrent of crimes, if the gleaming sword in its hand was not always raised to threaten, strike and punish the guilty. It is thus principally by the exercise of criminal justice that civil order exists and is preserved.[15]

According to this vision, all persons were subject, at least momentarily, to malicious or anarchic passions, and therefore had capacity for sin and crime. Most were restrained from acting on those passions by internalized disciplines other than fear of punishment; many others were not so restrained. Punishment, as dissuasive threat, was addressed explicitly to the latter, to the actually criminal and imminently criminal. But as warning, its didactic reverberations were wider and more subtle: it was suspended over every honest bourgeois momentarily tempted by fraud, over every dutiful official or clerk tempted by peculation, over every obedient journeyman or domestic servant tempted by pilferage, over every needy plebeian tempted to riot, over every ordinary man and woman seized by lust or jealousy, over every respectable subject inclined to avenge personal insults by direct violence. its prescriptive audience was universal.

For threat and warning to be credible, thus dissuasive, punishment of the guilty had to occur publicly—especially in a civilization without media of mass communication, one intensely local where popular cognition was visual and aural. Whenever possible, legal punishments were inflicted publicly in the locality where the crime had been commited, for immediate deterrent example, for the shaming and correction of the malefactor within his or her community, and to give consolation to victims. The State incurred considerable expense to accomplish punishment *in situ:* for example, a person convicted of theft at Limoges was most commonly transported under guard to Paris for final judgement on appeal by the Parlement; if the Parlement upheld the conviction and decreed even a sentence as banal as whipping and exposure in the iron collar, the convict was transported back to Limoges for execution of that sentence.

Parades of the infamous, theatres of defamation: spectacles of punishment punctuated the quotidian life of every eighteenth century French city. Inner Paris on both banks of the River was traversed by processions of the chastised, most of whom wore placards with their names and crimes in bold letters. They wound, in fixed trajectories, from the Châtelet, Parlement and other law courts, through densely populated and commercial quarters to the sites of punishment: the Place de Grève, the Portes Saint-Martin and Saint-Denis; the "Croix du Trahoir" and Pilory in the "Halles;" the squares of the Palais-Royal, Saint-Michel, Maubert, the Montagne Sainte-Geneviève, and the "carrefour de Buci." Those spectacles were equally intrinsic to criminal justice and to the public life of the metropolis. Brandings, whippings, "amendes honorables," exposure in the iron collar or pilory, convoys to the prisons of the Salpetrière and Bicêtre, chain-gangs on their way to the galleys at Marseille or the hard labor penitentiary at Brest, the corteges of executions, all alternated, competed for attention and space, and often intermingled with a multiplicity of other public ceremonial events, both religious and secular.[16] There was an average of approximately six hundred public chastisements or displays of punishment each year in Paris between 1735 and 1789.[17] Close to one-half involved more than one malefactor. That meant one person punished for about every 600 to 700 inhabitants of the metropolis. Only those who lived perpetually indoors could avoid witnessing legal punishments.

Each punitive event was invested with spiritual value. Old Regime legal punishment was grounded in a Roman Catholic conception of humankind, in which conscience and rationality were in permanent struggle with impulses to sin and crimes. Conscience and rationality were immanent capacities, but they had to be nurtured, educated and reinforced for they were continually besieged by destructive passions. Moral personality was malleable during an entire lifetime. No one was predestined to either salvation or damnation. By faith, contrition, the agency of the sacraments, and atonement even the worst of evil-doers could attain grace and salvation—even in the very last period of life, on the gallows or the breaking-cross. Legal punishment—like catechism, the mass, and practice of the sacraments—was a pedagogy in conscience, for those who suffered punishment and those who witnessed their suffering. A crime punished was the simulacrum of a sin expiated. The punitive intervention of the law occured when all other normative agencies had failed to prevent the delictual action. That law was the final temporal guardian of morality. Its magistrates—professional, dynastic and proprietary of their offices—regarded themselves as ethical counterparts to the clergy, in the secular domain. They had the ethos of "juristic theology," described by Edward Peters.[18] It exalted them both socially and morally. Nicolas Delamare wrote of the magistrates of the Châtelet, the principal tribunal of Paris and its region:

> The dignity of this Tribunal, premier of all the ordinary courts of the Realm, and the eminent qualities of its Magistrates have always attracted candidates of distinguished merit to form its Council... One may justly say of this Company that it is one of the most savant among the entire judiciary of France and a veritable Seminary of Magistrates.[19]

Jean Domat insisted that the virtuousness of the judge needed to be superior to that required of all other public servants, because of the "infinite consequences" of his actions:

> They have need of a rectitude so pure, so delicate, and so complete that it is far above that required for the good exercise of all other offices. This is to say that they must have the moral strength and courage necessary for their function, fear of God, knowledge and love of truth, and an aversion to greed that amounts to hatred... these qualities consist principally in a spiritual disposition, and only secondarily in intellectual disposition.[20]

Judgments and punishments were occasions and sites for interventions of priests with malefactors. Priests were on permanent duty inside jails, prisons, the galleys, and the hard labor penitentiaries of Old Regime France. They had literally captive audiences for the sacraments and for sermons during obligatory mass. They ministered to those who were condemned to death from the beginning to the end of the executionary ritual. Just as lesser defaming and afflictive punishments were always penitential occasions, the death sentence was always a salvational opportunity for the condemned. Should he or she believe and repent, Divine Grace could, in the words of Jean Domat, "reach into the midst of his suffering, as happened with the thief crucified with Jesus who in the final moment of his life made of his torment a passage to Heaven."[21]

Jurists and magistrates gave correction by punishment (short of the death penalty) a double meaning. The first was instruction by aversion: "this shameful, dolorous or privational experience is the consequence of your evil intention and action; you will endure a more intense version of this experience if you commit another such action." The second was penitential instruction aimed to persuade the guilty that their crimes were wrong and to induce a change in ethical attitude. The recurrent sight of punishments was expected to produce similar effects on audiences, via empathetic identification with the punished.[22] Exemplary punishment was expected to compensate for chronic weaknesses: in human nature; in the disciplining powers of religion, family, corporation and profession; in policing. Jurists and magistrates could insist that such punishment had didactic effets on audiences, precisely because the actual effects could never be measured. They did so vehemently, despite constant increases in the volume of serious crimes and increases in the number of recidivists convicted during the second half of the century—and at rates higher than the growth of population in the vast jurisdiction of the Parlement of Paris. From mid-century onward, Paris and its tribunals were increasingly populated by the migrant poor—transient, unemployed for long periods, motile and socially anonymous. They were described in bitter and fearful language by Nicolas Des Essarts:

> It is certain that the provinces depopulate themselves every day in order to swell the population of the Capital, and that it is almost always the dregs of the provinces that abandon them; the immense abyss of the Capital is the repair for the vices of the provinces. Who are the instruments of these public calamities [riots and criminality]? They are always persons whose names and residences are unknown, individuals who seem foreign to the very city that provides their subsistence; creatures who live only for the moment and who disappear with the same ease with which they appear; men who belong to nothing, who have no property, and who flee with the speed of lightening to avoid judicial pursuit... The majority of laborers, hod-carriers, messengers and porters exist in a kind of anarchy and dangerous license in the midst of a civilized Capital... Bound by no ties to the City, their emigration is as rapid as it is obscure.[23]

Such subjects and others convicted of major crimes had obviously not been deterred by spectacles of punishment, for they had all witnessed such spectacles. Their persons, however, were transformed into a resource for the law, for they were made into examples to dissuade other, anonymous persons. Social good was thereby produced by the law from social evil. Exemplary punishment was a tenacious practice because it was both a strategy of desperation and an incomparable display of authority.

Legal punishment brought into harmonious union the two supreme and interdependent moral systems of Old Regime civilization: the monarchical State and its magistracy; Catholic dogma and its Church. In virtually every public chastisement or display, the symbolic union of the judicious paternal state and the redeeming Church was produced. This was so whether the penalty was several hours in the stocks at the "Halles" for small-time commercial fraud (a petty crime and venal sin) or execution at the "Place de Grève" for premeditated murder (a statutory capital offense and mortal sin.) Legal punishments celebrated the virtuous by parading and chastising the vicious. The parading of vices—the offenses declaimed by court criers, descibed by placards around the necks of criminals, advertised on posters and handbills—belonged to the same moral pedagogy as the ceremonies and literature that exalted the lives of saints. So long as the highest purpose of life was preparation for salvation, which required atonement for sins, the criminal law offered a good, a spiritual resource, to the guilty who suffered appropriate punishment. That resource was the crafted opportunity for penance, purgation and moral change through the experience of punishment, even when the punishments had social or physical finalities. The offer—administered conjointly by magistrates and priests—mitigated, at least in principle, the severity of hard penalties, whether or not the criminal inwardly accepted the offer and whether or not correction or deterence ensued from the penal action.

The death penalty was, paradoxically, the supreme expression of these legal and spiritual values. It was comparatively rare in both law and enactment. During the eighteenth century, within the *corpus* of Royal statutory law and jurisprudence, there were only about forty mandatory death offenses; there were more than seventy other crimes punishable by death, but only according to the particulars of the case and the defendent. The most important restraint on the death sanction, and other severe penalties, was intentionality. A crime was not simply an action that was prohibited and penalized by a law. It was also the malicious disposition—knowledge of wrong and intent to harm—that preceded and produced the action. Crime was intention and action (including action attempted, but not accomplished); both elements were required for a crime to exist and for punishment to ensue. Malicious intent - "dol" in French, from the Latin "dolus"—without any prohibited enactment or attempt was sinful, but not criminal. An illegal action performed ignorantly, without intent to harm, or with justifiable motive was not a crime, even if it caused major injury.[24] This conception of criminal intent derived from the medieval Christian theory of moral personality. The capacity for "dol" was an expression of free will. Human beings were divinely endowed with the capacity to discern and to choose between good and evil. At ages of maturity they were responsible for using that endowment. The 1543 Declaration on Faith and Edict of Francis I gave that principle legal force: "One must believe that man has free will, by which he can do either good or evil, and also by which, even though he be in mortal sin, he can rise up to grace with God's help."[25] But the capacity and attendant responsibility for rational choice were not considered absolute, for they were vulnerable to other forces: maladies, deficiencies of reason; momentarily strong passions; errors of judgment; accidents. Those forces belonged to the "fallenness" and impefectibility of humankind.

Every criminal trial was an attempt to resolve two basic questions through one investigation: (1) did the defendent perform the incriminated action; (2) did he do so knowingly and deliberately (or "wickedly" in the language of guilty verdicts), ignorantly or accidentally, or intentionally but under either extreme provocation or momentarily passionate compulsion, or with justifiable motive? Ascertaining intent had three main effects on criminal trial and judgment: it individuated each defendant; it determined his penal liability or immunity (as with children and the insane); it influenced the assessment of his culpability, and the selection of punishment.

The various forms of the death penalty were at the summit of a graduated scale of some twenty-five distinct penalties; incarcerations for terms of three, five, or nine years in the "Hôpital-Général," the galleys at Marseilles, or (after 1750) the hard labor compounds at Brest, Toulon and Rochefort occupied the broad middle range in that scale.[26] The salient characteristic among those twenty-five penalties was shaming, not corporal punishment. Most crimes and offenders were subject to discretionary penalties; this usually meant one main penalty selected by judges from a range of three or four that were applicable to the case.

Subsequent to the Procedural Ordinance of 1670, the surpassing majority of penal sentences rendered by lower courts were automatically appealed for final judgment by the Parlement, or superior court of the jurisdiction. Judgment in lower courts had to be by a minimum of three judges. Appellate judgments by Parlements had to be by a minimum of seven, which was also the number required in all cases not subject to appeal. Ten judges formed the bench for every case judged in the criminal appeals chamber of the Parlement of Paris. That is only two less than a modern American criminal jury. The basic rule for judgement was set forth in Title XXV, article 12 of the 1670 Ordinance:

> Judgments will be according to the most benign opinion stated if the most severe opinion stated does not prevail by a majority of one voice in cases subject to appeal, or if it does not prevail

> by a majority of two voices with cases judged on appeal or in last resort.[27]

This meant that when a defendent was judged by a lower court, whose verdict was subject to appeal, for the most severe sentence opined to prevail—for example, conviction and penalty instead of acquittal, incarceration for three years instead of banishment for five or nine, death instead of incarceration for life or for nine years—that opinion had to be voted by a majority of one in a panel of judges. Otherwise, the most benign verdict or penalty opined among them would prevail automatically. When judgment was final, for the most severe sentence opined to prevail that sentence had to be voted by a majority of two—five of seven, six of eight, or seven of ten judges. Otherwise, the most benign sentence opined among them automatically became the judgment. This rule made severe sentences—and especially the death sentence—statistically difficult to obtain on an appeals bench, and rare in practice. Roger Blumberg, of the Columbia University Heyman Center for the Humanities, has mathematically calculated the probabilities of severe, moderate and benign outcomes within this system of final decision by seven judges, among a range of four penalties in a given case: the probability for severe outcome was 4% to 11%, for moderate outcome (the median two penalties of four) 23% to 37% for each, for most benign outcome 33% to 35%. The system of final or appellate judgment was biased to moderation and leniency.

During the fifteen years 1735-1749 inclusive, the Parlement of Paris judged more than five thousand criminal defendants on appeal, some 90% of whom had been convicted by lower courts—within a jurisdiction that encompassed almost one-third of the geographic realm and a population of some eight millions, which was roughly the population of England and Wales at mid-century. The Parlement rendered 413 death sentences during those fifteen years; 9% of its total judgments; an average of 28 death sentences a year for the entire jurisdiction.[28] The primacy of violence: 195 of the 413 death sentences were for crimes of lethal personal violence, attempted or accomplished (premeditated murder, intentional murder, homicide, abortion or infanticide, and duelling); another 38 for injurious assaults, rape, poisoning, and suicide; another 49 for murderous or violent thefts and arson. Thus, 68% of death sentences were reserved for those who wantonly killed, maimed, or robbed assaultively or with weapons. Only 31% of death sentences were for thefts or larceny without violence: half of those were burglaries by breaking and entering, an implicitly violent and life-endangering crime; a further one-third were thefts from households by servants and employees, a form of personal treason for which the 1724 Royal Declaration on Theft commanded the death penalty.[29] Yet 101, or almost one-fourth, of those death sentences were remitted or commuted by

Royal letters of *grâce* that were ratified by the Parlement.[30] Three-fourths of pardons were for those convicted of intentional (but not premeditative) murder, homicide, and injurious violence (usually in the course of brawls). None of the remissions and only 22 of the commutations, were for thefts. Old Regime justice executed primarily for violence, just as it reserved mercy principally for those guilty of violence—when they could establish that they had acted without evil and premeditative intent, thus accidentally, in self-defense, under intense provocation, or in transient rage. Only 312 persons actually suffered capital execution by judgment of the Parlement of Paris during 1735-1749.

Hanging was the most common method of execution in eighteenth-century France. The technique was primitive; it involved a rough physical encounter between the executioner, his assistants and the victim. There was no scaffold with a trap-door, a dead-fall and a broken neck for the hanged. There was only a wooden gallows post, twelve to fifteen feet high, with a single beam at the top, and a ladder that the executioner climbed with his victim.

Execution on the wheel, or breaking, was the most prolonged and agonizing of capital punishments. It was inflicted in two stages: breaking and exposure. A high platform was erected, on which a large wooden Saint-Andrews Cross was placed. The victim was tied horizontally to the Cross. The executioner struck two blows to each limb and two or three to the kidneys or stomach with a long, heavy iron rod. The shattered body was then removed from the Cross and tied horizontally, arms and legs bent back, to a carriage wheel that was fixed on a ten-foot pole. The pole was raised and set in a pavement hole. The victim remained on the wheel until he expired or, in the unvarying formula of the sentence, "his face turned to the Heavens, to remain there so long as it shall please God to conserve his life." Women were never broken. Executions by the full duration of breaking and exposure were very rare in eighteenth-century Paris. The Parlement customarily issued secret instructions, or *retenta*, for the executioner to strangle the victim rapidly with a leather garrot, that was attached to the cross and wheel, after striking a few blows with the rod or after a specified time on the wheel. *Retenta* were issued for a spiritual reason: the pain of breaking and the wheel was intense, and easily provoked blasphemous curses that sabotaged the ministrations of the priest. Every execution both extinguished a physical life and gave a salvational opportunity to a soul. Those who died blaspheming were doomed.

Burning was at an eight foot stake, around which kindling and wood were piled in a pyramid, with a hollow space near the stake and a passage for the executioner; only the victim's head protruded from the pile. Virtually all burnings were also executed with *retenta*, for the same reason as with breakings. Just before the fire was started, the executioner either garroted the victim at the stake, inside the woodpile and beyond sight of the crowd, or thrust the pointed wood hook into his heart.

Decapitation was the most rare of executionary methods. It was reserved for nobles and done with a heavy sword.

Old Regime magistrates had some discretion in selecting the form and site of execution. But each time they pronounced the death sentence against a malefactor who did not receive the King's pardon, they ordered the enactment of a ritual that was both inexorable and immutable. a ritual all of whose elements were fixed by tradition.[31]

The Place de Grève was the principal site of the Parisian execution. This small trapezoidal place was a central iconographic site—directly before the "Hôtel de Ville," or municipal hall, closely equidistant from Nôtre-Dame Cathedral, the "Palais de Justice" and the Parlement of Paris, and the criminal court of the Grand Châtelet near the "Halles." Adjacent to one of the most important River ports, the "Grève was at the heart of the most densely inhabited and trafficked zone of Paris.

Early in the morning of execution day, the two officiating judges announced sentence to the condemned person. He was led from his cell in the Conciergerie or Châtelet either directly to the prison chapel, to receive the sacrament of confession, or to the torture room for the "question préalable"—or interrogation under duress of water or leg braces to learn his accomplices in crime. This interrogation immediately preliminary to execution was frequently decreed when evidence suggested accomplices and the condemned had not revealed them during trial. Then he was taken to the chapel for confession. After confessing him, the officiating priest sang twice the *Tantum ergo sacrementum* and gave benediction; he was not given the sacraments of communion or extreme unction. The entourage then proceeded to the gate of the prison, where trumpeters and drummers played a *chamade*—the drumroll used in the Royal Army to announce that a besieged garrison was preparing to surrender. The court crier loudly read the sentence at the gate, and the placard on which the name and crime of the condemned were inscribed was suspended from his shoulders.

If the *amende honorable* had been decreed, he was escorted on foot through the streets to the portals of a main Church (usually Nôtre-Dame) to perform that penance. Afterwards, he mounted the executioner's one horse open cart and sat on a rough bench, holding a small crucifix, facing backward with the priest at his side holding a large crucifix. The strange convoy—an emblazoned black carriage for magistrates and clerks, following a shambling cart, all ringed by mounted guardsmen, wound its way to the Grève, along streets thronged with crowds. On the way, the priest continually exhorted the condemned to confess his crime at the site of execution, reveal accomplices, and to die in submission, contrition, and supplication of Divine grace. The priest would continue that exhortation to the final moments of execution. At the Grève, judges and clerks sat at a table near the main portal of the Hotel-de-Ville, close to the gallows, the cross and wheel or the stake. The guard formed a circle, facing inward. Beyond was the crowd. The sentence was read again to the audience.

There now began a series of protracted transactions. Magistrates summoned the condemned to fully recount his crime and reveal his accomplices, to make what was was known as the death testament. If he refused, the priest intervened with spiritual threats. Magisterial and ecclesiastical pressure converged to elict final revelations from him, virtually in public. Very often, the spiritual pressure was effective. Men and women who had denied guilt during trial and the preliminary question confessed and revealed accomplices in death testaments. They were faced with death and Pascal's Wager. Clerks loyally recorded the death testament. Always for a second time, and often for a third, judges summoned him to further avowals. There was no economy of time. Death testaments often went on for hours, with an initial statement being followed by longer ones. The transaction was symbiotic: the condemned could prolong his life, betray disloyal comrades or enemies, divert attention from true accomplices, cunningly subvert judicial authority by giving false or contradictory information, or, if he chose truth, purge his conscience in the shadow of the gallows; when the testament was a true confession and denunciation of accomplices, the state got public validation of its sentence and a propaganda of justice, along with vital evidence for further prosecutions; the Church could display its spiritual power over the condemned. Testaments had probative force; if the condemned denounced accomplices in Paris, the ritual was suspended, frozen in place at the Grève, while police searched them out and, if possible, brought them for confrontation with the condemned and questioning by the judges. Finally, the text of each testament was read back to the condemned person and he was invited to sign in authentication. It was countersigned by the judges and clerk. When this transaction was completed, the condemned was conveyed in the cart, along with the priest, a short distance to the gallows or cross. Only his wrists were bound and with rope; it was not even customary for them to be tied behind his back. The priest led in the following prayer:

> Lord, You who have left us a memorial to your miraculous Passion, in the form of the sacrament, cause us, we beg, so to venerate the sacred mystery of your Body and Blood that we will straightway feel the fruit of your redemption in us, O Lord who rules and lives forever.

If death was by hanging, two ropes were sling-tied over the gallows beam and their nooses fixed around the condemned person's neck while he remained in the cart, held by the executioner's assistants. A third, smaller noose—the *jet*—was placed. The executioner used it to tug him up the ladder and to jerk him into the air. The executioner mounted the ladder to the top, drawing the ropes taut as the condemned followed him, guided backward by the assistants. The priest climbed to a position just below the condemned, holding the crucifix high before his eyes.

The spirituality of the execution how reached its culmination. The priest gave final blessing and began chanting the *Salve Regina* . His song of mercy was joined in rippling, mounting waves of voices by the entire population of the ritual at the Grève—judges, clerks, guards, crowd, executioner and condemned:

> Hail, O Queen, Mother of Mercy; our life, our sweetness, and our hope, hail
> To Thee we cry, poor banished children of Eve
> To Thee we send up our sighs groaning and weeping in this valley of tears.
> Hasten therefore, our Advocate and turn your merciful eyes toward us
> And show us Jesus, the blessed fruit of your womb after this exile
> O merciful, O pious, O sweet Virgin Mary.

This was meant to be more than a prayer for someone about to die. For the entire assemblage, it was communion, around his person, in praying for redemption from suffering and sin. During the last verse of the *Salve Regina*, the executioner yanked the condemned into the air or, in breaking, struck the first blows with the rod. No profane time was to elapse between the ending of that communal prayer and the onset of dying. The priest continued to lead in prayer, directly below or beside the condemned through and beyond his agony:

> O Lord, mercifully hear the prayers of your people,
> So that we who are justly afflicted for our sins,
> Will be freed for the glory of your Name, by the
> Lord Jesus Christ.

This essentially Marian liturgy was a heritage of the Counter-Reformation. It predicated a community, an entire realm, of sinners—and the redemptive power of Christ through the intercession of the Virgin. The victim of execution—sinner *in extremis*—symbolized the power of that intercession and redemption.

Executions, and especially breakings, often lasted through the night. In polite language, this was "la nuit des derniers aveux" or "la longue station avant la mort;" in popular language, it was to "faire la nuit blanche." They were accomplished in the spectral illumination of torch-light and phosphorescent reflections from the River, or in the penumbral mists of dawn. They were particularly frequent in December and January, because of the judicial calendar. That was the period of the winter solstice, of shortest days and longest nights, of skies bleak and glacial in the Ile-de-France. Nature collaborated with State and Church, for in popular experience that was the season of deprivations, suffering and fear.

The sovereignty enacted on the Grève was theocratic, the fusion in power of State and Church. Catholicism was omnipresent in the execution. According to Church doctrine, the condemned was not killed; he was changed, from matter to spirit. Liturgical in language and action, impervious to time and weather, the event was meant to transcend all secular experience. The State manifested on the Grève and the other executionary sites of France was not an absolute, militaristic monarchy. It was sacral Catholic kingship—a rule endowed by the Divinity and grounded in the coronation oath taken by every French monarch from Louis XI in 1462 to Louis XVI in 1774:

> To this Christian people subject to me, and to the end that the entire Christian people of God's Church shall preserve for all time true peace according to the desire of all, I promise in the name of Jesus Christ:
>
> To forbid all conditions and ranks of persons to commit any and all crimes and iniquities. To instruct all judges to use equity and mercy, to the end that a clement and merciful God will grand me and you His Mercy. I shall make every effort, and in good faith, to eliminate from my land and from any jurisdiction subject to me all persons denominated 'heretics' by the Church. All these things said above I solemnly swear.[32]

The execution was also a theatre of mysteries. No one could predict the behavior of the condemned, perhaps not even himself. No one could know what would happen at its consummation in dying and the passage of a soul, for no living being can know death and its aftermath. The priest dramatized the mysteries, the Christian enigma of death and offered the only sureties—the possibility of salvation for the repentant malefactor, and the certainly of damnation for the unrepentant. Mystery: the long ritual contained durational openings for subversive or heroic defiance by the condemned, for multiple forms of public *agon* against the authority of magistrates and priests, against the imminence of death. That possibility, not only fascination with dying or sadistic curiosity, also magnetized crowds. Eighteenth-century plebeians lived in the omnipresence of death—by sickness, accidents, and violence. They were connaisseurs of stamina, courage, strength, and humor at deadly moments. For many of them, executions could also be celebrations of life-force and lessons in the art of dying.[33]

Agonistic behavior by condemned persons was increasingly frequent during the second half of the century, especially after 1770: defiant refusals to make death testaments; insults shouted at magistrates and the executioner; self-justifying appeals to the crowd; stoic endurance and mocking disdain of suffering on the cross and wheel; and, most seriously, loud, dramatic spurning of the priest's exhortations and prayers. On the Grève, royal and ecclesiastical authority had little actual power over the condemned. He was going to die, only spiritual threats could restrain him from agonistic behavior, but penitential behavior could not be enforced on the unrepentant, the unbelieving, or the enraged. Here was the great paradox of the Old Regime execution: the actual power of State and Church over the condemned—power as measured by capacity to determine behavior—was at a nadir inside the ritual of execution. The victim had an extraordinary, public freedom. He could stage his own death. That fact figured prominently in late Old Regime critiques of the death penalty and its execution. Behind the humanitarian arguments of reformist authors, there were anxious concerns about state authority and efficacy, about order in and through legal punishments. They were expressed pithily by François Vermeil, barrister of the Parlement of Paris: "Whoever does not fear death is above the law."[34] When impenitent defiance of death was acted out at the Grève, before a large popular audience, the authority of the law was compromised.

We are far removed from the spirituality of the Old Regime execution—from its faith in redemption, respect for dying, and investment of free will in the condemned. So too were the legislators of the Revolution who authored a new criminal justice, death penalty and capital execution in 1790-1792. Our modernity in the matter of judicial death dates essentially from them. They were utter secularists who followed the intellectual lead of Beccaria and Voltaire. They freed definitions of crime from conceptions of sin and human imperfectibility, invented the citizen (a rational and voluntarist being), then postulated a near-absolute personal responsibility for criminal action.[35] They aimed systematically to repress crime and the criminal.

The 1791 Penal Code replaced discretionary sentencing and the individuation of defendants with fixed statutory penalties—which were generally more severe than the penology of the Old Regime. Pardon was abolished. Most modern commentators have emphasized the predominantly carceral nature of the new penology.[36] The Penal Code was indeed centered on mandatory terms of imprisonment (usually at labor), for most crimes. But it was also more implacably thanatocratic than the old criminal law.

There were more than forty mandatory death penalties, all executed by machine after March, 1792. The advent of the killing machine was celebrated by the official *Moniteur*:

> The innovation of putting a mechanical device in the place of the executioner... is worthy of the century in which we shall soon live, and of the new political order into which we are entering.[37]

This statement was prophetic. From its first use in April 1792 (a year before the beginning of the Revolutionary Terror) to the abolition of the death penalty in the early 1980s, the guillotine served as the exclusive instrument for the death penalty in France. It did so without significant mechanical improvements. In that sense, it had perhaps the greatest longevity of any eighteenth-century European invention.[38]

The guillotine was an edifice 28' feet high; a 10' scaffold and the engine whose uprights measured 18'; the window of decapitation was 12' from the ground. The action of the blade was visible from the distant fringes of crowds. The entire structure was painted scarlet red. Ritual was virtually eliminated from the new public execution. There were no death testaments or spiritual intercessions. If he chose, the condemned could be accompanied in the cart by a priest—but not on the scaffold. There, he was alone and mute. If he attempted to speak, his voice was drowned by the drums of the guard. The only voice at the site of execution was the solitary reading of the sentence to the crowd by the court clerk. Execution was accomplished in a rapid, nearly continous movement: the victim was led from the cart onto the scaffold and thrust on the plank, which tipped him forward face-down with his neck in the lower block; the upper block was fastened down; the executioner pressed a lever, releasing the blade that was set in an 80 pound weight. He then held the severed head high for the crowd. The segmented corpse was removed.

This new economy of time and motion foreclosed agonistic behavior and banished mystery. It transformed the criminal into a passive object, to be annihilated. The guillotine manufactured death, just as its designers intended and as the great serial executions of the Revolutionary Terror proved. The machine enacted absolute State authority, behind the fiction of a Rousseauian general will.

Death by technology, death without either self-affirmation or spiritual redemption, death without dying: the history of modern capital punishment is the history of such anonymous and abject death—by gas chambers, electric chairs, narcosis. That history, our history, began with the guillotine.

---

[1]Archives nationales (cited hereafter as A.N.) AD III, 8; X2b 1334. The issues discussed in this essay are treated extensively in my *Law, Magistracy and Crime in Old Regime Paris, 1735 - 1789*: *volume I The System of Criminal Justice*; *volume II*

The Action of Criminal Justice The work is forthcoming with Cambridge University Press.

2 Since the Royal Ordinance of 1579 at Blois (article 92), in Decrusy, Jourdan and Isambert (editors), *Recueil général des anciennes lois françaises, depuis l'an 420 jusqu'à la révolution de 1789* (Paris, 1821-1833), 29 vols., vol. XIV, p. 404 (cited hereafter as Isambert, with volume and page numbers.)

3 *Code criminel ou commentaire sur l'Ordonnance de 1670* (Paris, 1767 edition), 4 vols., vol. III, p. 1101.

4 A.N. AD III, 31. The procedure for trying the memory of a cadaver, or a deceased defendant, was set forth in the five articles of Title XXII of the 1670 Criminal Ordinance; such trials were restricted to deceased persons accused of capital crimes (Isambert, XVIII, pp. 414-415.)

5 Daniel Jousse, *Traité de la justice criminelle de France* (Paris, 1771 edition), 4 vols., vol. I, p. 55.

6 Article 121, Ordinance of Louis XIII (January, 1629), Isambert, XVI, p. 262.

7 Article 111, Ordinance of François I at Villers-Cotterets (August, 1539), Isambert, XII, pp. 622-623.

8 Pierre-Francois Muyart de Vouglans, *Les loix criminelles de France dans leur ordre naturelle* (Paris, 1783), p. 86.

9 Clément L'Averdy, *Code pénal ou Recueil des principales ordonnances, édits et déclarations sur les crimes et délits, avec un Essai sur l'esprit & les motifs de la Procédure criminelle* (Paris, 1765), p. v.

10 As with René Plé, who was condemned to the "amende honorable" and breaking on the cross and wheel by the Parlement of Paris in December, 1784 for poisoning and robbery. The placarded judgement read: "... comdanme le dit René Plé à faire amende honorable au-devant de la principale porte de l'Eglise de Paris [Notre-Dame Cathedral], ou il sera conduit dans un tombereau par l'Exécuteur de la Haute Justice, nuds pieds, nue tête & en chemise, tenant en ses mains un torche ardente de cire jaune du poids de deux livres, ayant écriteau devant & derrière portant ces mots: (*Empoisonneur & Voleur*); & là, étant à genoux, dire & déclarer à haute & intelligible voix, que méchamment, témairement & comme mal-avisé, il a, sous le faux nom de Dubois, de complicité avec Jacques Flatté, dit l'Oiseau, ci-devant condamné et exécuté à mort, & un quidam, fait entrer le nommé Paul Bourgeois, vigneron, agé de soixante-quinze ans, dans une Auberge de Châteaugaillard, sous prétexte d'une gageure qui avoit été concertée entr'eux, & dont le prix étoit une bouteille de vin, dans laquelle Auberge ils ont fait prendre audit Bourgeois, dans un vin chaud, que l'un d'eux s'étoit chargé de préparer, une liqueur narcotique, assoupissante & pernicieuse, au moyen de laquelle ledit Bourgeois, après être parti de ladite Auberge, a perdu connaissance sur la route à une demi-lieue de Chateaugaillard, est tombé dans une sommeil léthargique, dont ils ont profité pour lui voler onze cens & quelques livres en or, & une tasse d'argent qu'il avoit sur lui, & par l'effet de laquelle liqueur ledit Bourgeois a été privé de l'usage de la parole pendant vingt-quatre heurs, & grièvement incommodé pendant cinq jours, sans pouvoir se rendre chez lui, dont il [René Plé] se repent & demande pardon à Dieu, au Roi & à la Justice; ce fait, ledit René Plé, mené dans le même

tombereau en la Place de Grève, pour, sur un échafaud qui y sera à cet effet dressé, avoir les bras, jambes, cuisses & reins rompus vifs par ledit Exécuteur de la Haute-Justice, & à l'instant jetté dans un bûcher ardent, pour ce pareillement dressé en laditte place, pour y être réduits en cendres, & les cendres jettées au vent..." (A.N. AD III, 15.) Poisoning was made a mandatory death offense by royal edict in July, 1682 (Isambert, XIX, pp. 396-401.)

11 *Les loix criminelles de France*, p. 38.

12 Isambert, XVIII, pp. 371-372.

13 Jean Domat, *Le droit public* (Paris, 1702 edition), p. 196.

14 *Traité de la justice criminelle de France*, vol. I, p. ii.

15 *Vues sur la justice criminelle* (Paris, 1783), 2 vols., vol. I, p. 245.

16 On the extraordinary density of non-punitive ceremonial and processional events in Old Regime Paris, see Annik Parrailhe-Galabrun, "Les déplacements des parisiens dans la ville aux XVIIème et XVIIIème siècles: un essai de problématique," *Histoire, Économie et Société*, no. 2, 1983, pp. 205-253 and Arlette Farge, *La vie fragile: Violence, pouvoir et solidarités à Paris aux XVIIIe siècle* (Paris: Hachette, 1986).

17 Calculated from A.N. AD III, 6 - 17 (sentences of Parisian tribunals), Y 10514 - 10530 (registers of judgments by the criminal chamber of the Châtelet), Inventory 450 (appellate judgements by the Parlement of Paris.)

18 See chapt. 3 of this book.

19 *Traité de la Police* (Amsterdam, 1729 edition), 4 vols., vol. I, p. 213.

20 *Le droit public*, p. 125

21 *Le droit public*, p. 197.

22 Those were consenual purposes in legal doctrine. See Jousse, *op. cit.*, vol. I, p. iii, Muyart, *op. cit.*, p. 39, Domat, *op. cit.*, p. 205, Claude-Joseph de Ferrière, *Dictionnaire de droit et de pratique* (Paris, 1769 edition), 2 vols., vol. I, p. 345, Pierre-Jean-Jacques Guyot, *et al*, *Répertoire universel et raisonné de jurisprudence civile, criminelle, canonique et béneficiale* (Paris, 1784-1787), 17 vols., vol. XIII, p. 64.

23 *Dictionnaire universel de Police* (Paris, 1783), 8 vols, vol. VIII, pp. 460-461.

24 On the issue of intentionality, see Jousse, *op. cit.*, I, pp. 1, 10-11, Muyart de Vouglans, *Institutes au droit criminel* (Paris, 1757 edition), pp. 2, 9, Du Rousseaud de la Combe, *Traité des matières criminelles* (Toulouse, 1762 edition), p. 1. The language of royal criminal edicts was infused with this definition of crime: against highway robber and burglary (Francis I, January 1534) "... ceux qui par mauvais esprit, damnée et misérable volonté, se sont mis et mettent bien souvent par insidiations et aggressions conspirées et machinées, à piller et destrousser de nuict les allans et venans ès villes, villages et lieux" (Isambert, XI, p. 400); against dueling (Louis XIV, June 1643) "...ce crime détestable, qui, en violant tout ensemble le respect qui nous est dû par nos sujets, comme à leur souverain, et l'obéissance qu'ils dovient à Dieu, comme à leur créateur et juge, les pousse, par une manie prodigieuse, à sacrifier leurs corps et leurs âmes à cette idole de vanité qu'ils adorent au mépris de leur salut" (Isambert, XVII, p. 13); against begging (Louis XV, 18 July, 1724)"... ceux qui sont en état de subsister par leur travail, mendient par pure fainéantise... la dissolution et la

débauche qui sont la suite de cette même oisivêté les portent insensibilement aux plus grands crimes" (Isambert, XXI, p. 272)

[25] Isambert, XII, pp. 821-824.

[26] Those royal carceral establishments were fully developed in law and administration, and heavily populated by judicial sentences, long before the Revolution. Michel Foucault's famous thesis in *Discipline and Punish: The Birth of the Prison*, trans. Alan Sheridan, (New York: Vintage Books, 1979) that carceral punishment in France was first conjectured by the "philosophes" of the Enlightenment and then instituted by the legislators of the Revolution is fallacious.

[27] Isambert, XVIII, p. 417.

[28] A.N. Inventory 450.

[29] Isambert, XXI, p. 260.

[30] A.N. Inventory 449 (U 995).

[31] The following description of the ritual is based on the detailed accounts of eighteenth-century Parisian executions in A.N. AD III, 6 - 17 and X2b 1330-1334; the "Salut des criminels condamnés à mort" (in A.N. AD III, 28); and the works of aforementioned jurists.

[32] Isambert, IX, p. 458.

[33] On forms and perceptions of death among the popular and elite classes of Old Regime France, see the following: Francois Lebrun, *Les hommes et la mort en Anjou aux XVIIe et XVIIIe siècles* (Paris: Flammarion, 1975); Robert Favre, *La Mort au Siècle des lumières* (Lyon: Presses Universitaires de Lyon, 1978); Pierre Chaunu, *La mort à Paris, XVIe, XVIIe, XVIIIe siècles* (Paris: Fayard, 1978); George Amstrong Kelly, "Mortal Politics in Eighteenth-Century France," in *Historical Reflections/Réflexions historiques*, vol. 13, no. 1, 1986.

[34] F. M. Vermeil, *Essai sur les réformes à faire dans notre législation criminelle* (Paris, 1781), p. 136.

[35] The fullest statement of the new principles of criminal justice is Lepeletier de Saint-Fargeau's Preamble to the Penal Code of 1791 (A.N. AD III, 54.)

[36] See, for example, Foucault, *Discipline and Punish*; Peter Spierenburg, *The Spectacle of Suffering: Executions and the Evolution of Repression* (New York: Cambridge University Press, 1984); Gordon Wright, *Between the Guillotine and Liberty: Two Centuries of the Crime Problem in France* (New York: Oxford University Press, 1983).

[37] *Réimpression de l'ancien Moniteur,* Paris, 1847, vol. II, p. 410.

[38] On the origins, instauration and Revolutionary history of the guillotine, see Daniel Arasse, *La guillotine et l'imaginaire de la Terreur* (Paris: Flammarion, 1987).

Dickens and the Representation of Punishment

Steven Marcus

My title is itself vastly inflationary. No English novelist was ever more deeply involved in the problematics of punishment and their cognate issues than Dickens. And no English novelist's work, in this connection, has been the subject of wider or more intense dispute and discussion. Dickens touched upon these topics in almost every form of his writing, in his novels, letters, journalism, books of travel, and in his capacity as an editor. He was never very far from questions of crime and punishment; of the law and its many sub-institutions; of the police; of capital punishment; of guilt, judgment and retribution; of debt, theft, embezzlement, fraud, burglary, and murder; of imprisonment, transportation, redemption and reform; of lawyers, beadles, aldermen, commissioners, magistrates, judges and Lord Chancellors; of violence legal and illegal. As an adolescent he had begun work in a solicitor's office and had moved on from there to become a reporter in courts both civil and criminal. Toward the middle of his life he even entertained the extraordinary idea of becoming a lawyer and magistrate himself, but eventually gave it up. His writings on these matters were famous in his own time and were even regarded as exerting an influence on public opinion: for crime and punishment and everything that was connected with both were matters of continual debate and concern in the Age of Reform with which the age of Dickens coincided. To make some coherent sense then out of a subject that is so extensive and that, at the same time, has been so variously discussed, one must perforce be extremely selective. I have therefore chosen two texts out of the multitudinous abundance of Dickens's work on these topics and will juxtapose them in the hope that their being so placed will throw new light on their meanings.

In January, 1842, just before his thirtieth birthday, Dickens sailed for America. He had many reasons for making this trip; one of them was to see for himself "the public institutions" of America. The United States was at the time universally regarded as the leading force in certain institutional reforms, and Dickens, who was acquainted at first hand with the prisons, work-houses and charitable foundations of his own country, joined a relay of other pilgrims and investigators (most notable among them, of course, was Tocqueville) from Great Britain and the Continent to visit the new country and examine these social experiments. He was already the most famous and popular novelist in the English language (if not in all languages) and was welcomed in the New World as a celebrity, was treated with great respect, and was the subject of virtually unremitting public scrutiny during his stay here. He repaid these attentions in long letters that he wrote back to England and that he used in preparing *American Notes*, which was published later in 1842 after his return. This volume caused something of an uproar in America since Dickens was outspoken on a number of matters that were offensive to American sensibilities—among them were slavery, the American habit of spitting tobacco juice in public, and America's most advanced penal undertaking. It is this latter with which we are here concerned.

But before he got to that discussion Dickens had to prepare the scene. The chronology of his journey helped him in this connection, for the first American city that he visited was Boston, and it was Boston's public institutions that he first described. The first of these was a privately run public charity, "The Perkins Institute and Massachusetts Asylum for the Blind," and Dickens was impressed by what he saw there. He was extremely impressed with a twelve-year old girl named Laura Bridgman, who was in his description of her a precurs of Helen Keller.

> I sat down in another room, before a girl, blind, deaf, and dumb; destitute of smell; and nearly so of taste: before a fair young creature with every human faculty, and hope, and power of goodness and affection, inclosed within her delicate frame, and but one outward sense—the sense of touch. There she was, before me; built up, as it were, in a marble cell, impervious to any ray of light, or particle of sound; with her poor white hand peeping through a chink in the wall, beckoning to some good man for help, that an Immortal soul might be awakened. Long before I looked upon her, the help had come.[1]

It had come in the form of a physician who had taught her to communicate in a manual sign language and to read letters and to write, who had in fact "made her what she is." In this passage Dickens is alluding to the story of Pygmalion and Galatea, as well as, unconsciously, to Pyramus and Thisbe in Shakespeare. But he is also representing the blind and deaf mute girl as an actual human being, as a soul imprisoned in a marble block or cell that is lightless and silent, who appeals to be awakened into fuller life. The child has been punished by Nature for no wrongdoing, and it is therefore the duty of her contemporaries to redeem her from this unmerited incarceration and bring her into fellowship in a community, a communal membership defined precisely by communication, in other words by its fundamental humanity.

Dickens takes us next to South Boston where "several charitable institutions are clustered together."[2] The first of these is the "State Hospital for the insane," which is run along impressively enlightened lines (*in re* Dorothea Dix)."Evince a desire to show some confidence and repose some trust, even in mad people," remarks the resident physician, as he and his guest make their way through "patients flocking around us unrestrained."[3] And at meal-times, entrusted with knives and forks, the imprisoned insane have been rendered altogether harmless:

> moral influence alone restrains the more violent among them from cutting the throats of the rest; but the effect of that influence is reduced to an absolute certainty, and is found, even as a means of restraint, to say nothing of it as a means of cure, a hundred times more efficacious than all the strait-waistcoats, fetters, and handcuffs, that ignorance, prejudice, and cruelty have manufactured since the creation of the world.[4]

Dickens's attitude is plain enough. Here too is a population deprived perforce of liberty; it seems possible and is certainly desirable to restrain them without cruelty, since they are not mad by choice or will and hence are not responsible for their errant, annoying or even dangerous behavior.

He then visits the local "House of Industry," where "old or otherwise helpless paupers" are kept in relative "peace and comfort" in one part of the institution and "orphans and young children" in an "adjoining building." The author of *Oliver Twist* needs to do no more than invoke the prospect of how English Poor Law Commissioners would respond to the idea of the furniture for orphan paupers having arms and back, and he has his readers with him. From there he moves to two neighboring "establishments for boys." The first of these, "the Boylston school," was "an asylum for neglected and indigent boys who have committed no crime, but who in the ordinary course of things would very soon be purged of that distinction if they were not taken from the hungry streets."[5] This asylum was in fact run as a school, and Dickens as a distinguished visitor questioned the boys about what they knew about England and got more satisfactory answers than anyone would expect today. The second institution was a "House of Reformation for Juvenile Offenders." It was under the same roof as the school for neglected and indigent boys (neither could have been very large), but, Dickens testifies, perhaps too hopefully, that "the two classes of boys never came in contact." But perhaps he was right, for in this place he saw "many boys of colour." The boys in the reformatory both labored at simple make work and got some instruction; they sang a "chorus in praise of Liberty," for their visitor, which he failed to appreciate—it was, he wrote, "an odd, and, one would think, rather aggravating, theme for prisoners." The boys were divided into classes, numbered and badged, in order to allow them to work their way toward freedom, and on the whole Dickens approves of the regime.

> The design and object of this Institution is to reclaim the youthful criminal by firm but kind and judicious treatment; to make his prison a place of purification and improvement, not of demoralization and corruption; to impress upon him that there is but one path, and that one sober industry, which can ever lead him to happiness...in a word, to snatch him from destruction, and restore him to society a penitent and useful member. The importance of such an establishment, in every point of view, and with reference to every consideration of humanity and social policy, requires no comment.[6]

The purpose of such an institution was to rehabilitate these young offenders and to restore them to society where they might occupy a useful place. And it is quite clear that Dickens approves of this purpose and of its practical possibilities. It was in point of fact the same line of policy that he pursued a few years later when he undertook to supervise and indeed actually run a home or homeless women, which he named Urania Cottage. This refuge, and what we would call today a halfway house, was financed by the philanthropist, Angela Burdett-Coutts, and was conducted with the aim of removing "fallen women" from the ranks of prostitution and returning them after a period of rehabilitation to respectable life, and then largely through emigration to Australia. Dickens believed that rehabilitation was possible for some of them because they were mostly still young, because they were female, and because they were not for the most part thorough criminals. But he did not set his hopes very high, calculating on the reformation of something less than half as a successful result.

We can see then what up to now Dickens has been doing. He has arranged these holding or enclosing institutions along a gradient. He begins with those who have been organically handicapped by nature, the blind and deaf, and an institution that cares for and even attempts to make up for their physical deficits. He proceeds to those who have been physically or spiritually disabled, the insane, and an institution that restrains them without further punishment and in which some remission might be hoped for. He then takes up the very old and the very young who are dependent both because of their age and their indigence; nature and society have conspired together in their helplessness, and what they require is an institution to shelter them and to provide in a civilized way for their fundamental human needs. Young boys who are neglected and impoverished come next; their injuries are altogether social, and what they need is compensatory nurturing in the form of a live-in school. And then come the delinquent young; they have already committed offenses against the law and society, but they are still of susceptible age and so the treatment for them entails restraint, punishment in the form of deprivation of liberty plus various visible emblems of stigma, plus efforts at remediation through rudimentary vocational tasks plus lessons in penitence. Thus far Dickens's descriptions and judgments are generally in line with what was widely regarded as liberal and enlightened reforming opinion during the 1830s and 40s.

There is one more institution to be included in this opening survey or catalogue of enclosures. And this was the State prison or "House of Correction." This institution in Boston followed at the time a version of what was then called "the silent system" of penal policy or, as it was then called "Prison Discipline." In this regime, prisoners were supposed to maintain strict silence at all times but were allowed to see each other and to work side by side, although they had to eat their meals in solitude. In America, as well, they were put to gainful labor, such as weaving, carpentry, blacksmithing, or cutting stone. This system, which originated in America, had already been imported into England with one substantial change. In order to avoid competition between free and forced labor, the work of the prisoners was removed from the market by transforming it into labor without a product—English prisoners on this system were set to walking on the treadmill, travelling rapidly to nowhere, to turning a crank handle with nothing attached to it, to passing cannonballs back and forth, or to picking oakum, that is to say taking apart old and discarded strands of rope. Dickens approved of this English variation, and not only for economic reasons. He thought that ordinary labor performed by these convicts in American jails was inappropriate to their justly stigmatized and degraded condition. Indeed, he goes on—

> In an American state prison or house of correction, I found it difficult at first to persuade myself that I was really in a jail: a place of ignominious punishment and endurance. And to this hour I very much question whether the humane boast that it is not like one, has its root in the true wisdom or philosophy of the matter.[7]

This passage may appear surprising to those who do not know Dickens's writings fairly well, but it is not at all inconsistent with his general views on these matters, views which were themselves no model of consistency. Above all, however, they were not consistent with Dickens's customary generosity. Moreover, whether we like it or not, Dickens was not what we would think of today as an orthodox liberal, nor a member of that herd of independent minds to which most of us in these contexts belong most of the time. He was aware that this opinion of his represented a deviation from accepted advanced and enlightened attitudes and was concerned quickly to cover his flank, which he does. He remarks at once that he is no supporter of the repudiated English "bloody code," "the good old customs of the good old times which made England" until recently "in respect of her criminal code and her prison regulations, one of the most bloody-minded and barbarous countries on the earth."[8] And he is aware of the great symbolic social importance of this matter, that "the subject of Prison Discipline is of the highest importance to any community," and that in this connection, through "sweeping reform and bright example," America has in general shown "great wisdom, great benevolence, and exalted policy."[9] Indeed he goes on, despite this one reservation, he has been so impressed by the institutions of Boston that he means "to take them for a model," a standard of comparison.

In these establishments taken as a whole, "the unfortunate or degenerate citizens of the State are carefully instructed in their duties both to God and man; are surrounded by all reasonable means of comfort and happiness that their condition will admit of; are appealed to, as members of the great human family, however afflicted, indigent, or fallen; are ruled by the strong Heart, and not by the strong (though immeasurably weaker) Hand."[10] America regarded itself as something of a social experiment, and Dickens was more than willing to endorse the results of these particular experiments with the dependent and the deviant that he observed in Boston.

There is no reason to doubt the sincerity of Dickens's remarks in these passages—he was as a rule straightforward in his opinions. At the same time, he was a writer. In this section about Boston he has carefully prepared the way for what he is going to undertake subsequently. After travelling through southern New England and visiting New York, Dickens moved on to Philadelphia, in part with the express intention of visiting Cherry Hill, the Eastern Penitentiary as it was called, at the time the most famous of American prisons, if not the most famous in the world. This prison embodied the most advanced, enlightened and widely-approved system of penology—it was named the "Separate System," owed much to the thinking of certain Quaker reformers, was intended to lead to the reformation and rehabilitation of its inmates, and was based on the idea of virtually unrestricted solitary confinement. Dickens was horrified by what he saw, attacked it at length, and became himself the subject of counter-attack by the experts and supporters of the system, a development that was neither unexpected by him nor in some sense unwelcome. The polemics were still being carried on more than fifty years later, for the Philadelphia experiment had some die-hard supporters.

The system, Dickens, wrote consisted of "rigid, strict, and hopeless solitary confinement." And he went on to say that he believed that it was "in its effects" both "cruel and wrong." It was, to be sure, freighted with good intentions and was "meant for reformation," but Dickens was certain that

> those benevolent gentlemen who carry it into execution, do not know what it is they are doing. I believe that very few men are capable of estimating the immense amount of torture and agony which this dreadful punishment, prolonged for years, inflicts upon the sufferers; and in guessing at it myself, and in reasoning from what I have seen written upon their faces and what to my certain knowledge they feel within, I am only the more convinced that there is a depth of terrible endurance in it which none but the sufferers themselves can fathom, and which no man has the right to inflict on his fellow-creature. I hold this slow and daily tampering with the mysteries of the brain to be immeasurably worse than any torture of the body.[11]

This punishment of the spirit of the subject was "immeasurably" worse than physical mistreatment. Dickens meant this literally; indeed he was not, as a rule, opposed to harsh physical treatment, sometimes including flogging, of convicted criminals. He was, however, horrified by the sights that he observed at Cherry Hill. He did not need to take notes, he wrote to John Forster a few days later, for those sights "are written, beyond all power of erasure, in my brain." He saw men and women who had been confined there for up to eleven years, and he began his description in his letter to Forster with the ritual of initiation that every new prisoner had to pass through.

> Every new prisoner who comes into gaol, comes at night; is put into a bath, and dressed in the prison garb; then a black hood is drawn over his face and head, and he is led to the cell from which he never stirs again until his whole period of confinement has expired. I looked at some of them with the same awe as I should have looked at men who have been buried alive, and dug up again.[12]

This systematic assault on the self is characteristic of what a modern commentator, Erving Goffman, has called "total institutions." What

Dickens emphasizes in this passage are the death-like attributes of the experience—the darkness, the ritual bathing (as much as in a laying out of the dead as in a baptism)—the black hood which reminds one of the scaffold and hangman, and the grave-like cell. And if he was not responding to Poe, Dr. Manette was already germinating in his mind. What is so terrible for Dickens is the deprivation of social, if not of all, psychic life—it is a death without surcease of pain. Once in his cell, the prisoner

> never hears of wife and children; home or friends; the life or death of any single creature...He is a man buried alive; to be dug out in the slow round of years; and in the meantime dead to everything but torturing anxieties and horrible despair.
>
> His name, and crime, and term of suffering, are unknown even to the officer who delivers him his daily food. There is a number over his cell-door, and in a book of which the governor of the prison has one copy, and the moral instructor another: this is the index of his history. Beyond these pages the prison has no record of his existence: and though he live to be in the same cell ten weary years, he has no means of knowing, down to the very last hour, in which part of the building it is situated.[13]

There is some slight hyperbole here, since there were numbers of occasional visitors, including Dickens, but the emphasis he lays upon depersonalization and disorientation seem right enough. And if prisoners did survive and manage to outwit the system and communicate with one another, it was a result of circumstances that were beyond the control of the reformers' intentions, which were as Dickens describes them.

The inmates had access on request to the Bible and certain other reading matter and to writing materials. And they worked, again on request, at the customary useful tasks in their cells. Dickens goes on to describe a number of those he visited. One of them, a burglar, impressed Dickens with his unsurpassable and "unmitigated hypocrisy," and he "blessed the day on which he came into that prison"—not a word of which Dickens believed. More typical, however, were the prisoners who suffered under these circumstances; the most famous of them he described as follows:

> In another cell, there was a German, sentenced to five years' imprisonment for larceny, two of which had just expired...he had painted every inch of the walls and ceiling quite beautifully. He had laid out the few feet of ground, behind, with exquisite neatness, and had made a little bed in the center, that looked bye-the-bye like a grave. The taste and ingenuity he had displayed in everything were most extraordinary; and yet a more dejected, heart-broken, wretched

> creature, it would be difficult to imagine. I never saw such a picture of forlorn affliction and distress of mind. My heart bled for him; and when the tears ran down his cheeks, and he took one of the visitors aside, to ask, with his trembling hands nervously clutching at his coat to detain him, whether there was no hope of his dismal sentence being commuted, the spectacle was really too painful to witness. I never saw or heard of any kind of misery that impressed me more than the wretchedness of this man.[14]

We know a good deal in addition about this prisoner, since Dickens's opponents went to great lengths to dispute this account and discredit Dickens's sympathy for him. He was an inveterate recidivist, tried to commit suicide at least twice, etc., etc. All of which, as well as other matters, suggests that the system didn't work for him, even if he was humbugging Dickens. In the main, however, Dickens was clearly right in his indictment of both the inefficacy and the inhumanity of this benignly-intended form of punishment.

After he has completed his description of the inmates with whom he spoke at Cherry Hill, Dickens tries to imagine what it must be like to be imprisoned in these conditions. He spends several impressive pages at it only to conclude that the anguish of the experience must be "so acute and so tremendous,that all imagination of it must fall far short of the reality"—this being, I believe, one of the few occasions on which Dickens confessed that he was unable to realize in his imagination and through words a particular reality and puts us immediately in mind of certain characteristic twentieth-century experiences of extremity.

He steadfastly believes, however, that the effect of this punishment on those who suffer it must be to render them "morally unhealthy and diseased," by which he means mentally disabled. And he has not an iota of faith in it "as a means of reformation." He has, in addition, one more observation to register about this world of "unnatural solitude." "On the haggard face of every man among these prisoners, the same expression sat....It had something of that strained attention which we see in the faces of the blind and deaf, mingled with a kind of horror, as though they had all been secretly terrified....It lives in my memory, with the fascination of a remarkable picture."[15] Dickens in fact remarked to the prison officials who were conducting him about Cherry Hill on his impression "that the criminals who had been there long, were deaf," and his interlocutors stared at him in disbelief at this notion, "which they regarded as groundless and fanciful."[16]

At this point, the attentive reader can begin to make out what Dickens is up to, for he has returned us at the far end of this spectrum of institutions to something like the place at which he began. This institution of extreme punishment, the creation of enlightened, benevolent and reforming minds, completes a cycle and somehow touches on the institution, the result of equally benevolent intentions, in which the random and indifferent, terrible punishment dealt out by nature is ameliorated if not undone by society. In both punishment takes for Dickens its characteristically most cruel form—deprivation of human and social connectedness. This is not the first occasion, nor will it be the last, on which radically benign social intentions lead in self-contradictory and objectionable directions.

The Separate System of prison discipline makes further appearances in Dickens's writings. In an article of 1850 in *Household Words*, called "Pet Prisoners," he attacked it yet again; but its most famous representation, and one that wider audiences have continued to respond to, occurs at the very end of *David Copperfield*. The Pennsylvania system had, so to speak, won out, and even before Dickens had travelled to America, decisions had been taken in England to adopt and adapt it in both existing and new English prisons. And indeed an experimental Model Prison at Pentonville was built—it opened at the end of 1842—in which this system was to be embodied; during the 1840s fifty-four new prisons on the Pentonville plan were built. The incorporation, however, entailed compromises from the beginning and even more compromises as time went on, as the harmful mental effects of extended and severe solitary confinement as an agent of reform, instruction, probation and improvement became manifest to the medical and penal authorities. At the end of the novel, you may recall, David has become a famous novelist, and among his large, unsolicited correspondence in London is a letter from his old, brutal schoolmaster, Mr. Creakle, the one-time owner and head of Salem House. He has retired from his educational pursuits and has been commissioned as a Middlesex Magistrate and member of the board that controlled Pentonville, though the prison is not explicitly named in the novel. He writes to David to invite him to inspect "'in operation, the only true system of prison discipline; the only unchallengeable way of making sincere and lasting converts and penitents—which...is by solitary confinement."[17] This is the same Creakle who once in the past, when his own son had "held some remonstrance" with him "on an occasion when...discipline was very cruelly exercised," turned that son "out of doors," "'discard[ed]'" him, as he said. This loathsome creature has "reformed" himself and is now as mindlessly dedicated to the idea of solitary confinement as salutary and reclamatory discipline as he was once to beatings and banishment.

Indeed he has now become as tender-hearted "'to prisoners convicted of the whole calendar of felonies,'" as he was once to Steerforth, the charming and transgressive, if not felon-like, head boy of his old school.

These contradictions reappear in the prison itself, to which David and Traddles duly repair to visit their former schoolmaster. The building itself is "immense...solid" and very costly, and David compares it to the Tower of Babel, explicitly because of its massive construction, but less overtly because of the unintelligible nonsense of its ideology and because the enjoined silence and non-communication of the system is violated with impunity and flouted on every side. He does not fail to notice the superior dietary of the prisoners—expressing one of Dickens's long-standing peeves—and remarks on the "striking contrast between these plentiful repasts, and the dinners, not to say of paupers, but of soldiers, sailors, labourers, the great bulk of the honest, working community. But I learned that the 'system' required high living; and...put an end to all doubts, and disposed of all anomalies."[18] The high point of the episode of course comes when David is introduced to a "Model Prisoner," the phrase alluding to Carlyle's intemperate polemic, "Model Prisons," published earlier in 1850 as one of the *Latter-Day Pamphlets*. That prisoner, known, in accordance with "the system," as Number Twenty-Seven and renowned because "of his pious admonitions to everybody around him, and of the beautiful letters he wrote to his mother (whom he seemed to consider in a very bad way)" is discovered in his cell "reading his Hymn Book." He is of course Uriah Heep, who responds to Mr. Creakle's question by saying that he is "'far more comfortable here, than ever I was outside. I see my follies now, sir. That's what makes me comfortable."[19] He goes on to make a request:

> 'I would umbl ask, sir,' returned Uriah, with a jerk of his malevolent head, 'for leave to write again to mother....I am anxious about mother. I am afraid she ain't safe....Immortally safe, sir....I should wish mother to be got into my state. I never should have been got into my present state if I hadn't come here. I wish mother had come here. It would be better for everybody, if they got took up, and was brought here.'
>
> This sentiment gave unbounded satisfaction—greater satisfaction, I think than anything that had passed yet.
>
> 'Before I come here,' said Uriah, stealing a look at us, as if he would have blighted the outer world to which we belonged, if he could, 'I was given to follies; but now I am sensible of my follies. There's a deal of sin outside. There's a deal of sin in mother. There's nothing but sin everywhere—except here.'[20]

He then addresses David directly.

> 'You knew me a long time before I came here and was changed, Mr. Copperfield,' said Uriah, looking at me; and a more villainous look I never saw, even on his visage. 'You

> knew me when, in spite of my follies, I was umble among them that was proud, and meek among them that was violent—you was violent to me yourself, Mr. Copperfield. Once, you struck me a blow in the face, you know.'
>
> General commiseration. Several indignant glances directed at me.
>
> 'But I forgive you, Mr. Copperfield,' said Uriah, making his forgiving nature the subject of a most impious and awful parallel, which I shall not record. 'I forgive everybody. It would ill become me to bear malice. I freely forgive you, and I hope you'll curb your passions in future. I hope Mr. W. will repent, and Miss W., and all the sinful lot. You've been visited with affliction, and I hope it may do you good; but you'd better have come here, and Miss W. too. The best wish I could give you, Mr. Copperfield, and give all of you gentlemen, is, that you could be took up and brought here. When I think of my past follies, and my present state, I am sure it would be best for you. I pity all who ain't brought here.'
>
> He sneaked back into his cell, amidst a little chorus of approbation; and both Traddles and I experienced a great relief when he was locked in.[21]

A second Model Prisoner is encelled next to Heep. He is, Littimer, Steerforth's servant and procurer, and he too makes a wonderful, accusatory profession of repentance. Both convicts are being renovated while awaiting transportation to Australia, on which continent they will join Mr. Peggotty and Emily, the Micawber family, Martha Endell, Mrs. Gummidge and all the other problems that Dickens, in analogy with the English penal system at that moment, shipped out of his novel in order to achieve some sort of resolution or closure.

The scene is unforgettably funny and far more vivid and effective than Dickens's journalism on these topics. There are, however, some unanswered questions that attach to it. What, in the first place, is it doing there? And why should the system that was in America a horror and a nightmare for Dickens become a laugher when it was translated across the ocean? Commentators have tended to answer the first question by regarding the entire episode as irrelevant to the novel's inner structure, as a contrivance that allowed Dickens to bring forward these two marvelously villainous characters one more time and give them their last innings at David and for the reader.[22] Furthermore, it permitted Dickens another ride on one of his hobby horses. And the second has been explained away by pointing to the "soft" version of the radically punitive American system of penal reform that had been, temporarily only to be sure, instituted in England.

There is naturally some merit in both of these readings, but they both also miss part of the point. That scene in prison is a kind of final hint to or signal for the reader, and serves to foreground unmistakably what has been from the outset a steadily developing theme and indeed structural element in the novel as a whole. That thematic element is to be located in the notion that England as it is represented in this extraordinary original novel has become for Dickens, dramatically and in a general sense, a punitive culture, a culture of punishment. The signifying venue of punishment, however, is not for Dickens at this juncture to be found in prisons or its origins understood through them. And Dickens's attitude toward and understanding of the vengeful impulsions in that culture are more complex, articulated, and ramified than he is customarily given credit for. In order to get some sense of that attitude and how it is concretely developed, we must take a cursory look at the novel itself.

David Copperfield opens with a series of problematicalities. In the very first sentence David wonders "whether I shall turn out to be the hero of my life," and the events of the first chapter, about which he has been, as he says, "informed," are in large measure represented as if they were experienced and remembered by him. Those events have to do with David's birth and what preceded it. And just as the problematics about the heroic character of this protagonist and his life refer in part to the recently published *Vanity Fair* ("a novel without a hero") , so the retelling of his birth at midnight on a Friday—"the clock began to strike, and I began to cry, simultaneously"—alludes in a fastidious way to the "key" episodes that make up the opening movement of *Tristram Shandy*, namely Tristram's conception and birth. It is all done with a lightness, certitude and apparent directness that make relevant at once George Orwell's recollection, in his essay on Dickens, that when, at the age of nine, he read *David Copperfield* for the first time, he found "the mental atmosphere of the opening chapters...so immediately intelligible...that I vaguely imagined they had been written by a child."

Neither David's parents nor David himself are the central characters at his birth. David's father has been dead for six months already, and David himself, Dickens cleverly and deliberately writes, is a "posthumous child." His mother is perforce present in the scene, but she is, as we will learn, more or less a stranger to it. The character who presides over and dominates the episode of David's birth is his father's aunt, and therefore David's great-aunt, Betsey Trotwood. Almost the first thing we learn about this "formidable personage" is that she "had been married"—and in point of fact she is still married. She was married to a "very handsome" man, younger than herself, who was said to have beaten her and tried once to throw her out of an upper-story window. Convinced by these events "of an incompatibility of temper," Miss Betsey pays off this handsome scapegrace of a husband with whom she had fallen in love, effects a "separation" from him, immediately takes "her maiden name again," buys a cottage on the sea-coast and "established herself there as a single woman...and was understood to live secluded, ever afterwards, in an inflexible retirement."[23] Well, not quite, since she remains involved with her nephew, David's future father, who had been "a favourite" of hers. When she learns that he is going to be married, she is "mortally affronted." Her ostensible grounds for affront are that David's mother-to-be was "a wax doll." She has never met Clara Copperfield but knows only that she "was not yet twenty." Why twenty should equal wax doll is not entered upon, especially since Betsey herself, misalliance or not, could never at any age have been mistaken for one. Moreover, her nephew is twice the age of his bride. The upshot is that Miss Betsey breaks with her "favourite" and the two "never met again." It is quite evident that her excuses for her behavior in this context are pretexts, and that in acting as she does she is displacing her outrage over her own marriage and its injuries onto her nephew and punishing him for what happened to her. And indeed as "principal magnate"of the family, her rupture with her nephew has larger consequences than simple personal repudiation and retribution. Moreover, she no longer believes in marriage, and doubts whether "'any two people *can* be equally matched.'"

It is with such lively sentiments animating her bosom that Miss Betsey descends out of the blue on David's mother on the eve of David's birth. She at once finds fault with the names—or identites—of things. Blunderstone Rookery is an insult aimed directly at her by her late nephew's lack of ordinary sense:

> 'David Copperfield all over....David Copperfield from head to foot! Calls a house a rookery when there's not a rook near it, and takes the birds on trust, because he sees the nests.'[24]

Peggotty is equally offensive: "'Do you mean to say...that any human being has gone into a Christian church and got herself named Peggotty?'" And when she is straightened out on this score, she is barely mollified. There is one name, however, that brings her unalloyed satisfaction. The girl who is about to be born will be named Betsey Trotwood Copperfield, after her godmother.

> 'There must be no mistakes in life with *this* Betsey Trotwood. There must be no trifling with *her* affections, poor dear. She must be well brought up, and well guarded from reposing any foolish confidences where they are not deserved. I must make that *my care*.'

> There was a twitch of Miss Betsey's head, after each of these sentences, as if her old wrongs were working within her, and she repressed any plainer reference to them by strong constraint.[25]

These wrongs are only exacerbated, and her "presentiment" falsified, when instead of Betsey Trotwood Copperfield, David Copperfield the Younger puts in his appearance in the world.

> 'The baby,' said my aunt. 'How is she?'
>
> 'Ma'am,' returned Mr. Chillip....'It's a boy.'
>
> My aunt never said a word, but took her bonnet by the strings, in the manner of a sling, aimed a blow at Mr. Chillip's head with it, put it on bent, walked out, and never came back.[26]

In short, David's punishment begins with his being born, and he is in truth punished for being born. Furthermore, the punishment is not a negligible one, since his Aunt Betsey is not there to offer him her care when he most needs her, which will be soon enough.

In this extremely brief and radically incomplete reading of the opening of *David Copperfield* one can make out how the conception of punishment, already in several variations and species, is dramatically present from the beginning. It remains near the forefront of the novel's workings and undergoes the kind of transformative developments that such themes in Dickens customarily do, a process that is best suggested briefly by a reference to the way thematics are developed in Shakespeare. That is to say the range and detail of that evolution are beyond the scope of any single essay of appraisal or commentary, and one can only offer indications about the directions in which to look while reading.

David's pre-Oedipal paradise (he actually has two mothers, both named Clara) is broken into by the appearance of Mr. Murdstone, who at once interposes himself between David and his mother. In the interval before the marriage, David, unconscious of the impending change, is sent off with Peggotty to visit her brother in Norwich, and there on the wall of Mr. Peggotty's boat converted into a house he sees pictures of "Abraham in red going to sacrifice Isaac in blue, and Daniel in yellow cast into a den of green lions."[27] These anticipate what is almost immediately to occur. David and Peggotty return home, David learns that he now has a father (whom he momentarily mistakes for the ghost of his natural father risen from the dead), and that his bedroom has been moved to "lie a long way off" from his mother. He also learns that downstairs the old "empty dog-kennel was filled up with a great dog—deep-mouthed and black-haired —and he was very angry at the sight of me, and sprang out to get at me."[28] The young boy is naturally upset by these changes, cries himself to sleep, and resists his mother's timid efforts to console him for his loss. At which point Mr. Murdstone steps in decisively, sends the ladies out and has his first interview with his new step-son:

> 'David,' he said, making his lips thin, by pressing them together [which anticipates Rosa Dartle] 'if I have an obstinate horse or dog to deal with, what do you think I do?'
>
> 'I don't know.'
>
> 'I beat him.'
>
> I had answered in a kind of breathless whisper, but I felt, in my silence, that my breath was shorter now.
>
> 'I make him wince, and smart. I say to myself, "I'll conquer that fellow"; and if it were to cost him all the blood he had, I should do it.'[29]

Nothing could be more open or candid. The relations of authority between parent and child are expressed uninflectedly as those of domination and punishment. From this moment forward, David says, something unfortunate took place in him, within himself; in addition, Blunderstone Rookery is no longer, for him, "home."

What it has become is made manifest at once with the appearance on the scene of Miss Murdstone, her brother's completing counterpart.

> She brought with her two uncompromising hard black boxes, with her initials on the lids in hard brass nails. When she paid the coachman she took her money out of a hard steel purse, and she kept the purse in a very jail of a bag which hung upon her arm by a heavy chain and shut up like a bite.[30]

Miss Murdstone's jewelry consists of "little steel fetters and rivets."[31] She is in her own person the very embodiment of the culture of punishment. She is a kind of walking prison, a hard, metallic enclosure, that shuts and grasps and bites. Along with her brother, she figures as a combined negative Oedipal parent for the growing David. The "grand quality" on which both Murdstone's take their stand is "firmness," a familiar Victorian cultural term. This firmness, which we have already met with in Aunt Betsey, translates in this particular context into harshness, coldness, and unkindness—firmness of character being, among many other things, unflaggingly exacting in its demands upon the behavior of others. It also finds cognate expression in the Murdstones' religion:

> The gloomy taint that was in the Murdstone blood, darkened the Murdstone religion, which was austere and wrathful...its assuming that character was a necessary consequence of Mr. Murdstone's firmness, which wouldn't allow him to let anybody off from the utmost weight of the severest penalties he could find any excuse for....I well

remember the tremendous visages with which we used to go to church....Again the dreaded Sunday comes round, and I file into the old pew first, like a guarded captive brought to a condemned service. Again, Miss Murdstone, in a black velvet gown, that looks as if it had been made out of a pall, follows close upon me....Again, I listen to Miss Murdstone mumbling the responses, and emphasizing all the dread words with a cruel relish. Again, I see her dark eyes roll round the church when she says 'miserable sinners,' as if she were calling all the congregation names....Again, if I move a finger or relax a muscle of my face, Miss Murdstone pokes me with her prayer-book, and makes my side ache[32]

The Calvinist God of their Evangelical creed is the model of their conception of a responsible, caring parent. That this conception of God and parenthood happens to coincide with a little boy's (or girl's) worst fears of parental powers is, as we say nowadays, not their problem, anymore than it is their problem that their religion tends to represent our existence in this world as a form of penal servitude.

In the "gloomy theology" of the Murdstones "all children [were] made out to be a swarm of little vipers," and it was believed that "they contaminated one another."[33] Hence David is kept relentlessly at his lessons, at which he "blunder[s] on" hopelessly, and deprived of "recreation with children my own age."[34] (This is Dickens's earliest, though by no means his last, prophetic anticipation of the fine details of John Stuart Mill's *Autobiography*.) After six months of this treatment, he has become "sullen, dull, and dogged...daily more and more shut out and alienated from my mother....almost stupefied."[35] He is delivered from stupefaction by two circumstances. First, he discovers his dead father's semi-secret hoard of novels and stories; "they kept alive my fancy, and my hope of something beyond that place and time," and he recalls "reading as if for life."[36] Second, Mr. Murdstone unconsciously acts so as to move David away from his settled, dug-in, boyish, silent and passive resentment. He comes to David's lessons one day armed with "a lithe and limber cane,"and in a climactic scene, excruciatingly built up with menace that increases with each of David's scholastic failures, finally takes to flogging his step-son.

He had my head as in a vice, but I twined round him somehow, and stopped him for a moment, entreating him not to beat me. It was only for a moment that I stopped him, for he cut me heavily an instant afterwards, and in the same instant I caught the hand with which he held me in my mouth, between my teeth, and bit it through. It sets my teeth on edge to think of it.

> He beat me then as if he would have beaten me to death....Then he was gone; and the door was locked outside; and I was lying, fevered and hot, and torn, and sore, and raging in my puny way, upon the floor....How well I remember, when my smart and passion began to cool, how wicked I began to feel....My stripes were sore and stiff, and made me cry afresh, when I moved; but they were nothing to the guilt I felt. It lay heavier on my breast than if I had been a most atrocious criminal.[37]

In this great, complex scene David has been bitten by Mr. Murdstone's cane [or rod] and has bitten back with his young dog's teeth. He has for the moment behaved like the frightening watch-dog that greeted him when he returned to find his mother newly-married; and he has also, for the moment, and in part, identified with his chief antagonist and enemy in rebelling against him and giving him a taste of his own medicine. Yet the identification goes even deeper and in other directions; however justified David's insurrection against punitive authority may be (and indeed it is justified), what he feels afterward is inevitable and intractable wickedness, guilt, and criminality. Whether it is the rebellion or the punishment or both combined that induce or set off these responses is not for us at this moment a topic for discussion; what matters is that they are there, and that almost all of us have felt like criminals when we have resented and chafed against the constraints of childhood. David has already internalized a strong and growing super-ego—he is between eight and nine at this moment—which has no mercy on him. And yet his resentment has not, now, been limited to thought or gloomy feelings alone; he has actively resisted; and although this brings down further physical violence on him, his ability to strike out in his own behalf is the beginning of the way out for him. This to-ing and fro-ing, moving back and forth, many-sidedness and ambivalence are characteristic of the inner movement of the entire novel, as they are of experience itself.

David has indeed committed a domestic crime and is imprisoned for it. The imprisonment is separation, Philadelphia-style, solitary confinement for five days.

> I saw no one, Miss Murdstone excepted, during the whole time—except at evening prayers...where I was stationed, a young outlaw, all alone by myself...and whence I was solemnly conducted by my jailer....my mother was as far off from me as she could be, and kept her face another way, so that I never saw it....
>
> The length of those five days I can convey no idea of to any one. They occupy the place of years in my

> remembrance...in my solitude and disgrace...the depressed dreams and nightmares I had...the strange sensation of never hearing myself speak...all this appears to have gone round and round for years instead of days, it is so vividly and strongly stamped on my remembrance.[38]

From this detention David is sent away to a school that specializes in harsh abusiveness—one did not have to look far to find one in the England of the first part of the nineteenth century—and as a further "punishment for my misdoing" is sent there during the holiday time.

Word of him has been sent on before, and he is at once stigmatized with the famous placard, and, he remarks, what he suffered from wearing it "nobody can imagine....I recollect that I positively began to have a dread of myself, as a kind of wild boy who did bite."[39] The school itself is quite overtly a penal institution in the old style; it is carried on by "sheer cruelty" and makes no bones about it, though boys' bones have literally been broken there. Yet that cruelty is for David—and for Dickens—only less dreadful than the ideas that rationalize and justify it. When David returns home on holiday he begins to discover more about these ideas. And he learns about them first from the mouth of his poor, oppressed and lame-brained mother, who tells him that Mr. Murdstone treats him as he does out of "love" and "solely" for David's own "good." This is of course a classic, salient instance of murderous bad faith—that we punish and torment others for their own welfare.[40]

Mr. Murdstone himself is more to the point on these matters. David's disposition, he declares, is sullen and withdrawn and needs "improvement." The one sure path to improvement is through absolute "obedience" to the Murdstones.[41] Obedience to authority is the goal; and the objects of legitimated cultural aggression and extinction are those spontaneous impulses towards preference, judgment, likes and dislikes, and even autonomy in children. On this account children are treated not merely as subordinates, dependents and apprentices in life but as deviants and delinquents whose behavior must be radically modified. They become indeed the cultural paradigm for the incarcerated criminal, if it isn't indeed also the other way around as well. This modification is thought of, as Mr. Murdstone says, as "correcting" a wayward or refractory "disposition."

> 'no greater service can be done [to it] than to force it to conform to the ways of the working world, and to bend it and break it.'
>
> 'For stubbornness won't do here,' said his sister. 'What it wants is, to be crushed. And crushed it must be. Shall be, too!'[42]

In other words, in ideological terms it has to be annihilated. This extinction, however, is to be effected not primarily though physical but by means of mental or psychic punishment:

> And now I fell into a state of neglect, which I cannot look upon without compassion. I fell at once into a solitary condition,—apart from all friendly notice....
>
> What would I have given, to have been sent to the hardest school that was ever kept!—to have been taught something, anyhow, anywhere!....
>
> I was not actively ill-used. I was not beaten or starved; but the wrong that was done to me had no intervals of relenting, and was done in a systematic, passionless manner. Day after day, week after week, month after month, I was coldly neglected.[43]

Neglect leads inexorably to its next, its final, and catastrophic stage, abandonment, and that essentially is what Murdstone does to David. He gets rid of him. He sends him, at the age of ten, to London, to work in the warehouse of Murdstone and Grinby. This section of *David Copperfield* is the most famous part of the book; it is based directly on Dickens's own recollected experiences as a boy, and represents in part a kind of quasi-therapeutic effort of recall, retelling and interpretation. These cannot be gone into here. What happens is that David passes into abandonment, a punishment that represents both radical inner solitude and displacement downward in social class.

> From Monday morning until Saturday night, I had no advice, no counsel, no encouragement, no consolation, no assistance, no support of any kind, from anyone, that I can call to mind, as I hope to go to heaven!...I know I do not exaggerate, unconsciously and unintentionally...the difficulties of my life....I know that I worked from morning until night, with common men and boys, a shabby child. I know that I lounged about the streets, insufficiently and unsatisfactorily fed. I know that, but for the mercy of God, I might easily have been, for any care that was taken of me, a little robber or a little vagabond....
>
> My rescue from this kind of existence I considered quite hopeless, and abandoned, as such, altogether. I am solemnly convinced that I never for one hour was reconciled to it, or was otherwise that miserably unhappy; but I bore it...and...never revealed the truth [of his misery][44]

Yet it is on this downward spiral that David runs into another partial version of his father, Wilkins Micawber, the essence of both improvidence and resilience under adversity, who throws himself continually onto a social world that just as continually rejects him, and who, along with his family, provides David with some amusement and human company in his solitude and neglect.

Inevitably, however, Micawber is thrown into prison for debt, and his family joins him there, where they live more comfortably than they had on the outside, thank you. David now feels that he is reaching the bottom of the spiral of his experiences of punishment—of separation and abandonment. "Secretly unhappy" in all his waking hours, and "lonely" yet "self-reliant" in his manner, he decides to run away to his only living relation, who had welcomed him into the world by walking out on his birth. Robbed of his "half-guinea" and few small possessions on the streets of London, he sets out with "three half-pence" on foot for Dover. He is forced to sell the clothes off his back to get there, and he finally arrives at his Aunt Betsey's cottage, half-naked, half-starving, and half-dead. He is taken in, fed, washed or baptized, renamed and adopted. *Incipit vita nuova*. The first movement of the novel has come to an end.

This movement takes up less than one quarter of the novel's extended length. But it is not excessive to state that the remainder is in considerable measure a set of expansions, augmentations, deepenings, and epicyclic variations and developments on the themes that I have summarily touched on. For the way to respond appropriately to the culture of punishment of which the Murdstones are merely one embodient is not by profligate or promiscuous kindness or passive acquiescence and submission. We see this complication most clearly in the two partial versions through splitting and variation on David's personality and history that Dickens characteristically spins off. These two surround David and illuminate the problematics that, in this connection, his personal history dramatizes. They are of course Steerforth and Uriah Heep. Steerforth represents a young, charismatic, handsome, heroic and sexually vivid upper-middle-class male,who has been brought up, deliberately, without appropriate or adequate "constraint." He has been raised with virtually insane permissiveness by his widowed mother and he has become a charming, aggressive, snobbish, rapacious and sadistic youth and young man. His relation with his mother's young dependent and companion, Rosa Dartle, is indeed represented with surprising openness as sexually sadistic—and on her part as both hysterically sadistic and masochistic—and his seduction and subsequent treatment and abandonment of Emily is also dramatized within the idiom of cruelty, aggression and punishment. He is conscious of these uncontrollable impulses in himself and early on confesses to David his hopeless inner state:

> 'David, I wish to God I had had a judicious father these last twenty years....I wish with all my soul I had been better

> guided....[I am a] torment to myself....I have been afraid of myself....I tell you, my good fellow, that it would have been well for me (and for more than me) if I had had a steadfast and judicious father.'[45]

Like the Byronic hero on whom he is in part—but only in part—based, Steerforth is aware that he suffers from an insufficiency of internalized interdictions and functions of regulation and control, and he leaves a swathe of destructive, cruel and vengeful behavior behind him throughout the novel—while remaining charming, bright, handsome and unfailingly attractive.

Uriah Heep represents a similar group of characteristics in an entirely different configuration. Writhing and undulating about in his "deferential servility," he is yet systematically punitive with his "cruel-looking hand" and its crushing thumb, as he schemes remorselessly after Mr. Wickfield's property and Agnes Wickfield's flesh. How did he get that way? His history is the negative analogue of Steerforth's:

> 'Father and me was both brought up at a foundation school for boys; and mother, she was likewise brought up at a public, sort of charitable, establishment. They taught us all a deal of umbleness—not much else that I know of, from morning to night. We was to be umble to this person, and umble to that; and to pull off our caps here, and to make bows there; and always to know our place, and abase ourselves before our betters. And we had such a lot of betters! Father got the monitor-medal by being umble. He had the character, among the gentlefolks, of being such a well-behaved man, that they were determined to bring him in. "Be umble, Uriah," says father to me, "and you'll get on." It was what was always being dinned into you and me at school; it's what goes down best. "Be umble, says father, "and you'll do!" And really it ain't done bad....I am very umble to the present moment...but I've got a little power!"[46]

David responds by remarking to himself that it had never occurred to him before he heard this bit of autobiography that "this detestable cant of false humility might have originated" not with the Heep family itself but outside of it in a larger culture, and that for the first time now he comprehended "what a base, unrelenting, and revengeful spirit, must have been engendered by this early and long suppression."[47] Discipline, enforced subordination, humiliation and submission breed hypocrisy, resentment, vengeance and still further punishment. Uriah has not had a judicious father either; the culture of the Murdstones has raised him, and he has done well by it. And yet he and Steerforth—apparent polarities—behave along similar ruthless, personally and sexually destructive and punishing lines.

These problems generalize themselves further and proliferate throughout this novel. *David Copperfield* focuses on essentially two kinds of relations—those between parents and children, particularly (though not exclusively) between parents and children of the opposite sex and those between men and women in specifically sexual or marital roles or combinations. And in both areas it finds that things have gone disastrously wrong. What has happened is that relations of authority and of mutuality have gotten out of control, and consequently relations that entail sexuality and aggressiveness are marked on every side with pathology and destructiveness. Both culturally and personally the internal controls on the impulses of both aggression and sexuality have been radically mis-set and/or misconstructed, and the ability satisfactorily to regulate or manage those impulses has been, for the moment, radically impaired. This is why, although one has to be firmly and explicitly against the Murdstones, it is not enough, it is indeed most unfortunate, to be simply the Murdstones inside out. And this is why Aunt Betsey, no altogether unimpeachable character herself, but right in this instance, counsels David to be morally

> 'a firm fellow. A fine firm fellow, with a will of your own. With resolution,' said my aunt, shaking her cap at me, and clenching her hand. 'With determination. With character, Trot. With strength of character that is not to be influenced, except on good reason, by anybody, or by anything. That's what I want you to be. That's what your mother and father might both have been...and been the better for it.'[48]

Mr. Murdstone in an unheard of mellow mood might have said the same thing. And that is the very point and the problem as well. As David says to himself, "What I had to do, was, to turn the painful discipline of my younger days to account, by going to work with a resolute and steady heart."[49] This Wordsworthian injunction is effective so far as David's work, his career as a young journalist and novelist, is concerned—for the Murdstone's values are generally syntonic with those that guided the socio-economic practices of the period. But that injunction does not apply without inflection to the life of the affections, where the terrible damage was in the first place done. As Annie Strong, another mismated young woman, says to David, she is thankful that she has been "'saved...from the first mistaken impulse of my undisciplined heart.'"[50] And David recurs to that notion in diagnosing and interpreting his own marital unhappiness.

> 'The first mistaken impulse of an undisciplined heart.' Those words...were constantly recurring to me...were almost always present to my mind. I awoke with them, often, in the

> night; I remember to have even read them, in dreams, inscribed upon the walls of houses. For I know, now, that my heart was undisciplined when it first loved Dora; and that if it had been disciplined, it never could have felt, when we were married, what it had felt in its secret experience.[51]

In point of fact there are no satisfactory resolutions to such circumstances available to Dickens at this juncture, and the way he deals with these insoluble problems in *David Copperfield* is to kill them off, as he does with Dora, Steerforth and Ham Peggotty, or ship them out, as he does with the whole gang that are dispatched to Australia. This makes the ending of the novel less than satisfactory, but it also serves to point up and accentuate the grave problems with which it struggles. This is why the episode in prison toward the end of the novel is such a piece of comic relief–Dickens has become aware by this point that the problematics of punishment are not to be centrally located in prisons–though prisons remain important expressions, one class among many others, of how we deal and treat with such matters. *David Copperfield* dramatizes those matters on a grand scale in the contexts of both personal and social existence. It is one of the early great cultural documents of a crisis of the superego that had begun to manifest itself in Victorian society–it is a crisis that has, to be sure, not yet played itself out. The circumstances of that crisis found one of its principal representations in the culture of punishment, and *David Copperfield*, of all Dickens's works, is both an important response to that culture and a witnessing expression and testifying artifact of it as well.

---

[1]Charles Dickens, *American Notes & Pictures from Italy* (London: Oxford University Press, 1957), pp. 31-32. All further references are to this edition, the New Oxford Illustrated, cited hereafter as *AN*.

[2] *AN*, p. 45.

[3] *AN*, p. 45.

[4] *AN*, p. 47.

[5] *AN*, p. 49.

[6] *AN*, p. 50.

[7] *AN*, p. 51.

[8] *AN*, p. 51.

[9] *AN*, p. 52.

[10]*AN*, p. 53.

[11] *AN*, p. 99.

[12] Cited in Philip Collins, *Dickens and Crime* (London: MacMillan, 1965), p. 121. See also John Forster, *The Life of Charles Dickens*, ed. J.W.T. Ley (New York: Doubleday, Doran, 1928). On nineteenth century prisons and punishment, see Michael Ignatieff, *A Just Measure of Pain: The Penitentiary in the Industrial Revolution* (New York: Pantheon, 1978).

[13] *AN,* 100f.
[14] *AN,* p. 102.
[15] *AN,* p. 108.
[16] *AN,* p. 109.
[17] Charles Dickens, *The Personal History of David Copperfield* (London: Oxford University Press, 1948), p. 848. All further references are to this edition, the New Oxford Illustrated, cited hereafter as *DC.*
[18] *DC,* p. 850.
[19] *DC,* p. 851.
[20] *DC,* 853f.
[21] *DC,* 854f.
[22] See , for example, Kathleen Tillotson, *Novels of the Eighteen-Forties* (London: Clarendon Press, 1954), p. 93n, and Collins, *Dickens and Crime*, p. 157f.
[23] *DC,* p. 3.
[24] *DC,* p. 6.
[25] *DC,* p. 7.
[26] *DC,* p. 12.
[27] *DC,* p. 30.
[28] *DC,* p. 43.
[29] *DC,* p. 46.
[30] *DC,* 47f.
[31] *DC,* p. 48.
[32] *DC,* p. 52.
[33] *DC,* p. 55.
[34] *DC,* pp. 54, 55.
[35] *DC,* p. 55.
[36] *DC,* p. 55.
[37] *DC,* p. 58.
[38] *DC,* 59f.
[39] *DC,* p. 78.
[40] *DC,* p. 114.
[41] *DC,* p. 119.
[42] *DC,* p. 151.
[43] *DC,* p. 149.
[44] *DC,* pp. 159-62.
[45] *DC,* p. 322.
[46] *DC,* pp. 574-75.
[47] *DC,* p. 575.
[48] *DC,* p. 275.
[49] *DC,* p. 520.
[50] *DC,* p. 661.
[51] *DC,* p. 698.

Dreading and Desiring Punishment: On Morality and Masochism

Robert Alan Glick

My purpose in this essay is to offer a psychoanalyst's perspective on the meanings of punishment in moral development. I shall argue that we are more or less "moral" as a significant consequence of the resolution and internalization of our earliest, intensely conflictual, relationships with those we desire and dread, with those who both care for us and punish us. In this enterprise, I am mindful of difficulties and the need for caveats. Any interdisciplinary effort faces the challenge of finding an appropriate language and a suitable voice. Words must be comprehensible, if not familiar, across the borders of intellectual worlds. My focus is on specific facets and functions of mental life, not on questions of forensic psychiatry—such as proper and effective punishment, whether punishment should be retributive, utilitarian, rehabilitative or deterrent, or how punishment might accomplish any of those aims. But with this disclaimer, I shall offer a suggestion as to why individuals perform actions which demand punitive societal responses, as to what makes punishment necessary.

Punishment is one of the central and most pervasive themes in the stories explored by patient and analyst. Its meanings and varieties occupy so much of the time my patients and I spend together that it seems to be inescapably on and in our minds. Since my patients come to me with punishment on their minds and with the desire to "get better" and "be better," how they "got worse" and "felt worse" becomes an essential question in their stories about themselves.

Consider the following clinical situations:

(1) A twenty-six year old graduate student is suffering intense despair and frustration because of a crippling inability to finish his thesis. Having been told by his advisor that his quite promising academic future is in serious jeopardy, he comes for consultation.

(2) A thirty year old unmarried professional woman has had considerable success in her career and painfully disappointing failure in her love relationships. Men turn out to be immature and uncommitting. Her internist refers her for consultation after reassuring her that the recurrent headaches she suffers are stress-related.

(3) A psychoanalytic candidate travels through an early morning severe snowstorm to his 8:00 a.m. analytic appointment only to find that his analyst did not show up for the appointment. Along with slight annoyance at the inconvenience, he feels oddly pleased.

(4) A patient reports the following dream: "I'm taking an exam, maybe in the Romance languages or in biology, and I'm caught cheating. I'm brought up to the teacher. I feel overwhelming dread, and I wake up extremely agitated."

Psychoanalysis can reveal the profound roles dreading and/or desiring punishment play in experiences such as these. It is an obvious but profound truth that we are all and always deeply conflicted about ourselves, although we may not necessarily experience that conflict directly. By conflicted sense of self, I mean that we live with a dynamic unconscious compromise, a form of adaptive synthesis, amongst competing and contradictory needs, desires, fears, emotions, attitudes and behaviors. Consequently, our self-esteem—what we live with as our sense of just how good we really are and what we truly deserve—remains always vulnerable and, for that reason, capable of growth. This conflict within ourselves is at the core of the meanings and power of punishment: relative success or failure in resolution of these inevitable conflicts about ourselves and those who care for and gratify us determine our self-esteem and our self-discipline; our conflicted sense of ourselves subsumes the entire history of relationships with those we desire and dread, or the internalization of our history of object relations. In my view, psychological health necessarily includes an implicit morality that has matured beyond the universal dreading and desiring of punishment. And yet, our moral development is a process of internalization and resolution that is never finished, never completed; it is always a working draft of a story, a "work in progress" of our lives.

A punishment is a penalty in some form of pain, suffering, shame, strict restraint or loss, for some fault, offense, or violation. Punishment derives its meanings, fulfills its purposes, and formalizes its practices within the relation of the punished to the one who punishes. It thereby codifies the history of that relation and remains embedded in our minds as our internalized object relations. Moral judgments are made within the real and imagined, concrete and symbolic, current and past, conscious and unconscious connections between the punished self and the punisher. Those intricate verdicts define our self-worth, values, ideals and ambitions. They become the elements in our "getting better" and "being better."

As a metaphoric illustration of internalizing the punishing relationship, Jean-Paul Sartre, in his one-act play *No Exit*, placed his three dead characters in their personal Hell, whose setting is a Second Empire style drawing room. They are damned to be eternally imprisoned there with each other, and to endlessly torture each other as punishment for their faults and offenses—which are revealed by what they desire from each other. Those needs and desires become the instruments of mutual torture. Sartre wished to teach us moral lessons: life is an inescapable moral dilemma; we are guilty of high crimes, our sins of vanity, sadism, deceit, cowardice; punishment is also ineluctable; we seek to define ourselves through others and those others provide the inevitable punishment. As he had his victims conclude: "Hell is other people."[1]

At the end of the nineteenth-century, Sigmund Freud created psychoanalysis from the study and treatment of the personal hell of "moral" symptoms. Highly respectable Viennese middle and upper middle class individuals, mostly women, consulted Freud because they suffered from symptoms of hysteria. He found that they struggled to remain unaware of seemingly "improper" or incompatible feelings and desires, and their symptoms expressed a disguised compromise between their desires and their self-punishment. Those patients were victims - of seductions, of their culture, and ultimately of their intensely conflicted wishes.

Dreading Punishment and Being Moral

Psychoanalytic theory is primarily a psychology of conflict, according to which our morality develops as our intra-psychic, unconscious conflicts are adaptively resolved. For Freud, biological humankind became civilized humankind through repression and sublimation of the mental representations of biologically driven impulses. The mind, or the "psychic apparatus," and civilization, including morality, religion, art and science, developed out of the resolution and sublimation of conflict among humankind's unconscious wishes and fears.

In his philosophic study of Freud, Rieff stressed the tensions and contradictions within Freud's insistence on a "duality of instincts." By recognizing Freud's novelist's eye and philosopher's passion, Rieff captured this creative tension in Freud's thought:

> Indeed, because the instincts are supposed to exist only in a mixed state, paradoxical emotions become the basis of the Freudian psycho-logic. Love is somewhat predatory, predation is partly an act of love. Freud's analytic taste was attracted, within the relatively harmless pathology of everyday life, to the exotic blends of character, the walking contradictions—the honest liar, the lascivious ascetic, the tender murderer, the pious iconoclast—relished by the sensibilities of such nineteenth-century writers as Dostoievski and Browning.[2]

That his work would be judged as inclining toward the poets and philosophers and away from the scientists remained a painful challenge to Freud throughout his life.

His psychoanalytic theory held that the threat of punishment is the major motivation for repression of dangerous and unrealistic drives. The origins of this threat are partly in our own lives and partly in the history of the human race. Embracing with great conviction the theory of evolution, he put it to extensive use in his systematic mental model-building. He was particularly fascinated with the parallels he discerned between primitive humans, the child, and the neurotic. He was convinced that the structure of neurosis reveals the developmental history of the individual and asserted that both in turn embody the history of humankind. Morality, along with religion, law and civilization, evolved according to a blend of Darwinian and Lamarckian principles. They rested on the bedrock of repressed desire to commit crimes of incest and patricide, on the oedipus complex and the feared punishment of castration. Our morality derives from taboos which are both "bred in the bone" and taught in the nursery. Freud was intrigued by the notion that at some time in our "prehistory" we actually committed these crimes. As he wrote at the end of *Totem and Taboo* (1913), his major work on the origins of morality: "In the beginning was the Deed!"[3] This unprovable conjecture sprang from Freud's passion to systematize the unrelenting, universal power of the Unconscious as a force in human life.

In our current, clinically grounded theories we retain the conviction that, in the unconscious mind, wish (fantasy) and deed are equivalent, and that our lives are profoundly influenced by the psychically real to a degree at least equal to, and perhaps greater than, the objectively real. The equation in the unconscious mind of wish and deed as dynamic conflictual forces constantly influences our self-esteem and, by extension, contributes to our doubts of others. This constant pressure drives our moral development and our adaptation.

In Freud's ultimate postulation (1923), moral development culminated in the establishment of the superego. This structure differentiated from the early ego and came to represent the internal moral institution in the mind. It was comprised of the conscience, the agency of punishment, and the ego ideal, the source of ideals and values.

This concept remains both incomplete in its reliance on drives and problematic in relation to gender. But it does assume and include ideas central to our contemporary understanding of punishment and morality. If we oversimplify for the moment and consider the superego as the source of our internal punishing mechanism, then the ego ideal exists in the mind as the repository of our idealizing narcissism, our unbounded infantile love and self-love, originally delegated to our parents from our infantile view of ourselves. As children we wish to be like our ideals, to be all-powerful gods once again, to have our parents for our pleasure, to be rid of all rivals for those delights to which we believe we are entitled. There are unconscious forces that make us resist renouncing any and all pleasures. We love who and that which pleases us; we hate and wish to destroy sources of pain and frustration. For Freud the dilemma is resolved through the "dissolution of the Oedipus Complex."[4] It was the obliteration of this biologically driven nexus of incestuous and murderous desires that resulted in the establishment of the superego. This monumental developmental event usually occurs at about age four, according to Freud. With it, the internal topography of the mind is altered forever and "innocence" ends. Under the threat of castration (or, for women the "fact of castration"), we renounce our wishes and identify with the powerful, narcissistically valued parent of the same sex. We install that parent's authority as the internal agency of praise and punishment, the internal regulatory of self-esteem, the source of shame and guilt, of pride and moral goodness. To be like the admired or idealized object creates a sense of well-being, of being good, better or best.

In reality, children are egocentric. All events in their world are about them and only have meaning in terms of them. They interpret all good and bad events in their lives in the currency of good and bad feelings about themselves, and therefore as potential judgments about themselves. Since childhood is punctuated by psychic dangers and traumas, all children juggle the pursuit of pleasures against the risks of calamities. We may describe children as optimists or pessimists, trustful or mistrustful about the world, partially by how they internalize the balance of hoped-for pleasures and inevitable pains. There is a developmental sequence to most of the fearsome calamities that confront a child's imagination. However, while new ones emerge, the old ones remain. These are: helplessness and fears of annihilation; abandonment or loss of the object (the mothering figure) who relieves tensions and insures safety; fall from a state of grace, or loss of parental love and approval; loss of sexual pleasure, castration or bodily injury; finally, shame and guilt, or the loss of self-esteem. Children can experience panic, terror and despair in the face of these dangers. As a form of self-protection, they project certain dangerous impulses outside themselves. They try magically to place unconscious qualities, motives, impulses and fears into others—parents, toys, heroes and villains—in attempts to master and resolve conflicts.

According to this schema, our morality always remains inherently, although most often silently, a construction based on our ambivalence. Ambivalence derives mainly from our competing sexual and aggressive drives and from the triangular nature of the oedipal relationship—the rivalrous struggle for exclusive possession of both parents. The aggression creates problematic ambivalence and problematic morality. Striking an adaptive balance between the loving and beloved superego and the hated and feared superego is a major maturational task.[5]

Developmental Perspectives on Morality

Developmentalists, those who watch mothers and their babies, offer insights from direct observation into the psychology of moral development, and into punishment. Modern child observation studies have shown that classical psychoanalytic moral theory has been wrong in its emphasis in at least two major ways. Moral development begins in the pre-oedipal phase of toddlerhood, well before the oedipal period of four to six years. More importantly, "dos" precede "don'ts" in formative and operational ways. Positive, approving, loving transactions between parent and child are profoundly instrumental in establishing early moral emotions. Emotions and reasoning are the two currents in moral development. But emotions are more evident and seem to precede what can be called moral reasoning. "Good" and "bad" have their origins in experiences of pleasure and unpleasure. "Feeling good" is the core equivalent of "being good," just as "feeling bad" equates to "being bad." The moral reasoning of all subsequent experience rests on this foundation. A sense of moral rightness comes initially from this emotionally-colored sense of self, and only later from moral reasoning which requires a developing cognitive capacity to logically and realistically assess good and evil, right and wrong, and to think in terms of the earliest of moral imperatives. It is across the "back-fence" of emotional, interpersonal experience—the moral emotions—that psychoanalysts and developmentalists can productively converse.

In healthy relationships, little children feel pride—the sense of well-being—before they experience shame, or loss of pride, for violating behavioral standards. To about age one, most children are constantly smiled at for almost everything they do; this reciprocity makes child and adult feel good about each other and about themselves. The child's emerging self is encouraged to be pleased and proud. Security, need-satisfaction, approval and sharing are the joys of this period. Separations, frustrations, the presence of strangers, and disapproving faces all make infants feel bad, and are therefore the earliest analogues of punishment. During these early months, the child's earliest aggressions and transgressions are generally accepted, ignored, or mutually pacified. It can be extremely difficult to punish a nine-month-old infant. Strict punishment of a child this age evokes moral outrage when observed. Abandonment, deprivation of nuturance, and bodily harm are our common-sense definitions of child abuse. We punish or attempt to treat parents who abuse their children in such ways.

During the second year, defiance and aggression become genuine issues for confrontation and negotiation. Freud called this phase "anal" because the instinctive pleasures involved with defecation became the battleground for control and socialization. The age of "don'ts" begins in earnest at about fifteen months, when the child has a new and favorite expression—"no!" This "no" is a milestone in conscience development. It expresses both identification with the parental "no" and the child's aggression toward the parents.[6] The once proud child can now be shamed for his aggression and for failing to meet parental expectations. This is the first obvious form of punishment. By age two, aggression, anger, and noncompliance are normal, and problems of control and ambivalence become manifest. The child is now aware of standards of behavior and begins to identify with the parent by saying "no" to himself, both in and out of parental observation. An internal representation of a "good" self becomes portable. Between ages three and four, a child can have private thoughts and therefore can have private bad thoughts. He believes that others can know his thoughts by reading his mind—as they always have done in choosing to meet his needs. He now inhibits his aggression in response to fears of parental punishment and internal self-condemnation.

Positive moral emotions evolve alongside this sequence of negative self-policing. These positive emotions generate and reenforce self esteem and contain the earliest elements of social conscience and responsibility—a phenomenon that has been notably underestimated in classical psychoanalytic theory. Little children show concern for others. They will commiserate with and endeavor to sooth the distress of other children, even share their toys with them (albeit only briefly when very young). They are capable of empathy, sympathy, and altruism. This behavior probably derives, at least in part, from the earliest, mutually pleasurable dyadic experiences of smiling and touching. One can observe toddlers inferring that what hurts them hurts another. The meaning of "me" and "mine" evolves alongside the sense of "you" and "yours." This is the beginning of "intersubjectivity" in child development—the evolving perception that there is another self, another self-conscious agent, there in that face.[7] The opportunity now exists for the growing "child-self" to feel and be good temporarily by behaving like a loving parent with another child.

Love is fine as far as it goes, but true morality has much to do with the crucial capacity to manage aggression. Psychological development is never smooth. There is a pivotal point in development that profoundly influences subsequent meanings of punishment. When internalization is still only partial, the child employs a new coping skill, a new mechanism of defense. This is "identification with the aggressor," which parallels identification with the protector.[8] This pre-moral operation, or "preautonomous superego schemata" in Sandler's formulation, reflects the internalization of parental punitive aggression, but now directed at others, not yet at oneself as self-criticism.[9] This is a very crucial moment, one at which identification with the aggressor or his aggression is a useful, limited, and temporary method of resolving internal ambivalences. It is a discharging of impounded aggression, a safe venting of frustrated anger, of desires for revenge or retribution. This pre-moral form of self-regulation is not yet true self-discipline. It is expressed when the child punishes others—his toys, sibs, other children—or has nightmares of monsters, in attempts at reestablishing psychological equilibrium. Self-discipline and true morality ultimately require the capacity and tolerance to turn the aggression, in appropriate measure, against the self, in self-criticism and self-control.

Gender and Moral Development

Female psychological development is perhaps the most glaring among the issues that Freud and classical psychoanalytic theorists underestimated and misunderstood. Males and females are two very different types of human beings, and there is much evidence to suggest important gender-related differences in moral development. Carol Gilligan has drawn attention to this question in considering morality and moral development from two distinct perspectives—justice and care.[10] In "justice- orientation," individuals are concerned primarily with equality and inequality, and the dangers of unjust or unfair treatment. In "care-orientation," individuals concentrate on preserving connections between themselves and others, on attachment and bonding, and on the dangers of detachment and abandonment. Her research suggests that, in our culture, women mature imbued with care-orientation over justice-orientation, whereas men are more concerned in their moral reasoning with justice than care and attachment. These processes are profoundly influenced by biological sex differences, gender psychology, and cultural values for masculinity and femininity.

The forms and meanings of punishment also differ in the moral development of boys and girls. Gender identity is established at about eighteen months. At that age, a child develops a fixed and essentially unalterable conviction of belonging either to the male or female gender of humankind, a conviction based on the attitudes and behavior of the parents. This is also the time when aggression gains a certain ascendency in moral development, when "don'ts" dominate control relations between parent and child. The far-reaching implications of Gilligan's work are beyond the scope of this essay, but the questions she raises are compelling. Are women taught to tolerate aggression for the sake of a "higher good"—preservation of the caring connection? Do women in fact have stronger consciences through identities as care-givers, rather than weaker superegos, because they supposedly suffered a castration complex (as Freud argued). Are more men than women in prison because men are more innately aggressive and women more nurturant? Is male moral development—like male embryological development—more fragile and contingent? Gilligan's work is also suggestive on "latency age" or school-age children, on that phase between early childhood and adolescence, the great epoches of sexual and moral change. It suggests that boys and girls both experience an intensification in consciousness of attachment or connection at that age. Being excluded by peers for failing to meet standards of behavior or for transgressing codes becomes an acutely painful form of punishment. To be ostracized from clique, club or team, to be left or forced out by one's friends, is then experienced as a fate worse than death. It can collapse self-esteem far more readily than can parental disapproval, and lead to antisocial or "immoral" behavior.

Punishment and Moral Pathologies

Problems, deviations, arrests and fixations in the internalizing of our early relations, in our moral development, become manifest as forms of moral psychopathology, as the problems we witness in prisons, hospitals, and analysts' offices. My inventory includes the amoral, the hypermoral, the paranoid, and the masochistic.

The amoral have no emphathetic identification with others, and are indifferent to the feelings of others—particularly as regards overt expression of their own aggression. Their "superego pathology" reflects failures in the maturation of defenses and internal representations needed to modulate aggressive impulses. Freud wrote a particularly gem-like paper in which he described the roles guilt and punishment can have in character structure.[11] What I call amoral he called the "exceptions"—those self-centered and guiltless individuals who are convinced that they have been made to suffer unjustly, and are entitled thereby to reparations and compensations for their injured narcissism. Freud used Richard III as a dramatic example of someone who believes he is "owed" because he was unjustly punished by Fate with deformity in childhood: unfairly victimized, he is entitled to victimize or punish others; moral rules do not apply to him. The vengeful hatred engendered by irreparable damage to the self negates guilt. There results a grandiose, megalomaniacal identification with the punisher, which is expressed in violence and sadism. Such persons rarely seek therapeutic help voluntarily, although they may drive others to do so. When they come for treatment, it is usually for profound, often suicidal depression.

The hypermoral fear being bad or wrong so relentlessly that they must constantly prove their worth and virtue. They are perfectionists, critics of self and others, who suffer from morbid fear of being mistaken, unprepared, messy or dirty. Analysts label this problem "obsessional." Such persons come to us because they are never good enough. They want to be the best. They live under the tyranny of the "shoulds," and by the principle that it is better to be right than to be happy. The internal world of the hypermoral obsessive is dominated by a harsh, forever vigilant punitive conscience. What sometimes appears to be mild-manneredness is the result of intense self-discipline. They must remain carefully controlled lest they become messy, impulsive, lustful or violent. They dread spontaneity. Their internal standards of self-worth are rigid and unattainable. Since wish and deed are equivalent currency in the unconscious mind, punishment is expected for all wishes that violate rules. These persons fear a private hell of guilt and shame. Analytic work reveals the flawed resolution of their ambivalences about aggression. In their narrations, they speak of the endless rules for containing infantile aggression, mess, and appetites. They seek to cast the analyst as parent or teacher who will praise their good behavior and grade their productions, or as the policeman who will punish them for real and imagined transgressions. Significantly, the hypermoral person usually has hidden zones of self-indulgence, mess, and moral failure which bring secret guilty pleasure.

There are persons whose hypermorality may seem obsessional, but on close examination it is seen to be paranoid. Among the paranoid, aggression is denied unsuccessfully and then projected onto others. The result is an inner conviction of moral superiority that others seek to attack, and a sense of culpability that demands punishment. The paranoid has created a tormenting reality in which his judges do exist and will punish him, whether justly or not. Yet, he believes himself innocent of evil impulses. Such is the plight of "K" in Kafka's *The Trial.* The aggression of the paranoid is always retaliatory.

Desiring Punishment and Masochism

Masochism obtains when there is a motivated and obligatory combination of pain and reward, or pleasure. The reward is most often unconscious; it takes form in fantasies, and is expressed in feelings, thoughts and behaviors. Masochism is not suffering endured realistically—the rational price paid for something of value, tolerance of a painful solution to a problem. It is not a matter of poor judgment, or simple obliviousness to the consequences of one's actions. It is not being stupid or unfortunate. It is not an occurrance of "when bad things happen to good people." It is rather the active seeking of some form of pain, humiliation, subjugation or wounding—of punishment—from oneself or from others. Whereas the suffering is usually apparent and sometimes dramatically obvious, the reward is usually hidden and secret. In the clinical analytic situation, analyst and patient explore the patient's stories to discover the satisfaction that the suffering or frustration provides. In these stories, the patient is always child-like, often problematically childism. He or she is always the victim of aggressions, whether unjust or just. Moral development becomes masochistic development when the dangers to the self are experienced as too real or too great, when life is viewed as an endless series of frustrations, disappointments, and failures. Those who must suffer will and do seek out punishment. They turn happiness into tragedy, victory into defeat. To those who know them, their suffering is rarely silent. They seek self-punishment, for it proves personal truths of embattlement and low self-esteem. When they come to treatment, ostensibly to get or be better, the process is very slow and painful. And the results often seem disappointingly limited. As in life, so in treatment: just when one might expect improvement, the self-punishing patient suffers further painful defeat. And the analyst shares in that defeat.

Certain concepts are milestones in the history of psychoanalytic thought. Masochism is such a concept. By seeing how it was understood at any given time, it is possible to place oneself in the evolution of psychoanalytic formulations of the mind. Every new idea in psychoanalysis has confronted the "litmus test" of masochism.[12] Freud used sexual perversions to explore and validate his general theories of normal psychological development. When he elaborated on Drafft-Ebing's description of the perversion depicted in Leopold van Sacher-Masoch's autobiographical novella *Venus in Furs*, he explained masochism as an infantilism, a developmental vicissitude of normal infantile sexuality.

Later, using Lady Macbeth and Rebecca in Ibsen's *Rosmerholm*, Freud described "those wrecked by success," whose unconscious guilt for their incestuous wishes is so powerful that any success in life represents a forbidden instinctual triumph and demands punishment. These are "moral masochists" who insist that life and circumstance punish them, and accordingly provoke mistreatment by others.[13] Their brethren in masochism are what Freud labelled "criminals from a sense of guilt," those who must do something wrong and are compelled to be caught for some offense in order to appease their unconscious need for punishment. As his mental models grew in complexity, Freud postulated masochism as a compromise between oedipal sexual wishes and defenses against guilt and aggression, including sibling rivalry.[14] The masochistic fantasy was a pathological regression from normal morality to an unconscious beating fantasy in which sexual pleasure and guilt for aggression are fused. This regressive resexualizing of the formation of the superego at the oedipal phase subsumed and organized all prior pre-oedipal trauma. Freud's "last word" on masochism emphasized the clinical problems of masochistic personalities, moral masochists, stalemates in treatment, and negative therapeutic reactions. He also recognized the failure of his metapsychology, and particularly his theories of psychic energy, to explain all of human hedonic motivation.[15] All subsequent psychoanalytic formulations of masochism have deemphasized guilt over sexual pleasure and instead emphasized pre-oedipal, narcissistic and object-related motivations.

Masochism can be seen as an adaptation to a disturbed, highly conditional, and/or dangerously aggressive early relationship. It can be a pathological way of loving a cruel or indifferent care-taker, an adaptive amalgam of passivity and receptivity to harshness or neglect. The result is frustrated aggression turned against oneself: "If I suffer, the infant or child is feeling, then mother will have to love me and care for me." This is seduction of the aggressor, the weapon of the weak according to Lowenstein, used to diffuse or control the aggression of the powerful.[16] It can be an attempt to recreate or maintain a magical power, a grandiose control over one's life by being the supreme author of tragedy, not simply its passive victim. This becomes a guiding principle in later life. It is easier to guarantee pain or frustration than pleasure.[17]

All formulations of masochism subsequent to Freud's suggest that unconscious sexual guilt can be a powerful motive for seeking punishments, although not necessarily the only one. The ambivalences and conflicts in self-worth that arise from very violent or conditional relationships with care-givers, or from particularly disjunctive early relationships, will lead to what we call empathetic failures. These failures create wounds in the healthy narcissistic organization of the self, wounds which lead in turn to excessive dreading or desiring of punishment in later life. The joy in the eye of the mother reflected back to the child creates the sense of feeling good, and therefore of being good. Failure to receive adequate doses of this experience—inadequate because of the child's excessive need, which is constitutionally determined, or maternal refusal—can lead to a life-long addiction to admiration. Life then becomes a series of narcissistic blows, of unjustified punishments which justify rage or withdrawal. By contrast, when a child grows up feeling responsible for the parent's emotional state punishment is sought to appease or sooth the parent and secure the bond. Bondage, thus formed, is at lest a protection against abandonment. Loss of the nurtrant object as punishment means psychological death.

In sum, one can unconsciously seek punishment because one wishes to prove that he or she is not alone, unloved or unlovable, not the passive victim of uncontrollable forces; or because one wishes to coerce others into guilty submission, to prove others worthless, bad or powerless; or because the pain is exciting and erotically sweet; or to gain absolution for sins of desire and sadism. These forms of the need for punishment become organizing principles in life, bases for self-definition and self-worth, and mechanisms of immature and perverse moral development.

Psychoanalysis as "Moral Treatment"

What of the four situations cited at the beginning of this essay? The roles punishment may have in the problems of those figurative patients, and how these might be uncovered through analyses, can now, hopefully, be more readily understood. For the blocked graduate student, his thesis represented a competitive transgression: by avoiding completion, he avoided an unconsciously more severe punishment, and as reward held on to his childlike, protective relationship with authorities. For the unhappy and angry professional woman, seeking out disappointing relationships with "bad" men provided secret satisfaction of and unconscious punishment for her desire to "have it all." The extremely conscientious analytic candidate needed to prove, against all odds, that he never failed to meet expectations, never broke a rule, and was therefore even superior to his elders. The dreamer caught cheating was beginning to "enjoy" her analysis and the gifts of insight from her analysis too much; she was cheating by finding forbidden pleasure in her work which might hurt or anger the mother whom she protected and on whom she unconsciously felt she still depended.

In the course of an analysis, the analyst attempts to facilitate the development of transference—that constellation of feelings, attitudes and behaviors which reflects past, childlike meanings of the analyst for the analysand. Freud's discovery of the transference and its ubiquity in analysis, as well as in love and life, was among his most powerful insights. Transferences are experiences that allow the analytic process to become real, immediate, and influential. As an analysis progresses, the narrative focuses increasingly on the analytic relationship itself. The analysand "becomes" a version of himself as a child in relation to the analyst. The analysis becomes various versions of psychic history, a history which includes moral development. Rieff noted: "All the issues which psychoanalysis treats—the health and sickness of the will, the emotions, the responsibilities of private living, the coercions of culture—belong to the moral life."[18] Patients do not in fact become children, nor do analysts become parents. Yet, in effective analysis, there develops a "split screen" in the narration: the analysand watches himself or herself at serious play, in an earnest fantasy of childhood. To his amazement, he becomes once again a good and bad child, a little and big criminal. Taboos are tested and transgressed. As if compelled, he becomes naughty, compliant, messy, destructive, dangerous, fragile, terrified, rebellious, virtuous, victim, victimizer, exceptional, forgotten, and, hopefully, with some reluctance, a wiser, freer, more tolerant and effective adult.

Conclusion

Why is punishment necessary? Obviously, people commit acts which society defines as wrong, bad, or injurious to individual and social values. An observation made by a contributor to this volume strikes me as especially relevant to this question. Contrary to what I would have anticipated, most victims of crimes desire or are even satisfied with recognition, not revenge or retribution, after the immediate impact of the crime.[19] Recognition suggests repair of the assaulted "person-ness," of the sense of self that has been injured by the crime. And I would suggest that behind this event there has been a failure of identification between victimizer and victim, a loss of shared beliefs and values, a fracture of early moral emphathetic bonds in the aggressor. People commit crimes, at least in part, because they experience themselves as insufficiently identified with, and connected to, their victims. They identify with the aggressor and his aggression; they become punisher, instead of victim. The criminal may believe that they are disenfranchised morally by the social system in which they live, and therefore justified in acting against it. The developmental notion of internalized relationships of punished and punisher and the social manifestations of those relationships merit further exploration.

We never escape our concerns with punishment. We are always prone to view events in our lives or problems in our relationships as punishments, just or unjust. The meanings we give to real and imagined, dreaded and desired punishments, self-inflicted or otherwise, always derive from intricate balances in self-appraisal. And self-appraisal subsumes the fundamentally conflictual history of our relationships to the objects of our desires and fears. This balance is a process of development, one subject to excesses and disturbances that eventuate in moral pathologies. Moral pathologies result from traumatic failures of nurturance, impaired impulse control, and parental moral immaturities. In consequence, persons fail to develop flexible and realistic self-discipline and self-appraisal. Heinz Hartmann cautioned against simple equations of psychological health and ethics. Pointing to the limitations of psychoanalytic moral theorizing, he stated: "No scientific psychology, even if it were perfected beyond what it is today, could take the place of personal responsibilities in these matters."[20] But psychoanalysis is not completely neutral or without bias in these matters. The goals of analysis are to be better, if only somehow good enough; to gain insight into oneself and one's life. The self-knowledge thus acquired is not liberation from moral constraint. It is rather a self-told moral story that can liberate from unconsciously driven dreading and desiring of punishment. It offers a form of personal wisdom and a sense of balanced moral self.

---

[1]Jean-Paul Sartre, *No Exit and Three Other Plays* (New York: Vintage Books, 1960), p. 47.

[2]Philip Rieff, *Freud: The Mind of the Moralist* (New York: Viking Press,1959), p. 54.

[3]Sigmund Freud, *Totem and Taboo*, Standard Edition (London: Hogarth Press, 1964) vol. 13, p. 161.

[4]*The Dissolution of the Oedipus Complex*, Standard Edition, vol. 19, pp. 173-182.

[5]Roy Schafer, "The Loving and Beloved Superego in Freud's Structural Theory," *Psychoanalytic Study of the Child*, vol. 15, 1960, pp. 163-188.

[6]Rene Spitz, *No and Yes: On the Genesis of Human Communication* (New York: International University Press,1966).

[7]Daniel Stern, *The Interpersonal World of the Enfant* (New York: Basic Books, 1985).

[8]Ann Freud, *The Ego and the Mechanisms of Defense* (New York: International University Press, 1946).

[9]Joseph Sandler, "On the Concept of the Superego", *Psychoanalytic Study of the Child*, vol. 15, pp. 128-162.

[10]Carol Gilligan, *In a Different Voice: Psychological Theory and Women's Development* (Cambridge: Harvard University Press,1982).

[11]Freud, "Some Character Types Met With in Psychoanalytic Work," Standard Edition, vol. 14, pp. 309-336.

[12]Robert A. Glick and Donald I. Myers, *Masochism: Current Psychoanalytic Perspectives* (Hillsdale, New Jersey: Analytic Press,1988), pp.1-25.

[13]Freud, "Some Character Types Met with in Psychoanalytic Work."

[14]Freud, "A Child is Being Beaten," Standard Edition, vol. 17, pp. 175-204.

[15]Freud, "The Economic Problem of Masochism," Standard Edition, vol. 19, pp. 155-172.

[16]Rudolph Lowenstein, "A Contribution to the Psychoanalytic Theory of Masochism," vol. 5, pp. 197-234.

[17]Arnold Cooper, "The Narcissistic-Masochistic Character," in R.A. Glick and D.I. Meyers (editors), *Masochism: Current Psychoanalytic Perspectives*, pp. 117-138.

[18]Philip Rieff, *Freud::The Mind of the Moralist* (New York: Viking Press, 1959), p. 300.

[19]Lois G. Forer, "A Trial Judge's View of Moral, Constitutional and Conventional Justifications for Punishment."

[20]Heinz Hartmann, *Psychoanalysis and Moral Values* (New York: International Universities Press), p. 102.

PART III

ISSUES IN CONTEMPORARY ETHICS AND JURISPRUDENCE

A Trial Judge's View of Moral, Constitutional and Conventional Justifications for Punishment

Lois G. Forer

There is a common belief that judges do not seriously consider moral dimensions of punishment. Professor H.L.A. Hart expressed that conventional wisdom when he wrote:

> No one expects judges—occupied in the business of sending people to the gallows or to prison—to have much time for philosophical discussion of the principles which make it morally tolerable to do these things.[1]

It requires temerity to take issue with so distinguished an authority. But I find that statement false in important material respects. First, judges are not engaged in a business. We are duly authorized public officials engaged in government. Second, our function is not sending people to prison or the gallows but upholding the law and, insofar as possible within the constraints of the law, doing justice. Third, many of us do indeed devote much thought to seeking moral grounds for the orders we are required to enter.

For sixteen years I served as a trial judge in the Court of Common Pleas in Philadelphia. In that capacity, I was obliged to sentence several thousand offenders. Although I presided over many murder trials, I never gave a death charge to a jury or imposed a death sentence. I believe that it is morally wrong to take a human life, and especially wrong when the killing is done by the state under the aegis of law. The authority of the state to kill is not immutable: it was not until the High Middle Ages that the state obtained a monopoly of the legal use of violence and executions. I believe that a death sentence is unconstitutional. The executed person is denied the equal protection of the laws because that person cannot in future petition for reconsideration on the basis of after-discovered evidence. The death penalty is wrong as a matter of policy because it brutalizes the public by pandering to desires for blood lust and vengeance.

In imposing other penalties, I was guided by the following principles: (1) my obligation to uphold the law; (2) avoidance of cruelty; (3) protection of the public. Although I sought guidance in libraries from the great minds of the past as well as from contemporary jurists, philosophers, and criminologists, they were of little help in my daily duties. Theories of retribution, deterrence, incapacitation, and rehabilitation appear to be logical and coherent, but when applied to specific human beings often proven irrelevant or in conflict with my moral beliefs. I was thus obliged to develop my own sentencing practices.

I do not use the word punishment in discussion of those practices. Punishment is customarily defined as causing pain. Historically, criminal penalties were designed to cause maximum pain. Disembowelling, drawing and quartering, maiming and beating, as well as public hangings were common. They were justified as being moral and appropriate because they would "right the wrong" done by the offender. As recently as 1922, Justice Holmes declared that requiring a prisoner to wear shackles was neither cruel nor unusual. Today, few of us would contest that such penalties are cruel and, indeed, barbaric. Like Richard Rorty, I believe that "cruelty is the worst thing" one can do—especially in the name of law.[2]

Punishment, whether inflicted by court order or privately, is an exercise of power by the powerful over the powerless. The most frequent and accepted imposition of punishment is within the family—parents exercising power over children, often through brutal beatings. Many a father who appeared before me on charges of child abuse filed by the hospital to which his injured child was taken justified his actions as "discipline." Only a few years ago the Supreme Court held the right of school teachers to beat pupils; in that ruling, it assimilated the authority of teachers to that of parents. The Court expressed no doubt that parents have such authority under some unarticulated principle of natural law. The Court also masked the brutality of the teacher's actions, which resulted in injury to several children, by using the euphemism "spanking," rather than the accurate word "beating." It should also be recalled that in Anglo-American law until the nineteenth-century husbands were authorized to beat their wives, although the size of rod was limited. Today, corporal punishment has been outlawed as a penalty for adult law-violators. And capital punishment is now restricted to murder without mitigating circumstances, instead of being applicable to more than 250 offenses as it was in England during the eighteenth-century. Yet, more than one thousand persons are now on death row awaiting executions that will inevitably be carried out in the near future because the appellate rights of the condemned have been drastically restricted. Many of those persons are young. Some are mentally retarded. Others are emotionally disturbed. Most are poor, undereducated, and from deprived backgrounds. These undeniable facts create serious equal protection issues.

Let us turn to the penalties legally imposed on the two million men, women, and children who were convicted of crime or delinquency in 1989 in the United States. Most of the misdemeanants and white collar felons among them were sentenced to probation, not prison. But more than 619,000 persons are incarcerated today. Both in absolute numbers and in proportion to the population we have more people behind bars than any other Western nation. And the numbers are steadily increasing. The number of prisoners is growing more rapidly than the crime rate because more judges are sending offenders to prison than ever before. I do not underestimate the tragic effects of drugs, particularly crack and angel dust, on criminality. However, the increase in the prison population is due primarily to sentencing policies and practices, in particular mandatory sentences and sentencing guidelines.

I was familiar with jails, prisons and juvenile lockups before I went on the bench. I had interviewed countless clients and witnesses in these places and visited many such institutions throughout the country. I will recount the experiences of three typical prisoners; the names are fictitious but the facts are true. Tony was a strong, handsome, black-haired man when I first saw him. He was married and had two children. He was convicted of theft of a $30.00 radio, a second offense. I could not represent him because I was then a deputy attorney general. Eight years later, after I had returned to private practice, Tony contacted me. He was still in prison for that theft. I entered the fortress-like prison. The first set of doors clanged shut behind me, always an unnerving sound. I proceeded to the second set of metal doors that were unlocked and then locked behind me. I smelled the familiar odor of age, urine and disinfectant. A frail, stooped, white-haired man shuffled slowly toward me. This was Tony. I obtained his release on parole, with some difficulty. Tony's wife had left him years before. He was never able to find his children. Billy, a slight light-skinned boy of nineteen who had stolen a car, was gang-raped his first night in prison. George, a state senator whom I had prosecuted for fraud, committed suicide in prison.

When I went on the bench I could not forget these people and scores like them whom I had known as defense counsel and as prosecutor. The old

Philadelphia prison that served, in the nineteenth-century, as a model of penology for the United States and much of the Western world is only a few blocks from my home. I saw its grim, forbidding walls from my windows, every morning and every evening. It was built in 1829 at a cost of $100,000. Today it stands idle, a monument to failed theories and to the arrogance and myopia of well-meaning ideologies.

Knowing what I did about the effects of prison on inmates and their families, I doubted whether I could fulfill the obligations of a judge without violating my conscience. The facile answer of an Eichmann that I would only be following rules did not satisfy me. After much soul-searching, I decided that I could uphold the law and avoid cruelty if I used prison as the penalty of last resort rather than the penalty of choice. Unless there was convincing evidence that the release of an offender would pose an unreasonable risk of harm to the community or individuals, I placed offenders on a probation conditional on their paying restitution and reparation to the victims of their crimes and a fine to the court. When I began this practice, I had no idea whether such sentences would be effective. There were questions to which I had no answers. Was such a sentence legal? The Supreme Court of Pennsylvania held that it was. Would the offenders cooperate? Most did report to their probation officers; only a few absconded. Would persons who were undereducated and had never held a steady job be able to make the required payments? It soon became apparent that when faced with the alternative of prison these offenders did find employment and did make the payments, although that often required some prodding. Would the crime victims consider that such sentences were not sufficiently severe? It was my practice to discuss the possible range of penalties with crime victims and to solicit their views. They appreciated the opportunity to be heard. Very few—even of those who had been injured or brutalized—expressed a wish for vengeance or cruelty against their aggressors.

When I retired in 1987, I wanted to know the results of this sentencing practice. I turned to Professor Marvin Wolfgang, an eminent criminologist at the University of Pennsylvania. He referred Elmar Weitekamp to me. Mr. Weitekamp, a doctoral candidate in criminology, made a careful study of the sentences I imposed over a ten-year period. The records of those cases became the basis for his doctoral dissertation.

Through exhaustive investigation, Mr. Weitekamp determined that I was the only American judge who had consistently used monetary penalties for all types of felons. No one else had regularly imposed such penalties on street criminals, although there had been several controlled experiments using restitution for misdemeanants, white collar criminals, and juveniles.

Mr. Weitekamp examined 605 consecutive cases of mine. He found that two-thirds of the offenders successfully completed their sentences, paid the restitution, reparations and fines, and had not been rearrested. This is a dramatic contrast to the national statistics on recidivism. They reveal that two-thirds of all prisoners are rearrested for other crimes after release from incarceration. There was nothing unusual about the offenders I sentenced. They conformed to national characteristics for metropolitan areas: 90.2% were male; 23% white; 74.2% black; 4.5% Hispanic; 78% high school dropouts. All were charged with serious felonies. From a strictly utilitarian perspective, my practice was successful: two-thirds of the offenders had been deterred from committing future crimes; they had also become gainfully employed. By such gross, but measurable, criteria, one could conclude that they had been rehabilitated.

General deterrence is an unreasonable goal for a just system of criminal law. There is no credible evidence that even the most draconian penalties, such as capital punishment, affect the crime rate. And my sentencing practices had no observable effect on the crime rate in Philadelphia. But their monetary savings were very considerable. The cost of keeping one person in prison for one year is $40,000. The cost of building one maximum security cell is $100,000. Unlike prisoners, the offenders I sentenced were employed and paid taxes. Many supported their families. Most of those families would have been on welfare if the offender had been imprisoned.

But these benefits do not, of themselves, morally justify punishment, and thus penalties. Even the minimal deprivation of liberty caused by a probationary sentence and the imposition of monetary penalties constitutes punishment. On what moral basis can the state wield such power over an individual? In addressing that question, I shall assume that every convicted offender has had a due process trial and was guilty of the crimes of which he or she was convicted.

There is a moral justification for imposing penalties on law violators. Every society must set reasonable limitations on individual, corporate, communal and governmental behavior if it is to maintain a functioning government and decent conditions of life for its members. Such rules and laws must be enforced, although I can find no categorical imperative to punish. The alternative to enforcement is anarchy, chaos, and a resulting loss of all individual liberty. But in enforcing laws, courts should adopt the least restrictive penalties possible to obtain compliance. This concept of the least restrictive conditions has been upheld with respect to mental patients but, paradoxically, it has not been extended to law violators.

No one today seriously questions two fundamental principles of criminal penalties: that the penalty should be imposed only on the wrong-doer; that the penalty be proportionate to the crime. Lip service is routinely paid to these principles. In fact, they are violated every day. When a mother who is the caretaker of her small children is sentenced to prison, the children are subjected to severe punishment. They are usually placed in a series of inadequate and often abusive foster homes. Wives and children of male offenders also suffer punishment when the breadwinner is imprisoned. But few sentencing guidelines consider the effects of a prison sentence on members of a family, nor do many writers on jurisprudence. The almost universal practice of sentencing white collar offenders to probation and fines that are not commensurate with their ill-gotten gains violates the principle of proportionality. When one compares the penalties imposed on street felons with the sentences imposed on Colonel Oliver North, the Watergate felons, and corporate offenders such as Smith, Kline & Beckman (whose failure to report the side effects of their products resulted in twenty-six deaths), the lack of proportionality and the denial of equal protection of the laws are blatant.

My third principle of sentencing was protection of the public from unreasonable risk of harm. This sounds like common sense, but it raises conceptual problems. Theorists such as Andrew Von Hirsch argue that the goal of protecting the public means punishment for future crimes.[3] I find this argument to be specious. No individual can be sentenced until he or she has been convicted of a crime. In determining sentence for that crime, I believe that it is appropriate to take into account the circumstances of the crime and the mental, emotional, and other conditions of the offender that indicate whether he or she will probably commit other offenses. Sensible individuals make educated prognostications in all aspects of life. I see no reason why judges should be denied such discretion.

The sentencing of irrational persons involves major problems. A reasonable individual—the paradigm on which the entire common law is predicated—will most probably be deterred from committing future illegal acts if he or she knows from previous experience that crime does not pay. The entire theory of deterrence is based on this presumption. However, irrational and mentally or emotionally disturbed individuals do not function in this fashion. Such people constitute an enormous danger to the public, a danger that the law does not recognize. It is a fundamental tenet of Anglo-American law that no one shall be held criminally responsible unless the person knowingly and volitionally violates the law. Customarily, this is phrased in what I would call ecclesiastical terms: an actor who is responsible for his actions "deserves" to be punished. The converse of this proposition is that a person who is not responsible should not be punished. That view was embraced by the Supreme Court in *Robinson v California.*[4] The Court held that "criminal penalties may not be inflicted upon a person for being in a condition he is powerless to change." This sounds humane—but it results in the release of scores of persons who have committed violent offenses and who most probably will continue to do so, not because they are evil, but because they cannot control themselves. The common law recognizes only two mental states: sane and insane. Enormous amounts of time and effort have been devoted to developing definitions of insanity. But comparatively little thought has been given to the appropriate treatment of offenders who fall in the broad continuum that exists between sanity and insanity.

I offer one example of that lacuna. The crime was unusual, but the consequences were not. Lemoyne, a fictious name but a real individual, forcibly raped his mother when he was twenty-three. He had a long history of psychiatric problems. But according to the McNaghten Rule in force in Pennsylvania he was not insane. He was examined by a court psychiatrist who reported that even with intensive psychotherapy his prognosis was poor. I sentenced him to the maximum penalty the law allowed: ten to twenty years in prison. I also ordered psychiatric treatment. But it was foreseeable that on his release Lemoyne would still be a violent and dangerous person. He was released for good conduct after eight years in prison. He raped an elderly woman within a few days. Lemoyne was convicted of that rape and again sentenced to ten to twenty years. It is most likely that he will gain be released at the end of his minimum sentence and will commit other rapes. If American jurisprudence were freed from notions of sin and punishment, courts could impose sentences on such individuals that would provide reasonable protection for society.

Two recent developments in American criminal law have created almost insuperable obstacles to the kind of sentencing I practiced: (1) widespread adoption of mandatory sentencing laws; (2) sentencing guideline statutes. I regard both as unconstitutional and unwise. They have resulted in an enormous increase in the number of prisoners. Mandatory sentencing laws usually state that for certain crimes a court must sentence the offender to five years confinement irrespective of the circumstances of the crime or the lack of danger that the individual presents. Other statutes require long prison sentences for three-time offenders, irrespective of the nature of the crimes. Under such a recidivism statute, the Supreme court upheld a life sentence for a person who had committed two non-violent thefts and one embezzlement. Those three crimes totalled less than $1000. Guideline sentences are based on a mathematical formula that gives a fixed number of points for each crime regardless of the circumstances and a fixed number of points for the prior record of the offender. Neither the background nor the mental condition of the offender is calculated in the sentence, which is fixed at a certain number of months or years in prison.

Arson is a good example of the folly of such guidelines. A person who sets a fire to collect insurance is a rational criminal. He can be deterred by a sufficiently high penalty of restitution and fines. A person who sets fires for the thrill of watching the blaze is irrational and cannot be deterred—even by a prison sentence.

It is commonly asserted that a prison sentence "incapacitates" an offender. This is a fashionable word, but an inaccurate one. Imprisonment does not incapacitate an inmate from committing crimes. The numerous assaults and fires in prisons dramatically demonstrate that capacity. A prison sentence only isolates the inmate from the general public for its term. This is desirable for habitually violent and irrational offenders. But it is unnecessary and undesirable for the majority of offenders who are reasonable and not violent. And because prisons do not rehabilitate, incapacitate or deter, the courts are trapped in a costly, frustrating recycling of offenders.

Aberrant sentences, a relatively minor problem could easily be corrected without the drastic remedy of mandatory or guideline sentencing. A system of broad appeals of sentencing, such as prevails in Canada, would suffice. Lawyers would no longer be required to comb through the record of a trial searching for a legal error on which to base an appeal, when the real ground for the appeal is the sentence, not the verdict.

In conclusion, I believe that when sentencing is individualized, and pain and cruelty are minimized, as far as is possible within the limits of rule of law, the offender can be rehabilitated and the victim can be aided. Such exercise of state power does not violate moral principles or public interest. In addressing the Polish Parliament, former President Havel of Czechoslovakia stated: "My program is to bring spirituality, moral responsibility, humaneness, and humility into politics." My aim as a sentencing judge was to bring those qualities to the criminal justice system.

---

[1]H.L.A. Hart, *Punishment and Responsibility: Essays in the Philosophy of Law* (New York: Oxford University Press, 1968), p.2

[2]Richard Rorty, *Contingency, Irony and Solidarity* (New York: Cambridge University Press, 1989), p.XV.

[3]Andrew Von Hirsh, *Past and Future Crimes: Deservedness and Dangerousness in the Sentencing of Criminals* (New Brunswick: Rutgers University Press, 1985).

[4]370 US 660.

Getting Even: The Role of the Victim

Jeffrie G. Murphy

> Not if his gifts outnumbered the sea sands
> or all the dust grains in the world could Agamemnon
> ever appease me—not till he pays me back
> full measure, pain for pain, dishonor for dishonor.
>
> *Iliad* (IX.383-386)

I. Introduction[1]

Achilles is vindictive; he wants to get even with Agamemnon. Being so disposed, he sounds rather like many current crime victims who angrily complain that the American system of criminal justice will not allow them the satisfactions they rightfully seek. These victims often feel that their particular injuries are ignored while the system addresses itself to some abstract injury to the state or to the rule of law itself—a focus that appears to result in wrongdoers being treated with much greater solicitation and respect than their victims receive. If the actual victims are noticed at all (other than to alert the state to a violation of its interests), they will likely be told that there is another branch of law—tort law—that has the job of dealing with private injuries and grievances and that, if they pursue this route at their own expense, they might ultimately get some financial compensation for the wrongs done to them. However, just as Achilles felt that mere compensation was inadequate to the kind of injury done to him by Agamemnon, many of these victims will often claim that the injuries they have suffered (brutal rape, perhaps) do not admit of financial compensation. How, they might ask, can a dollar value be set on the humiliation and degradation they have experienced? They might also note that those who injure them tend, unlike Agamemnon, to be judgment-proof—so lacking in resources as to be unable to make any meaningful contribution to any compensation package that the victim may win. From such a perspective and from such feelings has the "victims' rights movement" in part been born.[2]

In this essay I will address simply *one* of the many issues raised by this movement—namely, the issue of the legitimacy of hatred and desires for revenge as operative values in a system of criminal law. It is widely assumed—as a part of liberal culture, particularly Christian liberal culture—that such psychological states are either unambiguously evil or unambiguously sick and that, in either case, they deserve no place in the moral and legal outlook of civilized people. Thus opponents of the victims' rights movement will often characterize it as simply the institutionalization of vindictiveness—where such a characterization is supposed to serve as a *reductio ad absurdum* of the movement. Proponents of the movement will then generally take great pains attempting to show that the movement is *not* based on these admittedly evil feelings but on something else—social utility or justice, perhaps. Thus, both sides seem to agree that if the movement is indeed based on these feelings and the desire to institutionalize them, then the movement is a mistake.

Since I am skeptical that this agreement is justified, I will in this essay attempt to do two things: (1) I will suggest that the burden of proof should be placed on those who in principle *oppose* hatred, vindictiveness and revenge—that someone other than the champions of these responses should be put on the defensive for a change; and (2) I will suggest that this burden might not be as easy to bear as some might initially think. My purpose is neither to celebrate hatred and its close cousins nor to argue positively that this feeling and its associated practices should be built into the criminal law. I rather seek to expose some bad arguments against it and its institutionalization (but also to highlight some important arguments against it) in the hope that its possible role—and indeed the whole victims' rights movement—can be seen in a clearer and fairer light.

II. Who Has the Burden of Proof?

As a starting point in inquiry, I am inclined to accept what might be called a bias or presumption in favor of common sense—namely, that absent some good argument to make us withdraw our common-sense beliefs and attitudes, we should regard them as reasonable. We should not always feel obligated to defend our ordinary views, but should rather impose the burden of challenge on others—being honestly willing, of course, to abandon the comfort of the received wisdom if we are indeed provided with good arguments for so doing. The underlying assumption behind this bias or presumption can, I think, partly be understood in (loosely) evolutionary terms. Our ordinary views and attitudes must, at least at one time, have had *something* going for them—some useful and adaptive contact with our social world or with the world of nature. Otherwise, it would be hard to see why these beliefs and attitudes would survive and be so deeply entrenched in our psyches. Of course, some beliefs and attitudes that might have been adaptive at some distant time in our evolutionary history (e.g., racist beliefs and attitudes, perhaps) can properly be seen in present circumstances as maladaptive, irrational, and evil. But we come to see this, I assume, not because this was always obviously so (it clearly was *not*), but because we have listened to and been persuaded by overwhelming practical and moral arguments for a change in these beliefs and attitudes. Such an example, however, does not demonstrate the unreasonableness of a presumption in favor of common sense any more than the confident conviction of some guilty people demonstrates the unreasonableness of the presumption of innocence in criminal procedure.

In my role as armchair, anecdotal social scientist, I have come to the conclusion that most of us *do* accept, as a matter of common sense, the appropriateness of hatred and revenge in some circumstances—specifically, when these responses are exhibited by victims of serious wrongdoing and are directed against those who have wronged them. (In *Forgiveness and Mercy*, I call this "retributive hatred.")[3] Although most people pay a kind of general Sunday school lip service to the idea that even these hatreds are evil, their more casual conversations and practices will often fly in the face of these pious cliches. Give them the right criminal (e.g., John Mitchell for Watergate era liberals) and they will warm to shared fantasies of giving that criminal his "pain for pain, dishonor for dishonor." This also comes out rather clearly in people's entertainment preferences. For example, I recently resaw (with some equally civilized and equally liberal friends) the movie *Silverado*. In this classy Western, we are presented with four honest and decent men (and their friends and families) being subjected to unspeakable injuries by thugs of unspeakable evil. When, in the closing moments of the movie, these men take—and, indeed, *gleefully* take—their violent revenge on those who have wronged them, all who watched cheered them on and found this outcome not only aesthetically pleasing but morally satisfying. And I think that the vast majority of other normal people would have experienced a comparable reaction—otherwise, how could we explain the great popularity of revenge entertainment? We like to see the portrayal of evil people getting their painful but just deserts, and we particularly enjoy it when these deserts are administered by their victims. Portrayals are, of course, fiction and fantasy—and many of those who approve of the fictional portrayal of revenge might still have deep and even final objections to having it occur in the real world. (Perhaps, for example, they believe that we are never actually able to know that we confront the kind of genuine evil that is simply a given in the world of fiction—that, unlike The Shadow, we are unable to know what evil lurks in the hearts of men.) But this is a practical objection; it makes no contribution to establishing that all feelings of hatred and revenge are intrinsically, or inherently, or in principle irrational or immoral. Feelings that we genuinely regard as inherently depraved (e.g., racial hatred) we would not even welcome as fantasy or fiction; thus, I think, we would have great doubts about a person who applauded the fictionally portrayed successes of a Nazi deathcamp commandant—even if he followed up his entertainment by saying "But, of course, I would hate to see this happen in the real world." Thus I think that most typical, decent, mentally healthy people have a kind of commonsense approval of some righteous hatred and revenge (but not of simply unprovoked malicious hatred or racial hatred) and are in some sense willing publicly to admit this, at least symbolically—e.g., they will stand without shame in line to see such revenge movies as *Silverado*, but not to see a film that glorifies racial hatred.

So perhaps we can grant that those who are willing to take the trouble to present a case in favor of some hatreds and acts of revenge are really seeking not to challenge but simply to reinforce common sense—that most people, even if unwilling to provide verbal endorsement of such a view, do in fact find it acceptable in principle for victims to resent and hate those who wrong them and to seek revenge against those who victimize them.[4] (Perhaps Christianity's victory over pagan common sense here is largely verbal.) But, if this is so, then it looks as though we have the beginnings of an argument for the institutionalization of these feelings—an argument from *democracy*. For what is a democracy except a form of government in which the majority gets to have its dominant preferences enacted into law—even if those preferences are condemned by a refined and condescending elite? Thus, if most people want to create a system of criminal law that institutionalizes and expresses the hatreds and desires for revenge that crime victims feel toward those who have wronged them, what principle would allow anyone to say nay to the will of the people thus expressed?

This principle, perhaps: that the fundamental rights of citizens may not be abridged even when the majority so desires. Such a principle defines a *constitutionally constrained* democracy (as opposed to a pure democracy) and characterizes the kind of democracy at least theoretically present in the United States. Thus, since one of the presupposed principles of this society is that the government may not treat people (even criminals) in brutally inhuman ways, the United States Constitution imposes (in the Eighth Amendment) an absolute ban on such "cruel and unusual" punishments as torture.[5] This ban is not to be seen as an expression of the will of the people; it is rather a principled check, an absolute side-constraint, on what the people will be *allowed* to will.

I think that this constitutional excursion dramatically reinforces the point I want to make about burden of proof here. We may, I think, regard American society as one in which the majority may do whatever it jolly well feels like *unless* one can demonstrate that what it feels like doing is *fundamentally wrong in principle*. (I take it that the Bill of Rights seeks to provide an initial—but not a final—analysis of what it means to say that a governmental act is fundamentally wrong in principle.) To use my earlier language: the presumption is that the will of the majority should determine policy, and thus the burden of proof likes upon those who—for any majoritarian outcome—would seek to prevent it. My question, then, is this: can it be shown to be fundamentally wrong in principle for the suffering that criminals receive from the state to be contingent to any degree on hatreds and desires for revenge felt by their victims? Do criminals have a fundamental right to be shielded from the consequences of such feelings? Since I think I have shown that it is not obvious that they do (and that, in fact, people, tend to believe quite the contrary), those who would argue for the irrelevance or injustice of those feelings and their institutionalization should do just that—namely, *argue*. They have the burden of proof. I will thus now begin to explore what these arguments might be and the degree to which, if at all, they are successful.

III. Making the Case Against Hatred and Revenge

Those who condemn hatred and revenge can avail themselves of two different strategies of argument. They can argue (1) that the emotions involved in these responses are inherently irrational (like phobias) or inherently evil (like sadism or unprovoked malice). Or they can argue (2) that, whatever the merits of the emotions themselves (even assuming they are intrinsically splendid), it would either be unwise or wrong in principle for these emotions to have any effect on the administration of criminal punishment. (Some—e.g., Kant—have reasoned this way about compassion and mercy—suggesting that compassion, though a splendid and admirable emotion in itself and often productive of wonderful results in other contexts, may produce excessive acts of mercy—and thus undermine justice—if too influential on judges or those with the power of pardon.[6]) While (2) is my primary interest in this paper, it is so frequently tied in with (1) that I think it will be worthwhile to discuss and evaluate them both in the present context.

IV. The Rational Case Against Hatred

Surely hatred cannot be regarded as irrational simply because it is an emotion. Emotions (e.g., guilt, shame, fear, envy, jealousy, hatred, love, and compassion) are not like mere sensations (e.g., headaches): one sign of this is that we can speak sensibly of irrational emotions but not of irrational headaches or other sensations. (What is a phobia except an irrational fear? And what would it mean to call some fears irrational unless it makes sense to refer to others as rational?) Of course we sometimes speak of people themselves as being irrational if they allow emotions to dominate their personalities to an excessive degree—e.g., Spinoza's point about a rational person being one who is not *led* by a fear of death.[7] But is there any good reason to assume that hatred and desires for revenge are uniquely able to dominate or lead in a way that other emotions are not? Consider the character of Michael Kohlhaas in von Kleist's famous story.[8] Why will so many people say of a character such as Kohlhaas that he was so overcome, or dominated by, or in the thrall of vindictiveness—but would not tend to describe (for example) Mother Teresa as overcome, or dominated by, or in the thrall of compassion? (Is this anything more than a misleading way of noting that one like compassion and does not like vindictiveness? Is a moral point masquerading as a psychological point and a question thereby being begged?) The literature of hatred and revenge does, of course, tend to portray these responses carried to a pathological extreme, but this may tell us more about what makes literature interesting than anything basic about human psychology. (What a boring story it would have been had Kohlhaas simply beaten up a couple of people and taken his horses back.) Surely *any* emotion can be carried to a pathological extreme; does not the fact that we can identify pathological extensions of retributive hatred (e.g., Michael Kohlhaas's) suggest that there must be non-pathological instances of this emotion? And must this emotion have an inevitable tendency to provoke excessive behavior—as it did for Kohlhaas? What if the person is provoked by this emotion to seek only a level of revenge that we, on other grounds (utility or justice), would find acceptable? Are there no such people? Are all people who seek revenge really after consequences so extreme and socially disruptive that we must regard them as crazed? (It is, of course, question-begging to say that these feelings are irrational simply because they often prompt people to illegality only because we, not learning the lesson of Athena and the Furies, have refused to make a proper home for them and institutionalize them into the legal system.) And consider Nietzche's famous argument against *ressentiment* (a kind of hatred)—namely, that it tends to poison a person from within.[9] But why, according to Nietzche, does it so poison? It is because it is *repressed*; thus, Nietzche's point argues equally for getting rid of the emotion *or for expressing it*—e.g., through getting even.

We might, of course, regard an emotion as irrational if it lacks any point or purpose that we can understand or with which we can sympathize. John Rawls argues in this way, for example, about the emotion of (malicious) envy. For what is the point, Rawls asks, of simply desiring that another lose some benefit when that benefit was not wrongfully acquired and when the benefit, when lost, will not transfer to the malicious envier.?[10] Although I think that Rawls's position is not without problems, I will for present purposes grant it. Analogous arguments will not obviously condemn retributive hatred as irrational, however, since his emotion (with which, I have already argued, most of us sympathize) often has as its point the desire to annul (perceived) wrongful gains and to give people their (perceived) just deserts—in short, to "get even" through revenge. That, and not something further, is its point. Unless the desire to bring about these states of affairs is itself always wrong or irrational, then surely the emotion of retributive hatred—as a desire to bring them about—cannot be condemned as pointless and thus as irrational. (One would surely not want to give as one's argument against retributive hatred an appeal to some notion of pointlessness that would, if accepted, refute all deontological considerations in ethics.) But is revenge acceptable? I will explore this question in the final section of the paper, but it would, of course, beg the question simply to assume at this point that it is not.

The above considerations suggest to me that it is going to be very difficult to make a case that hatred (as a desire for revenge) is inherently irrational—the moral equivalent of a phobia. Though obviously (because by definition) pathological extensions of this emotion will not be present in a rational person, a lesser degree might well play some roles in the psyches of rational and healthy people—e.g., prompting them to seek restitution for injuries, liberating them from the bondage of resentment (through getting even), maintaining their self-respect, and even (by making themselves known as disposed to revenge) warding off some aggressors who might otherwise challenge their security and invade their "moral space." Thus if a case is to be made against the emotion of retributive hatred itself, the case will have to be *moral*—a case that the emotion, however rational it may be in some prudential or therapeutic sense for the person who experiences it, is still evil and would not be present in a truly virtuous person. It is to this moral case that I will now turn.

V. The Moral Case Against Hatred

The idea that hatred and desires for revenge are evil dispositions of character is linked, in our Christian culture, to the idea that these dispositions are *sinful*. God, through Jesus Christ, commands that we love and forgive our enemies rather than seek from them the "eye for an eye" that was characteristic of the older law.[11] If somebody embraces the Christian religion (so interpreted), then such a person does have—in my view—a sufficient moral reason to regard hatred as a vice and all acts based upon it as evils. All argument on the issue could thus stop here, as arguments have a way of doing when they collide with total faith.

My present inquiry, however, is this: does the moral case against retributive hatred essentially depend upon such faith or can a case that does not depend upon religious belief—a purely secular case—be made? I think that such a case may be possible and, indeed, that it might be possible even to draw a large part of the case from a secular interpretation of some Christian parables. This should not be surprising, since many Christians wish to regard their God as a supremely rational being. If so, He presumably did not command love and forgiveness of enemies capriciously (e.g., He did not flip a coin to get this command) but rather knew that such dispositions were of some benefit to us, His creatures. But if God had good reasons for issuing these commands, it is not impossible that we—with our reason—could discover at least part of the case that prompted Him and see its good moral sense for ourselves.

Consider, with this in mind, the story of Jesus at the stoning of the adulteress (there cautioning the crowd to "Let him who is without sin cast the first stone").[12] Think of this story in conjunction with the famous passage, "Vengeance is mine; I will repay saith the Lord."[13] Consider also the parable of the unforgiving servant.[14]

The fact that God reserves vengeance for Himself suggest that, in His view, the desire for vengeance is not an inherently irrational (or even inherently evil) disposition of character. (Otherwise, God would be condemning Himself.) It is rather that He has reasons for claiming that the disposition to vengeance is a uniquely divine prerogative. What might these reasons be? Presumably they are that only God *knows enough* and only God is *good enough* to seek vengeance reliably and without hypocrisy. His creatures lack these epistemological and moral qualifications; they must therefore wait and depend upon God to get the job done.[15] Thus these scriptural passages can be interpreted to mean that human beings, given their radical limitations, always manifest vices—specifically, the vices of *presumption* and *hypocrisy*—if they have and indulge feelings of retributive hatred.

Is this claim plausible? Are we too ignorant to be reliable retributive haters? Are we ourselves too morally flawed to hate, without hypocrisy, those who wrong us? Let us consider each of these questions separately.

What is it that we are unable to know about wrongdoers that poses no problem for God? We surely know what *acts* are unacceptable, and thus perhaps the problem is supposed to lie in some lack of ability we have in knowing the *mental states* and *dispositions of the will* present in wrongdoers. Kants, for example, claims that only God can "know the heart"; given his view that moral condemnation is addressed in the inner disposition of will, he argues (in his *Religion*, but not elsewhere) that human ignorance of such matters precludes the acceptability of the kind of harsh condemnation of others that legitimately hating them would involve.[16]

I think that this argument is important—one that should make us (as I stress in great detail in the book) *very cautious* of what we do in this area—but I am not convinced that it makes a fatal case against the moral legitimacy of all retributive hatred. For Kant is well known as being (to put it mildly) in favor of punishment; given his commitments to justice, he would want to condemn strenuously a system of punishment that employed only strict liability. This means, of course, that he would (like us) want a system of criminal liability that involves *mens rea*, excuse, and justification. But such a system can be administered only if, *in some sense*, we *can*, "read the heart." Thus those who would make flip arguments against retributive hatred based upon some supposed inability to determine the appropriate inner dispositions should note the massive (and certainly unwelcome) reforms in the criminal law—and perhaps in our whole moral conception of personal responsibility—that would flow from the literal acceptance of such a slogan.

So too, I think, for those who would make an overly ambitious use of the important insight that each one of us is morally flawed ("Let him who is without sin...") and often stands in need of some gentle response, such as forgiveness from others (a point of the parable of the unforgiving servant). For such things are in fact, of course, matters of degree. That I have certain vices (a certain lack of generosity, perhaps) does not mean that I ever have or ever would even contemplate treating another human being in the way that Michael Kohlhaas was treated by those who wronged him, or in the way that some rape victims are brutalized by their attackers. Thus it seems that although I may not be utterly without sin, I may well be without sin *in the relevant sense* in some cases. And why may I not, without hypocrisy, indulge retributive hatred in these cases? John Rawls has taught us the useful device in ethics of imagining ourselves in all possible roles that will be affected by the moral rules we adopt. As one who may sometimes need the love and forgiveness of others, I will of course want a world where retributive hatred does not reign unchecked. But as someone who may sometimes want to get even for terrible wrongs done to me, I might not want to create a social world wherein desires for revenge are utterly condemned—regarded as, in themselves, signs of irrationality or vice.

Finally, there is the argument from moral equality. According to this argument (often appealed to by Christians), all human beings are of equal moral worth—perhaps even absolute moral worth—and are to be equally loved, because it is both irrational and immoral for any one of these creatures to rule any of his equals outside the domain of benevolent concern—as hatred certainly does. (In religious terms, this Kantian point might be made by saying that we are all children of God and equally beloved in His sight; that God's perspective should then be adopted in our own dealings with our fellow humans.) To this argument I have the following response: that all human beings (no matter how morally vile) are to be loved strikes me as a claim whose *intrinsic implausibility* is staggering. Thus, I can imagine no reason for taking such a claim seriously unless one views it as a command of God—i.e., one therefore has an *extrinsic* reason for taking it seriously. Here, then, we perhaps have a good example of an ethical issue where a secular world view leads us in one direction and the Christian world view leads us in quite another—perhaps dashing any hasty optimism (present, I think, in some strands of liberal Christianity) about the ultimate compatibility or reconciliation of the two.[17]

I conclude from the above that the case against the rationality and morality of the emotion I have labeled retributive hatred has not been made. Thus, I think that we may properly retain our common-sense belief that this feeling is sometimes acceptable—and sometimes even laudable. Those of us who want to retain the concept of genuine evil—in discussing the Holocaust perhaps—the perpetrators of which merit hatred are not yet defeated. As noted earlier, however, this does not establish that it is ever permissible for us to act on such feelings or that the law should ever assist us in so acting. Desires for revenge are one thing; acts of revenge are quite another. Thus I shall now move to a consideration of the permissibility of revenge itself.

VI. The General Case Against Revenge and Its Role in Criminal Law (Especially Sentencing)

By "revenge," I will mean any injury inflicted on a wrongdoer that satisfies the retributive hatred felt by that wrongdoer's victim and that is justified because of that satisfaction.[18] I here assume again (for reasons earlier noted) that the burden of argument lies on those who wold oppose the legitimacy of revenge, and I assume that the arguments given will (like all arguments in ethics) be either consequentialist arguments or arguments of principle.[19] I also believe that the really impressive and important arguments will be those of the latter sort.

Why might revenge be disutilitarian—wrong on consequentialist grounds? The most common thing said against it is that it is socially disruptive—it is likely to provoke an unpredictable and destabilizing level of conflict. But this argument, of course, seems most impressive as an argument against *private* revenge—vigilante activity—and, if this is the only argument, really supports rather than undermines the claim that revenge ought to be institutionalized by the state: that is, that the state, taking on the personae of crime victims, should elevate (at least some of) the private grievances of individuals to the status of public grievances. If revenge is not intrinsically evil or wrong in principle, why should its public expression not be justified by these two consequences: (1) the satisfaction given to victims and (2) the resulting tendency to defuse the potentiality for private revenge and its resulting social turmoil?[20] (This does not mean that the state should take on all desires for revenge—some are excessive—but it does suggest reasons why the state might take on some of them.) And consider the standard utilitarian value of deterrence: might not potential criminals be given an extra incentive to remain law-abiding if they know that they live in a system where victim outrage (or, in murder cases, survivor outrage) might have a bearing on their level of punishment?[21]

The above considerations suggest that the purely utilitarian or consequentialist case against the institutionalization of revenge is going to be fragile. Some utilitarian arguments will tell against the practice, and others will tell in its favor; an impartial observer might well conclude that the latter arguments, on balance, win the day. This is, of course, often the case with utilitarian arguments on complex issues; we often, after all, lack the kind of hard empirical evidence that would be needed really to establish the probability of the claimed consequences. We thus often run the risk of lapsing into anecdotes and hunches that are often tailored to the outcome we want to justify. For this reason, those who want a *fatal* argument to block the institutionalization of revenge had better attempt an argument from principle, for one great virtue of such arguments is that they are invulnerable to the shifting winds of empirical guesswork.

Are there good arguments that institutionalized revenge is wrong in principle? I think that there are two that must be taken very seriously:

(1) The Argument from Retributive Justice. "All criminals have a fundamental right not to be punished in excess of their just deserts. A person is punished in excess of his just deserts if he is punished with greater severity than the blameworthy character of his conduct would justify. A person cannot coherently be held blameworthy for the degree to which he is hated by those he wrongs (very blameworthy for injuring thin-skinned victims and minimally blameworthy for injuring stoic victims?), and thus any criminal sentencing that take account of victim hatred (as any revenge system would have to do) violates a fundamental right, is unjust, and is thus wrong in principle."

(2) The Argument from Equal Protection and Due Process. "All criminals have a fundamental right to be protected against sentencing procedures that are inherently arbitrary and capricious. Sentencing systems based on victim hatred will inevitably have this feature and are thus wrong in principle."

These are very important arguments. (They were also the essential arguments at issue in the 1987 United States Supreme Court case of *Booth v. Maryland*—a case, regarded by many as a major setback to the victims' rights movement, holding that victim impact statements may not influence sentencing in capital cases.[22]) I take these arguments seriously, and I would like to consider them with some care. I will consider them in reverse order.

VII. The Argument from Equal Protection and Due Process

The best argument that revenge systems are inherently arbitrary and capricious lies in the fact that retributive hatred—the basis for such systems—is essentially a *subjective* response to being wronged; as such, it can vary enormously from one victim to the next. Thus, the very same injury that will be brushed off as trivial by those with a stoic disposition will generate anguish and deep hatred in the highly sensitive. Also, the level of hatred involved might well be a function of factors about the criminal that any reasonable person would regard as clearly irrelevant to culpability—e.g., the white rape victim who feels more deeply wronged if raped by a black person than if raped by a white person. If fairness requires that potential criminals receive accurate notice of the exact nature of the proscribed conduct and its attached penalties, it is hard to see how such notice could be given in a system where sentencing might actually depend upon factors that admit of such wide and subjective variation.[23] And if criminals have a right to be protected against mere prejudice (e.g., racial hatred), it might seem difficult if not impossible to give them this protection in a hate-based system, since hatreds often are a function of prejudices. I am by no means sure that it would not be possible to design procedures that would keep arbitrary and capricious sentencing at an acceptable level—i.e., at a level no greater than that already present and accepted at other points in the system—but we have at last found a principled objection to revenge that cannot simply be summarily dismissed. Those who look fondly upon revenge have an obligation to take this objection very seriously—i.e., seriously enough to recognize that the burden of argument may now have been properly shifted back to them and to take on the burden of formulating procedures to control these potential abuses. Of course, if it can be shown that criminals have a fundamental right to be sentenced in proportion to personal blameworthiness and that revenge is inconsistent with such a right, then we have the basis for an absolute ban on revenge (an absolute ban on its institutionalization) regardless of procedure. The procedural argument is thus secondary to what I have called "the argument from retributive justice," and it is to this most important argument that I shall now turn.[24]

VIII. The Argument from Retributive Justice

In *Booth v. Maryland* Justice Powell, writing for the majority, held that victim impact statements (VISs) are constitutionally impermissible in capital sentencing. Such statements—or actual testimony by victims if they are allowed to attend and speak at sentencing hearings—are very likely, according to Powell, to influence judges (or juries in states where juries have a sentencing role) to inflict cruel and unusual punishments. Their use and influence thus violates the Eighth Amendment.[25]

Powell essentially gives two arguments to support his view. One argument (a procedural one of the kind explored above) is that emotional appeals from attractive and articulate victims are likely to focus the judge's attention away from the legally relevant issues and produce arbitrary and capricious sentencing.[26] More fundamental than this procedural argument, however, is Powell's articulation of the principle that, in his view, defines what *is* legally relevant. Speaking essentially as a retributivist, Powell claims that criminal defendants in capital ases have a right that their sentence be solely a function of their personal *blameworthiness*—i.e., factors solely based on "the character of the individual and the circumstances of the crime" or on the defendant's "personal responsibility and moral guilt." Since VIS information may be, according to Powell, wholly unrelated to the blameworthiness of a particular defendant, and may cause the sentencing decision to turn on irrelevant factors such as the degree to which the victim's family is able to articulate grief and defend the victim's worth, such evidence will inevitably and improperly shift the focus away from the defendant and what he deserves. The essence of the argument, then, is this: sentencing should be based on what is morally blameworthy about the defendant; one is blameworthy only for that which is one's fault or which one brings about under one's own control; the degree to which a victim will be upset or outraged by what is done to him or will be able to articulate feelings is subjective and variable; it is thus not within the defendant's control; therefore, it would be wrong in principle to let sentencing depend to any degree on such matters.

Given the wide variety of penal purposes that are often articulated by judges in sentencing (see, for example, Judge Frankel's well-known sentencing opinion in *U.S. v. Bergman*[27]), it is odd that Powell should only emphasize the one retributive purpose of making suffering proportional to blameworthiness. (I will, for present purposes, ignore the special problems posed by the fact that *Booth* is a capital case, since I am interested in victim revenge and VISs in general.) We know that judges—both in sentencing and in approving plea-bargain agreements—typically weight such factors as jail crowding, likelihood of recidivism, impact on the defendant's family, the defendant's age and health, possible service the defendant might perform for the community, the need for special and general deterrence, the need for incapacitation, and the possibility of reform; none of these having any obvious connection with moral blameworthiness or any other valid retributive purpose.It is hard to see, if this long laundry list of (perhaps laudable) social and personal goals properly gets to play a role in sentencing, why it would be wrong in principle to find room for VISs as well.

Consider also the major (and, no doubt, quite unwelcome) reforms in the criminal law that a literal application of the moral blameworthiness principle would entail. As Justices Scalia and White noted in their dissents in *Booth*, we currently feel comfortable with making the penalty for successful murder more severe than that for an attempted murder that fails through a fortuity; yet it is obvious that the moral blameworthiness in the two cases is identical. We also punish reckless driving that kills much more severely than reckless driving *simpliciter*; yet, as Thomas Nagel would say, it is surely differences in "moral luck" rather than any differences in moral blameworthiness that distinguish the two cases.[28] Thus a decision to endorse some strong blameworthiness principle will not be cost-free; for it will force us to ignore other important factors—e.g., *harm* caused—that have typically been thought to be central to criminal liability. And with respect to the other factors, it is by no means obvious that VISs will be utterly irrelevant to them. For example: can the victim's personal response to the person who violated him tell us *nothing* about the degree of harm suffered? Is the revenge interest present in the victim worthy of no attention in a world where (for example) the community's supposed interest in service that the defendant might perform is regarded as relevant? All of this needs to be thought about much more deeply.[29]

But perhaps blameworthiness should be viewed simply as a *negative* retributive constraint on permissible punishment—a factor that sets an upper bound on the degree to which the state may legitimately pursue its other interests in punishing (e.g., crime deterrence). This might solve, for example,the puzzle about attempts. For even if attempters and succeeders have the same degree of blameworthiness, the state might have good reasons for punishing attempters less severely; no wrong will be done in such a system so long as the succeeders are not punished in excess of their just deserts understood as a function of their moral blameworthiness.

If we accept this weakened notion of retributivism, however, it is hard to see how this will form a principled objection to the institutionalization of victim revenge and the use of VISs. For, on this view, why not simply allow these factors to have influence—perhaps to counter sentimental tendencies to show mercy or make plans for community service—so long as their influence is capped off at the point when maximum just deserts for the offense is reached? This would, of course, simply be to restate Stephen's point: respect victim hatred and revenge, but institutionalize them so that their excesses can be constrained by other values equally worthy of respect in a system of criminal law.

IX. Conclusion

Let me close these ruminations on hatred and revenge by considering one final challenge to them. I can imagine a critic now arguing as follows: your case for hatred and revenge within the limits set by blameworthiness and desert has saved hatred and revenge at a very high price—namely, you have made them *redundant*. If these responses must operate within a context defined by retributive just deserts, then how does the account of punishment you call hatred-based revenge differ from what Kant, and Herbert Morris, your own previous self, and others have simply called retributivism?

My short response to this is the following: I have elsewhere argued that, given a traditional liberal-libertarian conception of the state (as modelled in social contract terms), it is hard to see why there is any important state interest served in securing retributive values—in seeing that wrongdoers get their just deserts—for the sake of these values themselves.[30] If rational contractors were forming a state, it is easy to see why they might give up some liberty and resources to protect themselves against assault (a basic human desire) by adopting a deterrence scheme of criminal law. It is very hard, however, to see why they would do this simply to achieve a state of affairs that seems of merely abstract worth—namely, one where wrongdoers get their jut deserts. In short: given the rarity of an intense sense of abstract justice, classical retributivism seems unmotivated within liberal theory.

If desires for revenge are basic and important to many people, however, this would provide some motivational grounds—in victim hatred—for those schemes of criminal justice we tend to call retributive; securing the revenge interests involved might, even in traditional liberal terms, prompt social contractors to be willing to make the sacrifices necessary to maintain a (constrained) system of revenge. Abstract concern for justice might explain the blameworthiness cap on punishment, but garden variety desires for revenge may generate—and quite properly generate - some of the values that drive the system up to that point.[31]

I will not, however, press this argument. If a consequence of my view is that it will ultimately be impossible to draw a sharp distinction between the desire for retributive justice and the desire for revenge, then this in itself will put revenge in better philosophical company than it normally enjoys. Perhaps it will achieve the kind of impartial re-hearing for hatred and revenge that it has been the primary purpose of this essay to provoke.[32]

Let me now close by summarizing the main thrust of my argument. Crime victims often want to influence sentencing, and their motives for this are often vindictive. Perhaps such motives are dishonorable; perhaps giving a legal role to victims so motivated would indeed produce deep harm to our system of criminal justice. I have attempted to show that this has simply been assumed and not demonstrated, however, and that—in fairness to those victims—it should be demonstrated before the state simply dismisses as irrational or evil the passionate claims of those whom it has failed to protect from criminal violence.

[1992 Note: In 1991 the United States Supreme Court, in *Payne v. Tennessee* overruled *Booth*—opening the way for the use of victim impact statements in capital cases.]

---

[1]The present essay is reprinted, with the publisher's permission, from *Social Philosophy and Policy,* vol. 7, no. 2 (Spring, 1990), pp.209-25. It builds on some ideas initially developed in ch.3 ("Hatred: A Qualified Defense") of *Forgiveness and Mercy*, by Jeffrie G. Murphy (Chapters 1, 3 and 5) and Jean Hampton (Chapters 2 and 4), (Cambridge: Cambridge University Press, 1988).

[2]The phrase "victims' rights movement" refers to those who advocate changes in criminal law and procedure that will (at least in their view) make crime victims more satisfied with the system. Rules of evidence that make it harder for defense attorneys to probe a claimed rape victim's sexual past, finding ways to allow claimed victims to influence criminal sentencing (e.g., by presenting victim impact statements to the sentencing judge) are examples of developments that may be viewed as victories for the victim's rights movement. The 1987 United States Supreme Court case of *Booth v. Maryland*, where victim impact statements were ruled unconstitutional in capital cases, may be viewed as a setback for the victims' rights movement. (This case will be discussed below.) It should be noted that the phrase "victim's rights" is importantly misleading as a characterization of some of the practices noted above. Since the use of a victim impact statement occurs after a criminal conviction (though prior to sentencing), the word "victim" here is appropriate. Prior to a conviction, however, we do not know for sure that we actually have a victim; all we know for sure is that we have an *accuser*. Thus it would be better if those who favor such things as shield laws to prevent unnecessary probing of an alleged rape victim's sexual past would refer to these practices as a matter of "accusers' rights." Also, is it correct to

refer to these practices as *rights* at all, or should they simply be characterized (by those who favor them) as good policy?

[3]Although I tend to support the legitimacy of what I call retributive hatred, I am inclined to agree with Willard Gaylin's claim that much anger and hatred in contemporary culture is — though understandable — irrational and maladaptive. See his *The Rage Within: Anger in Modern Life* (New York: Penguin Books, 1989).

[4]Those who have come out in support of some instances of hatred and revenge include God ("Vengeance is mine...etc."); Aristotle (*Nicomachean Ethics*, 1125b ff.); Adam Smith,*The Theory of Moral Sentiments* (Indianapolis: Liberty Press, 1982), p. 38; James Fitzjames Stephen, *A History of the Criminal Law of England* (London, 1883), Vol. II, pp. 81ff; Ernest van den Haag, "In Defense of the Death Penalty," *Criminal Law bulletin*, Vol. 14, No. 1, Jan.-Feb. 1978; Walter Berns, *For Capital Punishment* (New York: Basic Books, 1979); and Robert Axelrod (indirectly — as an endorsement of the strategy of "tit for tat" in iterated prisoner's dilemmas — in his *The Evolution of Cooperation* (New York: Basic Books, 1984). I also present a supportive case for these responses in *Forgiveness and Mercy*. In this book I suggest that, in addition to the social usefulness of these responses in some contexts, some considerations of *vice* and *virtue* also offer relevant support — namely, that a person's failure to resent wrongs done to him and to manifest retributive hatred toward the wrongdoer may be a sign that he has the vice of *servility* (a lack of proper self-respect and a lack of proper tendencies for self-defense). I would hate to have readers unfamiliar with the book conclude from the present paper that I see no moral and social problems with retributive hatred, however, so let me note that the book contains numerous qualifications and cautions with respect to my defense of this emotion — qualification and cautions that considerably constrain the domain of its legitimacy. No doubt the reader will want to check this out, and I recommend that he do so by purchasing — preferably in the hardcover edition — a copy of the book.

[5]Amendment VII of the United States Constitution reads as follows: "Excessive bail shall not be required, nor excessive fines imposed, nor cruel and unusual punishments inflicted." This has been interpreted by the United States Supreme Court to rule out such inherently barbaric punishments as torture, punishments that are radically disproportionate to the gravity of the offense, and the punishment of death when administered in an arbitrary and capricious fashion.

[6]Might not hatred and compassion stand or fall together with respect to criminal punishment? If it is wrong to increase a criminal sentence out of hatred, will it not also be wrong to decrease a criminal sentence out of compassion? Can one consistently be meticulous and strict about justice only in one direction? Perhaps we tend to be more lax about mercy because we think that the compassion on which it is based is, unlike hatred, an acceptable or even admirable emotion. But this, of course, needs to be shown. For Kant's discussion, see his *The Metaphysical Elements of Justice* (Indianapolis: Bobbs-Merrill, 1965), p. 107.

[7]*Ethics*, Four, LXVII.

[8]Heinrich von Kleist's 1810 story *Michael Kohlhaas* portrays a man who, when he fails to receive legal justice over a comparatively small injury done to him (theft and abuse of his horses), takes matters into his own hands. In his pursuit of revenge, he forms an army, kills large numbers of people, and nearly topples the government under which he lives. This story was retold by E.L. Doctorow in his 1975 novel *Ragtime* — wherein Michael Kohlhaas becomes Coalhouse Walker.

[9]*On the Genealogy of Morals*, Essay I, Section 10.

[10]*A Theory of Justice* , (Cambridge: Harvard University Press, 1971), secs. 80 and 81.

[11]Matthew 5:38-48. The older law is well represented in Psalms 58:10-11: "The righteous shall rejoice when he seeth the vengeancc: he shall wash his feet in the blood of the wicked. So that a man shall say, Verily there is a reward for the righteous." In Aeschylus's *Oresteia*, the Furies represent sentiments of this kind. Athena refuses to banish them, however, because she respects the impulses they represent and believes that, by institutionalizing them under due process of law, she can make them such valuable forces in support of community morality that they will become known as "the kindly ones."

[12]John 8:7.

[13]Romans 12:19.

[14]Matthew 18:21-35.

[15]God seems to promise that the job of vengeance will get done. Is this to reassure His creatures that their hated enemies may not go eternally unpunished? But why should He pander to His creatures' desires for vengeance, unless these desires are in some sense both rationally and morally legitimate on their part? May these creatures not even look forward with delight to the coming divine retribution on their enemies? May they not even have pleasing fantasies of it? When it happens, may they not look down from heaven with delight at the torments of their enemies below? Is God here in some sense promising (like Athena) to "institutionalize" (in His divine law) these legitimate feelings and thereby make their personal expression unnecessary? I raise these questions not to be impious, but simply to make the point that the "Vengeance is mine" passage can be read simply as a command that humans not *act* on retributive hatred — leaving open the possibility that *feeling* retributive hatred is neither an evil nor a vice. I do not believe that the simple command to love and forgive one's enemies is comparably ambiguous, however, for here feelings themselves are clearly the object of the command.

[16]For a discussion of those aspects of Kant's moral philosophy that appear to be in tension with his commitments to retributivism, see "Does Kant Have a Theory of Punishment?" in *Columbia Law Review*, Volume 87, No. 3 (April 1987).

[17]Suppose I am willing to grant that hatred would properly be addressed toward me if I performed (with full responsibility) certain evil acts. Perhaps I would even resent it and regard it as an insult (because it would challenge my status as a responsible moral agent) if such hatred was *not* directed toward me in these circumstances. If I then address such hatred to others when they (with full responsibility) perform such

acts, it is not clear that I violate any important equality demand. Saint Augustine tells us that we should "hate the sin but not the sinner." But if it is permissible to hate the act because it is bad, why is it wrong to hate the actor because he is bad? Of course, if the wrongdoer sincerely *repents*, this may block the legitimacy of hating or even resenting him — a theme I pursue in Ch. 1 of *Forgiveness and Mercy.*

18Revenge is not to be identified with vigilante activity, and indeed I will assume for purposes of this paper that anyone who seeks revenge in ways that are illegal acts wrongly (not to mention uncreatively). The issue that I mainly want to explore, of course, is if the law itself should find a way of institutionalizing some of this revenge and thereby perhaps eliminate some temptations to self-help. I will also be assuming throughout that we are dealing with cases where the victims are not fantasizing the wrongdoing but have accurate beliefs that they have been wronged, accurate beliefs about the nature and degree of the wrong done to them, and accurate beliefs that the wrongdoer is as fully responsible for that wrongdoing as any human being ever is for any wrongdoing.

19Some people might also suggest virtue arguments, but I am suspicious of their use in this context. For example: it is often suggested, as an argument against capital punishment, that it is wrong because of what it does to the characters of those favor and inflict it — namely, it degrades and debases and dehumanizes them. But this is by no means obvious. In my view, a person is debased by the doing of *X* only if *X* is wrong (unjust, say), and thus — absent an independent showing that *X* is wrong — the character debasement argument will not get off the ground. Similarly, engaging in revenge will debase people only if it can be shown, on independent grounds, that revenge is wrong. So too for the common "two wrongs do not make a right" cliche that is often trotted out here. Obviously, those who regard revenge as justified will not see it as a wrong; they will thus quite properly fail to see the relevance of the cliche to their claim.

20This, I take it, is the point of James Fitzjames Stephen's famous analogy between the criminal law and the law of marriage (see note 4). He argued that we deal in each case with a passion that is legitimate (the desire for revenge in the one case and sexual desire in the other), but we have also learned that the passion in question has high potential to provoke disruptive behavior. Thus, the way to honor the passion without risking serious social disruption is for the law to regulate that passion — to provide it with a proper channel for expression. Taking victim hatred seriously in this way (by building it into legal practice) may thus benefit both the community and the victims themselves, for the practice recognizes the validity of the hatred while placing important constraints on its excess. Such institutionalization might even help to educate persons on the legitimate bounds of hatred.

21One might, of course, argue that such a deterrent system is unpredictable — an acceptable consequence from the point of view of deterrence, perhaps, but a disutilitarian consequence from many other points of view (e.g., liberty). I think that this is an important argument. However, since I think that unpredictability is an evil essentially because of its *unfairness* rather than because of its potentially disruptive social consequences, I will treat this as an objection of principle in the next section.

[22]482 U.S. 496 (1987). A victim impact statement is a statement from the crime victim or some representative of the victim that seeks to influence sentencing by stressing the impact of the crime on the victim and the victim's desires (or perhaps the survivor's desires in a murder case) with respect to the sentence.

[23]Expressions of hatred might, of course, be *evidence* that something of assumed relevance to criminal liability — e.g., the existence of a certain level of *harm* - is present. I will explore this idea a bit later in the paper. As Ellen Paul has pointed out to me, one could argue that if criminals knew that they would face varying degrees of punishment based on the degree of hatred felt by their victims, they would factor this into their calculations of advantage/disadvantage before committing the crime. A rational criminal might then presume that his victim might be one with great capacity for hatred, and this might augment the deterrent value of the law. The criminal, by committing an illegal act, puts himself willingly and knowingly (but within limits, of course) in a kind of punishment lottery with respect to the harm that actually results from what he does. So why not a comparable lottery (again within limits) with respect to hatred and desires for revenge that might be felt by his victim?

[24]Had the United States Supreme Court held that capital punishment is, like torture, inherently cruel and unusual punishment, consideration of the procedural problems surrounding the administration of that punishment would never have achieved their current prominence. The reason why *Furman v. Georgi*a (408 U.S. 238 (1972) and most later death penalty cases have dealt primarily with procedural matters — the desire to avoid arbitrary and capricious capital sentences — is that the Court has held that the penalty of death is *not* inherently cruel and unusual — at least with respect to some crimes of murder. Thus, it is not surprising that, in America, most principled legal objections to the death penalty now take a procedural form.

[25]The Court did not clearly indicate what it will rule on VISs in non-capital cases. In capital case, of course, the VISs are not primary victim impact statements (the primary victim being dead) but rather statements from concerned survivors — e.g., family members considered as secondary victims.

[26]It is not made clear why this poses any greater problem than that posed when the same victim appears as a witness during trial. Freedom from cross-examination, perhaps? Might it not be possible to allow such cross-examination at a sentencing hearing?

[27]*United States v. Bergman*, United States District Court, S.D.N.Y., 416 F. Supp. 496 (1976). Rabbi Bergman, owner of several nursing homes, had been part of a scheme to defraud the United States government with respect to Medicaid payments. In his sentencing opinion, Judge Frankel explores a variety of punitive purposes that he believes must be weighed: retribution, community outrage, community support for the Rabbi because of his many philanthropic ventures, special and general deterrence. etc.

[28]Thomas Nagel, "Moral Luck," in his *Mortal Questions* (Cambridge: Cambridge University Press, 1979).

[29]The problem being noted here is that of the inconsistency of insisting on a blameworthiness basis for punishment in a system that gives the same weight to harm that most systems of criminal law currently do. This does not entail abandonment of a blameworthiness basis, of course, for one might instead avoid the inconsistency by arguing on retributivist grounds for the abandonment (or considerable qualification) of the relevance of harm. For an exploration of this issue, see Stephen J. Schulhofer, "Harm and Punishment: A Critique of Emphasis on the Results of Conduct in the Criminal Law," 122 *University of Pennsylvania Law Review* 1497 (1974).

[30]See my "Retributivism, Moral Education, and the Liberal State" in *Criminal Justice Ethics*, Vol. 4, no. 1,1985. For a skeptical attack on the common idea that there is a sharp distinction in principle between criminal law (with the state as injured party) and tort law (with individual victims as injured parties), see my "Why Have the Criminal Law at All?" in ch. 3 of *The Philosophy of Law: An Introduction to Jurisprudence*, by Jeffrie G. Murphy, chapters 1, 2 and 3, and Jules L. Coleman, chapters 4 and 5, (Totowa: Rowman and Allanheld, 1984).

[31]Even Herbert Morris's very abstract notion of criminal punishment as annulment of wrongful gains or unfair advantages (in his "Persons and Punishment," *The Monist*, Volume 52, Number 4, October 1968) may ultimately depend not upon some abstract sense of justice (the desire to see justice done for its own sake) but on something very like victim revenge. What, on Morris's theory, motivates me to want the criminal (as free-rider) punished? That he has taken an unfair advantage of those who have been law-abiding. But that means, given that *I* am one of those who has been law-abiding, he has taken unfair advantage of *me* — he has derived a wrongful gain at *my* expense. If this is what is most vivid in my mind (as it surely will be), then in what sense is my desire to see him punished impersonal and not a kind of victim revenge?

[32]Most philosophical defenses of retributivism (including some of my own previous essays) take great pains to distinguish retribution (which is taken to be just) form vengeance (which is taken to be unjust or evil in some other way). Perhaps such attempts at drawing a sharp distinction have been misdirected.

Just Deserts or Just Desertion? An Attack on Modern Retributivism

Nigel Walker

Like Jeffrie Murphy I am a retributivist at heart—but not in my head.[1] I experience strong punitive emotions when confronted with some kinds of crime; and I have no feeling of guilt about those emotions. That does not, however, make me a retributivist, since I do not regard emotions as a justification for action, and certainly not as a justification for official penalties. That is where I part company with retributivists. Their position may seem more consistent than my own combination of private resentment and official utilitarianism; but I see no merit in their consistency. Nor can I understand why some retributivists think that they stand on higher moral ground than utilitarians, who after all are more concerned about human welfare.

My subject is the variant of retributivism known as "just deserts". As a slogan it was popularized not by philosophers but by penologists: more precisely, by American penologists; and more precisely still by the Committee for the Study of Incarceration, in its report called *Doing Justice*, which was drafted by Andrew von Hirsch (1976).[2] In Britain it is sometimes called "modern retributivism," but since we have made no significant contribution to this particular variant it might well be called "American retributivism." The first question which I shall try to answer is "What distinguishes it from the 'classical retributivism' of Kant, Bradley *et al.*?"

I can see four differences. First, classical retributivists regarded the infliction of appropriate punishment as a moral duty. The "serpent-winding of utilitarianism," to quote one of Kant's translators, was an irrelevant consideration—perhaps even a pernicious one.[3] It didn't matter whether punishments deterred, eliminated or reformed people. What mattered was ensuring that they underwent the penalties they deserved.

Modern retributivism, on the other hand, is a reaction to disillusionment, and in particular disillusionment about the efficacy of utilitarian techniques. Postwar research was interpreted as showing that deterrents do not work and that efforts to reform or at least rehabilitate the undeterred are equally ineffective. As for techniques which are undeniably effective—elimination and prolonged detention—moralists raised objections which were rhetorically persuasive, if not always well-founded.

It can be argued that these criticisms of utilitarian objectives were excessive. All that research has demonstrated about deterrents is that they are less effective than our forefathers believed, and that reform and rehabilitation are seldom achieved, not because they are impossible but because we lack the skill to identify the offenders who will respond to specific regimes, and to provide these regimes with consistency. As for incapacitating measures such as long detention, the moral objections to them contain fallacies. My central point is simple: modern retributivism—or "just deserts"—is the child not of firm conviction but of a rather impulsive disillusionment, which says that if we cannot reduce crime we can at least punish it. "Just deserts" is a *pis aller*, a slogan of despair.

The second difference between classical and modern retributivism is another product of discouragement. Classical retributivists found it very difficult to explain why the infliction of punishment is a duty. Explanations were superstitious (the will of God), metaphysical (Kant's noumenal aspect of man), metaphorical (the metaphors being either the payment of a debt to society or the annulment of the crime—as if one could be unmurdered, unraped or unburgled), or, as a last resort, merely intuitionist.[4] One explanation for retribution did not have those qualities: law-breakers take unfair advantage of law-abiders; the advantage cannot be taken away from them; but they can at least be made to suffer a countervailing disadvantage, a penalty. This may not be a metaphor, but it is clearly inspired by the analogy of a game such as football, in which the rules decree penalties for fouls. It has flaws. It implies that all crimes can be viewed as instrumental, as directed to some desired advantage, whereas many—and especially many crimes of violence—are simply what is called "expressive," an emotional response to a situation. It also implies that if the attempt to secure advantage by illegitimate means is unsuccessful it need not be penalised: the referee can say "no advantage, play on" (as he can in British football). Where crimes are concerned, on the other hand, purists consider even unsuccessful attempts as deserving punishment, and, if they are very pure, as deserving as much punishment as successes.

I myself believe that the notion of man as a rule-making animal offers a better, and more completely literal, explanation of why some retributivists see punishment as a duty, and I have developed it elsewhere.[5] But it is not my task, in this context, to point out to "just deserters" where they have missed a trick.

Partisans of just deserts prefer to rely on what can be called "the symbolic function" of punishment—its capacity for delivering a message. It is now more than two hundred years since English lawyers first asserted this proposition, but it was probably Durkheim who elevated it to the status of a complete justification for punishment.[6] French sociology did not cut much ice in Anglo-American jurisprudence, and the idea did not begin to take root there until Lord Denning told the English Royal Commission on Capital Punishment that the denouncing of murder was—and I use his words—its "ultimate justification."[7] I am glad to be able to say that the U.S. Supreme Court, in deciding the case of *Gregg versus Georgia*, did not think much of Denning's justification.[8] But the idea was taken up by American philosophers and penologists, and what they have done with it is interesting.

The notion that penalties may convey a message which has a desirable effect on the attitudes of potential law-breakers is what I call penal McLuhanism: the measure is the message.[9] It is not new among utilitarians, although few have suggested that this is their fundamental justification for punishment. Durkheim and Denning seem to have thought so, but they were exceptions. In the United States, Hyman Gross, in his *Theory of Criminal Justice*, suggested that the justification for penalties is that they are part of "a system of liability ensuring that those who commit crimes do not get away with them." He called this message "anti-impunity." He recognized one awkwardness: such an argument makes it desirable to ensure that as many crimes as possible are followed by the penalising of *someone*, even if that someone were known by the penalisers to be innocent. Gross had difficulty in extricating himself from this implication.[10] Even more awkward, however, is the fact that most of us—and especially most potential law-breakers—know very well that a very large number of crimes *are* committed with impunity. Consequently the message which is actually delivered is not "You cannot break the law with impunity" but "If convicted of breaking the criminal law you may expect a penalty, unless of course, you can afford a good lawyer." This is more precise, but less impressive.

Penal McLuhanism makes a neat armchair theory, but it needs to be able to answer three practical questions. First, who are the intended recipients of the message? Durkheim seems to have had in mind every member of a society, however virtuous or wicked. Hyman Gross is more sensible: his message is directed at those whose respect for law is weak or non-existent. Second, whatever message is in the mind of theorists, what is the audience likely to make of it? I have suggested that Hyman Gross' message is almost certain to be interpreted in an unimpressive way by its recipients. Third, what effect does the message of punishment, as interpreted by its recipients, have on their moral attitudes? A few years ago I found what I think is a way of ascertaining this. With the help of Catherine Marsh, the British survey expert, I presented samples of English adults with faked newspaper cuttings about sentences for everyday crimes, varying the sentences for different subsamples. We then measured respondents' moral attitudes to those crimes, and found that even varying the sentence from probation to imprisonment made no difference: respondents' moral evaluations of those crimes were unaffected.[11]

Robert Nozick (1981) and Andrew von Hirsch (1986) try to have the best of both worlds.[12] They regard the message as one of moral "censure," (von Hirsch's word) or as what Nozick calls "connecting the offender to moral values." This may have a desirable effect on him, or even on other people: they hope that in some cases it will. But even if it fails to do so it remains the justification for the penalty. Nozick even seems to believe that it does not matter whether the offender gets the message, or accepts its justice: delivering the message is all that matters.

There is an important difference, however, between von Hirsch and Nozick. Nozick does not address the question: "Why is there a moral duty to deliver such a message?" He either does not see or does not care that his explanation conveys no sense of obligation. Von Hirsch does see this, and tries to supply the deficiency: "If the state is to carry out the authoritative response to such conduct [i.e., law breaking]—as it must if it visits any kind of sanction upon its perpetrators—then it should do so in a manner that testifies to the recognition that the conduct is wrong."[13] If I understand him correctly, he is saying that the obligation to do *something* about the crime rests on the state for reasons which are non-retributive, probably utilitarian, but that *what* the state does about the crime ought to convey censure. Ingenious as this is, it still doesn't explain why the form taken by the State's response to law-breaking *ought* (in the moral sense) to be such as to convey censure, especially if it needs have no practical utility.

In short, just deserts have either lost sight of, or failed to deal adequately with, a point which classical retributivists saw clearly: that any explanation of desert must show why there is a moral duty to inflict it.

My third criticism of modern retributivists concerns what is called "proportionality." They recognize the naivety of claims to achieve "commensurability"—that is, to match the severity of the punishment to the desert of the offender in a way of which the Recording Angel would approve. No one acquainted with the wide divergences between the severity of different penal codes can believe any longer in an objectively accurate match. Retributivists still want some offenders to be punished more severely than others, but for reasons which are not utilitarian. Hence, Hegel's invention of what has come to be called "proportionality."[14] For modern retributivists this means the construction and juxtaposition of two scales, which I will call ladders because the analogy will help to make my criticisms clear.

Consider first the penalty ladder. Each rung is supposed to be more severe than the one below and less severe than the one above. The intervals between the rungs need not necessarily be equal: we do not have to assume that the differences in severity between a fine of, say, $1000, a six-months' prison sentence and nine months' prison sentence are equal, so long as we can be sure that there are differences. The difficulty is that the differences may disappear, or even be reversed when the attributes and circumstances of the offender, are taken into account. They may have the result that Offender A prefers paying a $1000 fine to a short prison sentence, but that Offender B would rather go to prison. In Britain, quite a number of offenders show this preference by opting to go to prison by default. This makes a point of general importance: the ordering of the rungs cannot be taken for granted but depends on what Bentham called the offender's "sensibility." Unlike most retributivists before or since, he acknowledged that the degree of suffering which a given penalty entails varies according to the offender's age, sex, social status and other circumstances. The notion of a penalty-ladder which serves a whole society has to be replaced by the notion of a penalty-ladder for each individual. Proportionalists overlook this point. Since most proportionalists offer public price-lists for crimes, in order to deter or educate, they must, if they are honest salesmen, add a declaration that the listed prices are subject to variation in the light of individual circumstances.

The other scale is an offence ladder, on which each rung is essentially a legal definition: murder, rape, robbery, arson, burglary, theft... Here, problems of interval supervene. Is the interval between the heinousness of robbery and that of burglary worth one, two or more intervals in the penalty-ladder? Overlap is an even more serious problem. As soon as mitigating and aggravating considerations are taken into account nearly every offence overlaps with its neighbours. Some robberies are more culpable than some rapes, some rapes than some murders. Only the crudest sort of price-list, which deals in nothing but legal definitions, can escape this problem.

The proportionalist persists, however, in juxtaposing his two scales in the hope that they will tell him the appropriate penalty for a mercy-killing by an aged wife, a robbery by a mentally defective teenager, and so on.

They will not, of course. They may tell him that one crime should be penalised more severely than the other, although they cannot always do even that. They will certainly train sentencers to be less idiosyncratic in the reasoning which they apply to the choice of penalty. But that is all. The rungs on both ladders are too movable and elastic to provide firm footholds. Proportionality promises what it cannot possibly deliver.

An analogy will make this shortcoming cleaner. I was once a member of a group which was assigned the task of carrying pieces of a prefabricated hut up a mountain. The pieces were of different sizes, weights and shapes. And so were we. The man in charge was a pragmatist. He simply assigned the largest load to the largest man, and so on. No doubt his intention was a just one: to equalise so far as possible the effort demanded of each of us. He had no means, however, of knowing whether he would succeed, and some of us certainly felt that he did not. His solution was certainly proportional. But intellectually satisfying it was not .

My fourth criticism applies to both classical retributivists and just deserters; although the latter have less excuse for ignoring the realities on which it is based, because they claim some knowledge of penology. It concerns what can be broadly described as unintended punishments. How do retributivists propose to deal with the cases in which they regard offenders as clearly deserving of long prison sentences but realise that these sentences will impose considerable hardship on the offenders' dependants? The answer is that they prefer not to discuss this problem. If forced to do so, they are apt to reply that it is the offender who should have thought of his family before doing what he did. This reply ignores the fact that many offences are committed impulsively, or even—at the other extreme—in order to benefit the family. If the retributivist is an Oxford-trained philosopher (I apologise to my *alma mater*) his reply will be more sophisticated: he will say that what happens to offenders' families is not punishment because it is not intended, and punishment is, by definition, intended. But can one settle moral questions by definition?[15] One might retort that the harm to families is, at least, a foreseeable consequence of the sentence, and that if the sentence were not a sentence but an ordinary reckless action the law might well hold the actor liable for the harm which he foresaw. The retributivist's attempts to talk himself out of this problem are consolations rather than solutions.

The problem extends to unintended hardship suffered by the offender himself. Some, not all, convictions entail loss of jobs and stigma. Some sentences, notably custodial sentences, intensify the stigma, and make loss of job inevitable. Some sentencers take such effects into account, some do not. If they do so, they are taking into account what they cannot quantify. If they do not, they are ignoring factors which seem just as relevant as a prisoner's age and health, and which may sharply distinguish two equally guilty accomplices. The choice is between the almost impossible and the almost indefensible. But retributivists do not discuss this problem.

Few modern retributivists have anything interesting to say about the relevance of repentance, forgiveness and mercy to proportional punishment. There is a tendency to leave these topics to theologians, with the sort of dismissive tolerance which professional baseball players extend to softball. Yet Alwynne Smart (1969), Jeffrie Murphy (1988) and Jean Hampton (1988) have shown that there are very relevant questions.[16] For instance, can a retributive sentencer who believes that he knows how severely a given offender should be punished exercise mercy in his case without being inconsistent? As Jeffrie Murphy neatly puts it, "Is tempering tampering?"[17] If the sentencer has taken into account all that he should—proportionality, extenuating circumstances and the degree of suffering which the individual will experience as a result—what is left that can cogently prompt leniency? I have suggested an answer elsewhere.[18] Here I need only make the point that for utilitarian sentencers this is a non-problem. They can believe, for example, that Penalty X will maximise utility, and yet be willing, for respectable reasons, to sacrifice a little utility in order to impose less suffering.

Compromises between retributivism and utilitarianism are currently popular. I will attempt to classify the compromises. First—and most popular amongst sentencers—is emotional eclecticism: their sentences are utilitarian unless the crime outrages them, in which case they become retributive. Next is a more rational eclecticism, of the kind preached by the Supreme Court of Victoria, Australia. You sentence with utilitarian objectives unless the case turns out to be one in which none of these objectives seems likely to be attained, in which case you sentence retributively.[19] Eclectic compromises are favoured by practising lawyers rather than academics, who tend to prefer what I call "hybrids." An interesting example is offered by the Australian philosopher C.L. Ten:[20]

> Punishing a person is justified if and only if
>
> (i) he is an offender who has voluntarily violated a legitimate law, or [and this is one of his innovations] an innocent person whose punishment will inflict much less suffering on him than the suffering that at least one other innocent person would have experienced as an additional victim of crime had there been no punishment; and

> (ii) punishing him does not have serious adverse effects on others; and punishing those who have voluntarily committed similar or lesser offences is justified on utilitarian grounds.

An equally complex hybrid has been engendered by Paul H. Robinson (1988) of Rutgers University, as a result of his experience as a member of the U.S. Sentencing Commission. His hybrid

> "...uses desert as a determining principle and combines utilitarian purposes as a limiting principle. The limiting criteria is an 'intolerable crime rate' standard. The utilitarian purposes are also subject to contingent limitations based upon the reliability of any predictions of crime rates. Desert then serves as a second limiting principle, one that limits the application of the first limiting principle if the combined utilitarian purposes generate an 'in tolerable injustice'...Such a system requires both defining a point of intolerable crime and, if the occasion arises, a point of intolerable injustice. Recognizing the magnitude of this project, I leave it to others or to a future article..."[21]

A much simpler proposal, which stands Robinson's on its head, was originally offered by Lord Longford in 1961, but elaborated by Norval Morris in *Madness and the Criminal Law.*[22] Punishment is to be justified by utility, but with desert as a limiting principle. In other words, utility rules unless it suggests a punishment so severe that it seems retributively intolerable.

By way of a concluding thought, I want to pose the question: "Why compromise?" There are two kinds of compromise. One is voluntary, and usually political. The other is obligatory, and can be called intellectual, or at least logical. Compromises between retributivism and utilitarianism are certainly advisable from a political point of view. In England only about 40 percent of adults give retributive first choices when asked to justify penalties: the rest seem to be utilitarians.[23] The compromising retributivist maximises support from his constituents, and the same is true of the compromising utilitarian.

More interesting is the question whether a compromise is logically as well as politically necessary. To make it so there have to be serious weaknesses in the positions of *both* parties. If only one of the positions is weak, the other party need not compromise, and wins, as it were, by default. I hope I have demonstrated that retributivism suffers from serious weaknesses, which modern retributivists have, if anything, made worse. If so, the next question is whether utilitarians also suffer from weaknesses which they cannot rectify without help. Certainly, in the past their claims have been exaggerated, especially in regard to reform, rehabilitation, and the moral education of the public. On the subject of deterrence, elimination and incapacitation their claims had a sounder basis: they were exaggerated, but had a hard core of truth. It is true that moral objections have been raised to these expedients and I have addressed those objections elsewhere.[24] The only criticism which utilitarians seem to be unable to answer satisfactorily is that they cannot offer an acceptable form of proportionality. Bentham's "frugality-principle" (1789) sounds fine, but in practice might result, for example, in penalising illegal parking more severely than fraud.[25] At this point, the utilitarian is understandably apt to compromise by accepting retributivists' proportionality. But this need not be an intellectual compromise. Indeed, it cannot be, since no one can be genuinely satisfied with proportionality. He is, therefore, compromising voluntarily, for reasons of political utility, and not because logic compels him to do so. The utilitarian can hold out against any intellectual compromise, whereas the retributivist, classical or modern, cannot.

---

[1]See Jeffrie Murphy, "Getting Even: The role of the victim," chapter 8 of this volume.

[2]Andrew von Hirsch, *Doing Justice: Report of the Committee for the Study of Incarceration* (New York: Hill and Wang, 1976).

[3]Immanuel Kant, *Rechtslehre* (1796), trans. W. Hastie as *Philosophy of Law* (Edinburgh: Clark, 1887), p. 195.

[4]E.g. *Leviticus*, chapt. 20; *Numbers*, chapt. 35; Kant, *Rechtslehre*. It is a common mistake to think that Kant's main justification for punishing criminals was that if we fail to do so we share their guilt. His notorious passage in *Rechtslehre* about the need to execute the last murderer before dissolving the state was loose rhetoric. If we fail to punish were not are not guilty of the crime itself, but of refusal to obey one of Kant's categorical imperatives. *Rechtslehre* needs to be read in the light of *Grundlegung*.

[5]Nigel Walker, *Crime and Criminology* (Oxford: Oxford University Press, 1987).

[6]Emile Durkheim, *The Division of Labour in Society*, trans. G. Simpson (New York: Free Press, 1965), chapt. 2.

[7]*Minutes of Evidence taken before the Royal Commission on Capital Punishment: Ninth Day* (London: Her Majesty's Stationery Office, 1967).

[8]*Gregg vs. Georgia* (1976). Mr. Justice Marshall dismissed that justification in a few well-chosen words: "It is inconceivable that any individual concerned about conforming his conduct to what society says is "right" would fail to realize that murder is "wrong" if the penalty were simply life imprisonment."

[9]For a brief history of penal McLuhanism, see Nigel Walker, "The Ultimate Justification," in *Crime, Proof and Punishment*, ed. C.F.H. Tapper, (London: Butterworth, 1981), pp. 109-26.

[10]Hyman Gross, *A Theory of Criminal Justice* (Oxford: Oxford University Press, 1979), p. 401.

[11]Mike Hough and Nigel Walker, *Public Attitudes to Sentencing* (Aldershot: Gower, 1988).

[12]Robert Nozick, *Philosophical Explanations* (Chicago: University of Chicago Press, 1981), pp. 370-79. Andrew von Hirsch, *Past or Future Crimes* (Manchester: Manchester University Press, 1986), chapt. 5.

[13]Von Hirsh, *Past or Future Crimes*, p. 53.

[14]G.F. Hegel, *Philosophie des Rechts*, trans. T.M. Knox as *Philosophy of Right* (Oxford: Oxford University Press, 1942), pp. 37-38.

[15]For condemnation of this "definitional stop," see Herbert Hart, *Punishment and Responsibility* (Oxford: Oxford University Press, 1968), p. 6.

[16]See Alwynne Smart, "Mercy" in *The Philosophy of Punishment*, ed. H.B. Action, (London: MacMillan, 1960), Jean Hampton and Jeffrie Murphy, *Forgiveness and Mercy* (Cambridge: Cambridge University Press, 1988).

[17]Jeffrie Murphy, *Forgiveness and Mercy*, p. 167.

[18]Nigel Walker, *Why Punish?* (Oxford: Oxford University Press, 1990).

[19]*Report of the Victorian Sentencing Commission* (Melbourne: The Victorian Attorney General's Department, 1988).

[20]Chung Li Ten, *Crime, Guilt and Punishment* (Oxford: Oxford University Press, 1987).

[21]Paul Robinson, "Hybrid Principles for the Distribution of Criminal Sanctions," in *Northwestern Law Review*, vol. 82, pp. 19-42.

[22]Norval Morris, *Madness and the Criminal Law* (Chicago: University of Chicago Press, 1982).

[23]Hough and Walker, *Public Attitudes to Sentencing*, p. 179

[24]In Walker, *Why Punish*

[25]Jeremy Bentham, *Principles of Morals and Legislation*, ed. G. Harrison, (Oxford : Blackwell, 1948), chapter XV.

Punishment: A Communitarian Approach

Nicola Lacey

Over the last decade, communitarian themes have emerged (or perhaps one should say re-emerged) in many debates in political theory.[1] In a book published in 1988, I sketched and defended an approach to state punishment which I described as communitarian.[2] Since then, I have reflected further on communitarian contributions to social theory, particularly in exploring feminist critiques of orthodox political theory.[3] In this essay, I return to the issue of punishment so as to reassess the communitarian approach in the light of those further reflections. I shall begin with the communitarian conception which I developed in my book, and describe how it grew out of my perception of certain difficulties with traditional approaches to the justification of punishment. Then I shall raise some questions about the methodology of that work and the substance of its arguments, particularly their reliance on the insights of communitarian political and social theory. Finally, I shall suggest how my earlier arguments might be strengthened by being somewhat recast, and sketch how some of the critical difficulties of the communitarian conception of punishment might be addressed and at least partially overcome.

Rejecting Traditional Approaches to Punishment

The traditional philosophical literature on the justification of punishment is vast and yet oddly inconclusive. It consists of a long rally of arguments between retributive and utilitarian writers, resulting in a stalemate only imperfectly broken by recent attempts at compromise and synthesis. Most of the arguments which feature in this debate are very well known. I do not propose to repeat them here. Instead, I shall focus on what

I take to be important objections which confront all the traditional theories before moving on to describe a somewhat different approach.

Whatever arguments can be made in favour of practices of punishment set out, explicitly or implicitly, from a definition. Yet the task of definition is fraught with difficulty. Many definitions seem to be flawed in that they resonate decisively with a particular justifying argument, without at any stage articulating that link. At least a predisposition to the particular justification is therefore contained within the definition before it has ever been properly argued for. I shall return below to the question of whether it is possible, even sensible, to try to escape this dilemma. Since my particular interest is in punishment by the state, the definition which I favour identifies legal punishment as the principled infliction by a state-constituted authority of what are generally regarded as unpleasant consequences on individuals or groups. These individuals or groups must have been adjudicated, in accordance with publicly and legally recognized criteria and procedures correctly applied, to have breached the law. Penal consequences are inflicted as a response to that breach and as an enforcement of the law. A further definitional condition is that the response is not inflicted solely as a means of providing compensation for the harm caused by the offence. This idea of punishment as both response and enforcement seeks to be neutral as between the main contenders in the "great debate" about punishment—utilitarians and retributivists—whilst delineating a terrain which is sufficiently well-differentiated to avoid the discussion collapsing into a general treatise on political philosophy and the proper role of the state. Based on this relatively broad notion of state punishment, my argument for a communitarian conception of punishment is informed by three general theoretical commitments.

In the first place, I contend that questions about the justification of state punishment can be addressed adequately only by an approach which integrates consideration of them with that of other major questions of political philosophy. It seems to me quite impossible that one could come up with anything approaching a sensible or complete set of arguments in favour of state punishment without also considering questions of personal responsibility, notions of political and legal obligation, and the proper nature, functions and limits of criminal law. Since punishment is defined as a response to breach of criminal law, we must know something of the justifications for that institution before we can consider those of its sanction, just as we must consider the conditions under which it is appropriate to hold citizens responsible for their formal breaches of law. And if the justification for punishment is parasitic on that for criminal law, we must seek to understand the multiple ways in which laws impose or entail obligations or, contingently or systematically, generate reasons for action on the part of citizens and state officials. It is unfortunate that a majority of philosophies, especially in the twentieth century, have been ready to hive punishment off and to treat it as a discreet, textbook problem of political philosophy, as if capable of independent argument and resolution. Of the questions I have mentioned, only that of responsibility has consistently occupied the attention of writers on punishment. In my view, this has been a very basic flaw which has hampered the development of modern argument about punishment. The effective insulation of state punishment from developments in the mainstream of political philosophy has, I think, maintained the plausibility of unitary consequentialist and retributive accounts far longer than would otherwise have been the case.

Secondly, and flowing from this first contention, my argument for a communitarian approach is informed by a critique of certain aspects of the liberal tradition in political philosophy and its implications for the justification of punishment. During the last one hundred years, the predominance of liberal ideas in the Anglo-American academic world has been such that arguments about the justification of punishment have typically been defended in the context of a general commitment to liberal ideology. This ideology has a cluster of features, and these features of course affect the main traditions in the philosophy of punishment in rather different ways. But there are certain important common themes. In particular, the liberal commitment to individualism and the failure to develop an adequate account of collective values, public virtues and community interests have obstructed the development of a cogent analysis of state punishment. The liberal assumption that human individuals are invested with a set of pre-social rights, needs, interests and characteristics which remain fundamentally unchanged in and which must be acknowledged and respected by political society can be, and has been, criticized on a number of grounds. Feminist, Marxist and communitarian writers have argued that humans are essentially social beings whose interests, needs and values can only be understood in concrete social situations. Furthermore, liberal individualism sets up a particularly intractable problem of justification for punishment, in that any practice of punishment is likely to violate, *prima facie*, the rights of the individual. The liberal primacy of individual rights and interests sets up an unrealistic opposition at the core of arguments about punishment, an opposition in which the moral claims of the individual are seen as inevitably pitched against the claims of the collectivity represented by the state, whose powers are regarded with jealous suspicion by the liberal theorist.

Liberal emphasis on the moral claims of the individual leads to failure in developing a sophisticated account of public goods and collective values. These goods and values are often understood in non-liberal political traditions as intrinsically as well as instrumentally valuable. They can be and often need to be promoted and maintained by political organizations. State practices which have individually coercive aspects may in fact contribute to or even be fundamentally necessary to the maintenance of standards, goods or facilities which are crucial to the common living of a decent life. Certainly, more modern and social-democratic conceptions of liberalism are sympathetic to this insight, but the extraordinary insulation of modern debate about the justification of punishment from general developments in political philosophy has meant that these more sophisticated arguments have barely touched the punishment debate.[4] And because the strongest arguments which can be made for state punishment may well be precisely in terms of the more diffuse, collective, intangible goods and values on which liberalism has been silent, this has constituted a major obstacle to the development of adequate arguments for punishment, most of which remain firmly rooted in a form of liberalism which one might otherwise reasonably have assumed to have disappeared at the end of the nineteenth century.

This problem has been compounded by the liberal emphasis on a notion of rationality as the selection of instrumentally appropriate means to chosen ends. The possibility of rational action is a basic presupposition of liberal theory, just as its realization is a fundamental ideal in political life. The development of this narrow conception of rationality, particularly in the penal sphere, has been strongly influenced by utilitarian instrumentalism. It is set up as neutral and objective. Even apart from its extraordinarily unrealistic vision of criminal behavior, it has the consequence of marginalizing arguments about the symbolic, emotive or affective aspects of punishment. Commitment to this kind of rationality has led to "rationalization" of retributive arguments into the currency of utilitarianism, and dismissal of traditional retributive claims as mysterious, metaphorical and opaque.[5] Such dismissal is unsatisfactory, because it ignores the ethical views behind the widespread retributive attitudes which characterize many people's thinking about punishment. Finally, the typical liberal focus on a negative conception of freedom—the sheer absence of restraint—must be abandoned if we are to say the best that can be said for punishment. For some strong arguments for that practice flow from a commitment to a more positive conception of human autonomy—the actual capacity of people to develop their lives and pursue their goals and conceptions of the good. This positive conception of freedom relates closely to the provision of public facilities and to the recognition of public goods and collective provision.

Thirdly, I believe that the modern tendency to divide up discrete questions relevant to the justification of punishment in an attempt to accommodate the insights of philosophically opposed traditions is fundamentally flawed. Whilst an identification of distinct questions such as that of the "general justifying aim" of punishment and that of its distribution may be helpful in identifying different *aspects* of the justification for punishment, it is neither theoretically possible nor practically useful to give a utilitarian answer to one and a retributive or quasi-retributive answer to the other, as done in a famous article by H.L.A. Hart.[6] My argument here is rather technical but it is central to my ultimate claims and I must therefore flesh it out a little, using Hart's work as my model. Hart pursues the initially tempting and intuitively plausible strategy of drawing the best from the two main philosophical traditions in the history of justifying argument—retributive and utilitarian theories of punishment. He distinguishes between questions of definition, aim and distribution, and gives an essentially utilitarian answer to the second (the justifying aim of punishment is to reduce the amount of crime) and a quasi-retributive, or fairness-based, answer to the third (punishment should only be meted out to those who have committed an offence for which they are responsible in the sense that they knew what they were doing and had a genuine opportunity to do otherwise than they did). The major problem for such an account is that utilitarianism, which forms the basis for Hart's justifying aim, purports to be a complete theory of punishment, as does its retributive rival. Hart obscures this by talking rather as if the problem with utilitarianism is that it simply lacks a distributive principle. But of course it does have a distributive principle, the problem being that many people find the implications of that principle in the context of punishment (like elsewhere) deeply distasteful. Can we simply amputate the part of the theory of which we approve, and tack this on to part of another (also purportedly complete) theory coming out of a completely different philosophical stable, and flowing from a radically opposed (deontological rather than consequentialist) moral view of the world?

In case this sounds like an unduly abstract quibble, I should illustrate its practical implications with an example. Hart introduces the distinction by analogy with a system of taxation; the reasons why we have such a system, he argues, are separate from the question of how we distribute its burdens. But this is too strong a claim. If the rationale of a tax system is an egalitarian welfarist one of enabling the state to provide a threshold level of social security for the poor, at least some distributive strategies are ruled out. For example, a flat rate tax would be out of keeping with the general justifying aim. And questions of the aim and distribution of punishment are interrelated in just the same way: once we have determined our aim, certain consequences (albeit not entirely determinate ones) flow from this in terms of proper distribution. Thus if Hart sticks to his utilitarian aim, a solidly retributive rule of distribution is cancelled out in principle, even though in practice such a rule could operate as an absolute side constraint on the pursuit of the utilitarian goal. Yet Hart stops short of this practically feasible solution, because he contemplates the possibility of strict liability—albeit with a "sense of sacrifice of principle". This is precisely the kind of difficult area in which we expect principles of punishment to give us some guidance in designing our practice, but a theory composed of two unitary but oppositional principles cannot help us here. What is needed is a theory in which the logical relationship of questions of aim and distribution are acknowledged, and in which a more sophisticated, complex and pluralistic conception of the aim or rationale of punishment generates internal, logical constraints on the distribution and design of penal measures.[7] This entails abandoning both utilitarianism and retributivism as theories of punishment and resisting the apparently attractive but illusory simplicity of unitary theories. Although it does not mean that we have to abandon all arguments for punishment put forward by utilitarian and retributive writers, we do have to accord them a different weight and status within a different political and conceptual framework.

A Communitarian Approach to Punishment

The three concerns which I have described provide the intellectual and political context in which I argue for a communitarian conception of punishment. My starting point is a rejection of liberal individualism and a commitment to the idea that humans are essentially, necessarily, and primarily social beings. As persons, we are in an important sense constituted by our relationships with others and with social institutions. Relationships, interpersonal connections, understanding, mutual support and fulfillment of obligations are among the things which we tend to value most highly, and we are physically and emotionally dependent on each other and on social institutions. Indeed, our very identity is tied up with our social life: we define ourselves in terms of our relations with others and with the communities of which we are a part. This recognition of the ways in which our interests, needs and preferences—our very personhood—are socially constituted, leads to an important shift of emphasis in our thinking about punishment. For it suggests as centrally important not merely the moral claims of the individual, but the maintenance, stability and development of the societies which are necessary for the flourishing of people within them, and hence prompts us to think about the potential contributions of criminal law and punishment to this central value. The alleged moral boundaries which dictate that individuals never be used merely as means to social ends begin to dissolve once we recognize that people have a fundamental interest in the maintenance and development of a peaceful and just society to which they belong and in terms of which their social identities are realized.

In the light of this assumption and the change of emphasis which it engenders, it is possible to sketch a conception of what kinds of social functions the practice of punishment might fulfill in an idealized community into which a political society such as ours might develop. The ideal community which I am envisaging would be characterized by a certain threshold of shared goals and values, to be determined by a democratic process with a far greater element of political participation than is typical of modern liberal representative democracies. The extent and richness of the community's public culture and shared commitments can not, of course, be determined in the abstract. But we must not fall into the liberal trap of assuming a opposition between adoption of common goals and respect for individual freedom. For public commitments to the pursuit of shared goals, such as the provision of health, educational, sports, and artistic facilities, in fact enhance the development of different forms of life. I envisage a community in which human beings participate both directly and indirectly in the development of the social framework, policies and norms; in which they would be bound at some level by a sense of commitment to the maintenance and peaceful development of the community through acknowledgment of their investment in it and of its importance for themselves and others. It would be united by a second order commitment to the values and goals adopted through the process of public decision on democratic principles. Members would thus maintain a sense of themselves whilst creatively acknowledging their interdependence and mutual responsibility.

In such a community, the function of criminal laws would be to express, uphold and, if necessary, enforce only those democratically determined standards and norms which are seen as being of fundamental importance to the peace and stability of the community and the interests of its members. Criminal law would express and uphold the fundamental social values affirmed in the community. It would respond only to actions which directly violate citizens' socially acknowledged fundamental interests in welfare and autonomy. Given its peculiarly coercive means, criminal law in such a community would be stringently restricted to the preservation of norms and standards seen as *fundamentally* important to the welfare and autonomy of citizens. It would be used only as a last resort. Less coercive response to actual or threatened breaches of criminal law, for example mediation and persuasion, would be important and would have to be exhausted before recourse to punishment could be had. In ideal conditions of economic plenty and mutual good will, the actual infliction of penalties might be exceptionally rare, and their form of a less severe and more symbolic nature than is usual in existing societies.

I would argue, then, that a commitment to maintaining a community in which human beings can flourish, by developing their affective and productive capacities and achieving an adequate level of welfare, must be at the root of any justification of punishment. Punishment is justified to the extent that its deployment may contribute to the maintenance of a valued community and to the maintenance of publicly affirmed standards. These standards concern not just individual interests but also diffused common goods, which all citizens have reasons to uphold and in the formation of which all citizens have a real chance to participate. Once individuals are seen as social beings whose self-conception, development and welfare depend on their social environment and their relations with others, general reasons for them to uphold the values of a just community to which they belong are not hard to produce. In a community, whose general organization was conscientiously directed towards the autonomy and welfare of its citizens, arguments from responsibility, commitment to other citizens, and to the community as a whole would enable a persuasive, albeit minimalist, argument for "respect for law" to be constructed.[8] In such a community, criminal law and punishment might make a modest but important contribution to realizing an autonomy consisting in the positive autonomy of citizens and their welfare, conceived personal empowerment and the fulfillment of fundamental needs and interests. These would encompass goods such as shelter, physical integrity, nourishment, physical, intellectual and spiritual development, but would do so in ways which are socially and politically contingent. The needs and interests would be those democratically acknowledged by the community, and they would be met to a relatively equal level. Criminal law would be conceived as responding to, expressing disapproval of, and underlining social rejection of actions which directly counter the basic conceptions of autonomy and welfare. It would do so by specifying particularly interest-threatening forms of behavior as serious wrongs both against the direct victim and the community as a whole.

The social meanings and functions of punishment could be understood at a number of different levels within this communitarian framework. Insights from all branches of the traditional debate could be incorporated. At a basic level, the threat of punishment would be justified by its necessity as a means of making the standards of criminal law "*real*": as a way of stating that the meeting of those standards is a matter of duty or obligation, from the community's point of view. Punishment would meet the collective need to underpin, reaffirm and maintain the internalized commitments of the community's members to the standards expressed by criminal law, and to acknowledge the importance of those commitments to the existence and identity of the community. Flowing from this general argument from systemic necessity is a cluster of specific aims and goods which could and should be fostered by institutions of punishment. These include social goods such as the restoration of social cohesion, which may be disturbed by certain sorts of offending; the reaffirmation of the social values endorsed by political processes and entrenched in criminal law; the chance for reconsideration and possible modification of criminal law; the general educative effect flowing from the public affirmation of social values and the implicit or explicit denunciation involved in the process of conviction and sentence. Many of these ideas resonate, of course, with the insights of retributive theories of punishment. But the specific goals espoused by utilitarians would not have to be abandoned: punishment might also promote general or individual deterrence, reform, incapacitation, social protection, the prevention of resort to private vengeance or self-help (not to mention the consequent maintenance of respect for the legal system), and some satisfaction of victims' grievances.

In the communitarian approach, therefore, the functions of punishment would encompass a cluster of general and specific, direct and indirect, symbolic and instrumental values which go well beyond the ambit of any one of the traditional theories. The significance which punishment would have for the citizens of a community could serve the instrumental, practical ends which we have mentioned. General and specific, symbolic and instrumental arguments for punishment are interdependent, logically related, and mutually necessary to its justification. The core of a communitarian approach is the general argument from necessity, but that necessity itself flows partially from the potency of intuitions which are most obviously acknowledged in the traditional retributive theories. The idea of punishment as a significant and necessary symbol of the community's own entitlement to enforce its democratically determined central values, may be difficult to explicate purely in terms of instrumentally rational judgments about how particular social goals may be pursued. It does, however, form a central part of our moral thinking. The community conception reflects the role of punishment in our emotional and affective lives, whilst it restrains that role in a morally acceptable way.

Since this approach is explicitly pluralistic, I need to explain more clearly the important differences between the community conception and the mixed theories of punishment such as that of Hart. These are best illustrated by comparing their distributive implications. The community conception, like mixed theories, rejects a unitary approach and therefore implicitly accepts the need to balance different values and goals both in designing institutions of punishment and in making decisions about particular cases. However, the approach which I have sketched denies the appropriateness of responding to this complexity either by reducing different values to a common currency such as utility, or by simply according them invariable priorities, as is usual in mixed theories. Nor does it attempt to make such strategies manageable by dividing up different questions, thus confining balancing judgments to the trade-off between general aim and distributive principle. It acknowledges, on the contrary, that difficult balancing decisions also have to be made *within* the delineation of both functions and distribution. It therefore constructs the problem of punishment as even more fragmented than do the mixed theories. However, the fragmentation flows from a pluralism which is not fractured by the intractable oppositions which characterize Hart's theory. This is because the community conception recognizes that there are internal relations between the proper functions and fair distribution of punishment, the arguments for both being structured by the same, not competing, evaluative concerns. In my view, an adequate understanding of the justifying functions of punishment must be combined with a commitment to the idea that means as well as ends are of moral significance, and that intrinsic states of affairs as well as consequences are valuable. This understanding provides a richer set of guidelines to what is inevitably a morally complex reasoning process. The specific demands of politically concrete conceptions of welfare and autonomy would have to be balanced and accommodated when in tension, and this would be done in determining the proper functions as well as the fair distribution of punishment: both kinds of values inform the specification of both aspects of the question of punishment.

On the specific question of distribution, therefore, it is not difficult to see why punishment in a community of the kind I have described would be restricted to those who have been judged to have actually perpetrated criminal acts: any other solution would unjustifiably violate a value which the general functions seek to realize by denying respect for the welfare and autonomy of each and every citizen. Any practice of punishment which sanctioned victimization would thereby sacrifice its claim to be acting in the interests of the welfare and autonomy of each member of the community by legitimating penal responses which evinced no respect for and accorded no weight to autonomy. It would be. By emphasizing the importance of protecting autonomy as a function of punishment, we can see how an adequate distributive principle can actually flow from, rather than merely act as, a limit upon the justifying aim itself. Punishment, then, should be limited to those who are "dispositionally" responsible, in the sense that their actions genuinely express hostility or indifference to the values of the community which the law in question exists to protect and foster. The test of whether or not a particular action manifests a relatively settled disposition to carry out such actions, as evidenced by all the circumstances, including whether it was done intentionally, heedlessly or negligently, seems to be an apposite test of such hostility.

The internal relation between functions of and distributive limitations on punishment is clear. The limitation of punishment to those who are dispositionally responsible for their offences is entailed both by the lack of need to punish others, whose offences are in some sense fortuitous, and by the different reactions we have to someone who does wrong as an aberration, and one who does so in a considered, characteristic way. In a community, it seems overwhelmingly likely that social cohesion, reaffirmation of common values, and denunciation could only be served by penal responses to those whose actions exhibit a considered, settled rejection of some aspect of the community values expressed in criminal law. With other offenders, such a community can afford, and therefore ought, to adopt an attitude of toleration. But does a requirement of dispositional responsibility adequately respect human autonomy, given our limited ability to control our actions and dispositions? I would argue that it does so, because if humans are primarily social beings who must live in some form of community, a just community must have some entitlement to preserve at least its basic framework. In order to do so, the community's institutions have to take its citizens, in a manner of speaking, as they find them. If a certain number of them purposefully, heedlessly or negligently express themselves through hostility, opposition or indifference to the community's central values in the form of criminal behavior, whether or not they can help the relevant aspects of their disposition, the community must either assert itself or allow itself to be undermined.

Turning to the proper form of punishments, my argument emphasizes the social contingency of this question and, at least partly for this reason, my book did not develop a detailed account of what penalties would be acceptable or appropriate. But, especially given the possibility of abuses of political power, and in the light of the value to be attached to positively conceived human autonomy, I would emphasize the need to retain a residual area of autonomy by ruling out annihilating penalties such as capital punishment. I would also argue that more ideal social conditions might well render the imposition of penalties unnecessary, and could rely in the first instance on non-punitive, persuasive and conciliatory responses to actual or threatened breaches of criminal law. The argument from necessity justifies the community's assertion of its central norms, but this assertion does not have to be punitive in every case. Where punishment is necessary, my argument entails a much more lenient range of penalties and a heavier reliance on formal and symbolic measures such as the expression of conviction and condemnation. The design of penalties would be informed by the distributive and function-based considerations already discussed, and would involve a commitment to some notion of proportionality, on a variety of functional grounds. I have also suggested that my account of what meaning and justification punishment might have in an ideal community does have relevance for the justification of punishment in our less than ideal world, through the analogies of function and form which would be identified between real and ideal-world practices of punishment. However, many real-world punishments clearly can not be justified on this basis, even in the minimal sense of there being arguments for them just marginally stronger than those against. So the argument from ideal-theory by analogy should not be regarded as a *carte blanche* for punishment. The relationship between the actual and the ideal in the realm of punishment needs to be developed further.

Refining the Communitarian Approach

Some of my arguments for a communitarian approach require further analysis and differentiation. Two main themes need to be isolated. First, communitarian approaches adopt a social constructionist position: in other words, they assert that human nature and identity are in an important sense constituted by the particular social environment in which human beings live. This tends to lead into a form of ethical relativism: if human nature is itself open to social influence and construction, the idea of pre-social or "objective" ethical values becomes suspect. A more suitable approach seems to be to regard ethics as a practical project flowing from human debate, development and judgment in concrete social contexts. Moral judgments, then, are seen as grounded in particular communities and their practices. This social constructionist strand in communitarian thought is, of course, not peculiar to it: other political theories, notably feminist and Marxist accounts, have espoused strongly socially constructionist ideas. However, as developed in modern feminist and communitarian thought, the idea of the social construction of human nature has generated a trenchant critique of the traditional liberal conception of fixed, pre-social human nature and hence of basic human rights, needs and interests.[9] This, as I have described, became an important part of my critique of liberal theories of punishment, and in particular of the ways in which their unstated assumptions about human nature set up an unnecessarily intractable problem of justification for practices of punishment. I still hold very firmly to this kind of critique of liberalism, although I would certainly acknowledge that much more work in social theory remains to be done to explicate the social construction of human nature and identity. In particular, there are still unresolved questions of how the constructionist thesis is consistent with an adequately strong account of human subjectivity and with the possibility for acquisition of critical consciousness which militates against prevailing social practices and norms.[10]

The communitarian commitment to social constructionism suggests a somewhat different way of theorizing about punishment. The kind of ethics suggested by a socially constructionist approach to human nature and, hence, to moral and political value is a rather different one from the traditional self-conception of post-enlightenment, universalistic political philosophy. This philosophy, which characterizes much of the writing about punishment which I have been concerned to analyze and criticize, takes a classic "ideal observer" or "detached, objective" view; it purports to speak, in Nagel's famous phrase, "from nowhere." Standing outside a particular social institution, and working from an allegedly neutral definition, it aspires to produce a cogent and persuasive set of normative arguments which are only minimally grounded in or contingent upon the actual state of the world. Empirical questions tend to be regarded as marginal. This point relates closely to the difficulties already mentioned about definition—the practical impossibility of producing a definition which is not grounded in a particular practice in such a way as to reflect not just its empirical features but also the value judgments as to function and justification which inform the practice. From a socially constructionist perspective the classic distinctions between descriptive and normative enterprises begin to blur. From this perspective one begins with an analysis of the social meaning of a practice such as punishment—its actual features and the current social understandings about what justifies and explains the practice—and would then move to an incremental and immanent critique of the practice. The idea of a "neutral" definition would be recognized as a conceptual impossibility, and the evaluations implicit in social definitions would be explicitly identified and subjected to analysis and critique. To put it figuratively, the theoretical movement would tend from the actual to the aspirational, rather than the other way around. The theoretical framework would be more like the immanent critique of criminal law which I developed in chapter 5 of *State Punishment* than the idealized communitarian approach sketched and defended in chapter 8, and then later compared with actual practices. This kind of "interpretive" approach to ethical and political questions now characterizes a good part of modern social theory, including much feminist work.[11]

Current conceptions and practices of punishment fail to live up to values and standards which inform some, currently marginalized, political doctrines, which also have some support in culturally endorsed value systems. The communitarian conception would more adequately meet those values, particularly in the light of social constructionist insights about human beings and our "nature". The social constructionist thesis argues for a shift in the kinds of values and functions traditionally espoused by penal institutions and hence for a shift in the dominant culture. My argument is suggestive not only of a utopian vision of what criminal justice might become in a better world than ours, but of what particular conditions would have to change in order to get there or at least make some progress.

I strongly affirm the enterprise of imaginative, critical and even utopian political thinking. And despite the fact that I am not entirely persuaded by the interpretive approach to ethics and political argument, I do think that it also raises some very difficult questions which we are far from resolving. These have to do with the complex and fragmented notion of ideas such as "community" and "public culture" in any society as complex, large and heterogeneous as ours. If moral argument is simply the expression of different evaluations and political conceptions of a large number of competing viewpoints, criteria for judging between them are difficult to determine. I shall return to the problem of fragmentation below. Furthermore, even where it is possible to identify a prevailing, dominant and homogeneous culture, intractable problems arise not just about the status of moral arguments but also about the possibility of developing and asserting minority or critical consciousness.

Secondly, the social constructionist themes on which I draw need to be differentiated from what might be called value-communitarianism. This is the substantive communitarian argument that punishment, like other major social institutions, can and should aspire to further not simply individual rights, needs and interests but also community values, social goods, collective goals and even public virtues. Of course, this particular critique of liberal individualism and liberalism's failure to develop an adequate account of public goods is related to the argument that human beings are socially constituted. Once the opposition between individual and community is attenuated, the liberal focus on individual-oriented values begins to look distinctly dubious. Nevertheless, the argument that punishment can and should serve collective goals, that a communitarian conception embodies an enriched conception of what the functions and positive social contributions of punishment might be, is an important one in its own right. Two further points need to be made here. In the first place, in fleshing out the value- communitarian argument, I used a variety of expressions as if they were entirely consistent and indeed interchangeable. I spoke of public, collective and community interests, values, goods, commitments, goals and virtues, because all of these ideas represented a departure from the classical liberal conception of individual-oriented value. However, they do so in importantly different ways. Two meanings in particular need to be distinguished. The first meaning captured by these ideas is that of goods which have an independent value which can not be reduced to a set of benefits to or goods for assignable individuals. This collective nature may mean that the good in question cannot be distributed to some and not others, whilst still being something that individuals may benefit from directly or even, as in the case of a clean environment, necessarily. It may be collective in the sense that it benefits people indirectly by making certain actions, practices or ways of life possible, these being things which only some people may ever take advantage of, and thus benefit from as assignable individuals. These kinds of distinctions could be multiplied and refined. But the important defining feature of this sense of the collective, social or public nature of a good is its focus on *who* is benefited and *in what kind of way*: such goods tend to be diffused, and their value does not simply consist in the sum total of individually distributed benefits which they secure. My occasional casual reference to the notion of public virtue betokens the idea that some of these goods are regarded as intrinsically valuable, independently of their contribution to individual utility or other kinds of consequences. This first meaning is obviously different from a second sense in which goods may be public. The second sense refers to *whose* values, concerns and judgments they reflect; in other words, they may be not just public or community goods but goods and values of *the* community or *the* public—i.e., those of a *particular* community—identified by a particular kind of political process. In this second sense, community values may refer not only to collective but also to individual goods and interests. This important distinction is probably best captured by speaking of the first sense as public or collective goods, and of the second as community values or interests, and I shall adopt that way of speaking henceforth.[12]

Arguments about both collective goods and community values are important to my account of punishment, but they are important in different ways, and they raise different problems. Collective goods and the contribution which the practice of punishment may make to their realization is absolutely central to my substantive argument, and still seems to me a fundamentally important corrective to the impoverished view of the possible functions of punishment taken by the classical liberal theories. The main question which the notion of collective goods raises is that of their identification, but this problem is endemic to political argument and not a special feature of these kinds of goods. The notion of community values, on the other hand, is important not only to the substantive communitarian argument but also to the method which that argument employs. Here we touch on the problems I have already adverted to in discussing the status of socially relative ethical and political judgments. The basic problems inherent to the notion of community values are its naive presupposition that clear common commitments can be identified in modern heterogeneous societies and, even if this problem can be overcome, the status of an apparently prescriptive claim based on a descriptive generalization. Focussing on the first problem, one way of putting this would be that modern societies consist in a collection of communities which themselves overlap in the sense that members of society are also members of a number of different communities and groups, each of which structures our experience and generates its own set of norms, values and conventions. Because of our membership of these overlapping communities, our own identities, as well as that of society as a whole, are typically fragmented and complex. This suggests that the communitarian vision of the homogeneity and consistency apparently needed for the grounding of ethical and political judgment in particular communities is unrealistic. It is this very fragmentation, the diversity and contradictoriness of experience, which helps to resolve the problem of how critical consciousness arises (as in Marxist theory's account of crises of capitalism; critical theory's account of fundamental contradictions; feminist theory's account of consciousness-raising). Communities are not harmonious, consistent and homogeneous, and nor are their members transparent to each other, or even to themselves: social life is a constant process of conflict and challenge, out of which views and commitments are gradually developed. Given all this, can the second kind of communitarian claim about the social construction of value and the importance of community values in justifying and explaining practices such as punishment be maintained?

A further difficulty of the communitarian claim is not so much its lack of realism, but its potentially oppressive implications. More precisely, it has to do with communitarianism's failure to address the issues of oppression and subordination which flow from the social fact that in most societies some groups or communities have the power to enforce and impose their definitions of right and conceptions of justice on other communities which are relatively powerless in the political process. This problem is absolutely fundamental to any critical approach to criminal justice, practice of which in current American and British society, at least, has a starkly differential impact on politically powerless groups identified along racial and socio-economic lines. How is a communitarian approach to respond to the facts of heterogeneity, of inequality, and of unequal access to the dominant communities which have the power to objectify in legal form and hence to enforce their own meanings and interests?

Although I do not underestimate these difficulties, I still believe that something like the second kind of communitarian claim can be maintained. We have to begin by understanding that social practices such as punishment are grounded in the value judgments of particular communities. Arguments about their justification and for their transformation themselves flow out of social evaluations, albeit subjected to a critical scrutiny and an imaginative effort to think through how things might be otherwise, and better, than they are. The notion of community value has theoretical use notwithstanding its complexity and fragmentation; but it has to be understood in the light of two further arguments. First, in the chapter devoted to criminal law in *State Punishment*, I noted that current conceptions of criminal law pay lip service to the idea that it should only be used where strictly necessary, but fail to meet that prescription.[13] I translated this idea into what I called the principle of urgency, and argued that a better practice of criminal justice would involve only the absolutely fundamental framework values—the individual and collective interests acknowledged by the political process to be of ultimate importance. Only on this basis could the general argument for punishment from social necessity, buttressed by its more particular functions, stand. This conception, I think, does survive the insight about fragmentation, because even the most fragmented and heterogeneous society has to have some core common commitments, specified by democratic political processes, which hold it together. This argument justifies a criminal process far more minimal than, for example, the current British and American systems. As for the questions of power and oppression, the argument I have just made leaves open the possibility that any particular society is not in itself justified and should be allowed, or encouraged, to disintegrate or transform. It also suggests that a communitarian conception based on immanent critique can have teeth in criticizing actual penal practices in societies such as our own, where current practice clearly goes well beyond the dictates of any principle of urgency. But, more than this, because the minimalist necessitarian argument for punishment is parasitic on a justification for the perpetuation of that society in its present form, it is directly undermined by the very kinds of injustice and oppression which characterize penal practices such as our own. For a politically legitimate conception of community interests would have to flow from a legitimate set of political arrangements.

This would be a participatory democracy in which all groups and citizens have real power to shape their community and hence their social lives, and under which the radical material and political inequalities which still characterize late capitalist societies could not be maintained. The idea of a necessitarian criminal justice system geared to the pursuit and protection only of those interests absolutely fundamental to society's existence does still seem to me to constitute the core meaning of criminal justice. I would therefore hold to my communitarian argument for punishment, embracing its implications for a much more minimalist criminal justice system which would seek only to enforce values and standards widely shared and seen as essential to the perpetuation of society. This ideal vision is one in which the social definition of the framework values to be enshrined in criminal law is politically legitimate. In this respect, my arguments engender a quite radical critique of existing penal arrangements in countries such as the United States and the United Kingdom.

Conclusion

The communitarian approach to punishment contains some important insights and is susceptible to further development. I attach no real importance to that particular label, and do not mean by using it to affirm anything like even the major part of the arguments and positions defended by the wide range of modern theorists who have at one time or another announced themselves as communitarian. Much of this work is, I think, flawed, notably in its failure adequately to address the problem of fragmentation and in its silence on questions of power and access to the membership of dominant communities within larger nation-state communities. In thinking more concretely about criminal justice, these problems of power would have to be a central preoccupation, given the obvious social facts of the unequal impact of criminal justice on powerless groups in most societies. Were I ever to attempt a substantial development of my earlier thoughts I would start out from a more explicit reflection on interpretive methodology in social theory, and I think this would lead me into a much more detailed and thorough discussion of actual penal institutions and potential forms of sanction than I have so far undertaken. Such work would, I think, be able to generate more concrete prescriptions for change, because of its focus on analyzing and criticizing the actual rather than holding it up for comparison with a less explicit and socially grounded ideal conception. Along with a more analytically precise account of the notion of public goods and community interests, encompassing a fuller treatment of the former and a more concretely grounded account of the latter, I think that this methodological shift could push us toward an approach to punishment which accomodated the important insights of communitarian thought whilst avoiding its pitfalls. If this can be achieved, it would without doubt enable the philosophy of punishment to develop in a more constructive and critical direction.

[1]See, for example, Michael Sandel, *Liberalism and the Limits of Justice* (Cambridge: Cambridge University Press, 1982); Michael Walzer, *Spheres of Justice* (Oxford: Blackwell, 1983).

[2]Nicola Lacey, *State Punishment: Political Principles and Community Values* (London: Routledge, 1988).

[3]An agenda for this project is set out in Elizabeth Frazer and Nicola Lacey, "Communitarianism and Feminist Lives," in*Warwick University Working Papers,* 1989. The present paper was originally written in 1990. Since then, the critical analysis of communitarianism which I began to develop in the later part of this paper has continued to occupy my attention. See Elizabeth Frazer and Nicola Lacey, *The Politics of Community* (Hempstead: Harvester-Wheatsheaf, 1993). Whilst I still endorse the central claims of the present paper, I now think that the problems thrown up by communitarianism (in particular its potential conservatism) and the diversity of issues encompassed within the liberal vs. communitarian debate need to be more fully explained in developing a communitarian approach to penal philosophy.

[4]See, for example, R.M. Dworkin, *A Matter of Principle* (Cambridge, Massachusetts: Harvard University Press, 1985), Part III; V. J. Rawls, *A Theory of Justice* (Oxford: Oxford University Press,1971); J. Raz, *The Morality of Freedom* (Oxford: The Clarendon Press, 1986).

[5]See T. Honderich, *Punishment: the Supposed Justifications* (Harmondsworth: Penguin, 1984).

[6]H.L.A. Hart, "Prolegomenon to the Principles of Punishment," in his *Punishment and Responsibility* (Oxford: The Clarendon Press, 1968).

[7]See R.A. Duff, *Trials and Punishments* (Cambridge: Cambridge University Press, 1986), Chapters 6-8.

[8]See J. Raz, *The Morality of Freedom* (Oxford: The Clarendon Press, 1986), pp. 94-9; *The Authority of Law* (Oxford: Oxford University Press, 1979), pp. 250-61.

[9]See A. Jaggar, *Feminist Politics and Human Nature* (Brighton: Harvester Press, 1983), pp. 27-48.

[10] This question is discussed in more depth in Elizabeth Frazer and Nicola Lacey, *The Politics of Community* , chapters 5 & 6.

[11]See S. Benhabib and D. Cornell (eds), *Feminism as Critique* (Oxford: Blackwell, 1986).

[12] For further discussion, see Frazer and Lacey, *The Politics of Community*, chapter 4.

[13] Lacey, *State Punishment*, chapter 5.

CONTRIBUTORS

RICHARD MOWERY ANDREWS is author of *Law, Magistracy and Crime in Old Regime Paris, 1735 - 1789. Volume I: The System of Criminal Justice* (Cambridge University Press, 1994) and several essays on the French Revolution.

LOIS G. FORER is a former judge in the Court of Common Pleas of Philadelphia. She is the author of *Unequal Protection: Women, Children and the Elderly in Court* (Norton, 1991); *A Chilling Effect: The Mounting Threat of Libel and the Invasion of Privacy Actions to the First Amendment* (Norton, 1987); *Money and Justice: Who Owns the Courts?* (Norton, 1984); *Criminals and Victims: A Trial Judge Reflects on Crime and Punishment* (Norton, 1980).

ROBERT A. GLICK is associate professor of psychiatry at the College of Physicians and Surgeons of Columbia University. He has edited and contributed to the following works: *Rage, Power and Agression* (Yale University Press, 1993); *Pleasure Beyond the Pleasure Principle: An Integration* (Yale University Press, 1991); *Masochism: Current Psychoanalytic Perspectives* (Analytic Press, 1988); *Psychiatric Emergencies* (Grune and Stratton, 1976).

NICOLA LACEY is Fellow in Law of New College, Oxford University. She has written *State Punishment: Political Principles and Community Values* (Routledge, 1988).

BRIAN MCKNIGHT is professor in the Department of East Asian Studies at the University of Arizona. He is the author of *Law and Order in Sung China* (Cambridge University Press, 1992); *The Quality of Mercy: Amnesties and Traditional Chinese Justice* (University of Hawaii Press,

1981). He edited *Law and the State in Traditional East Asia: Six Studies on the Sources of East Asian Law* (University of Hawaii Press, 1981).

STEVEN MARCUS is Delacorte Professor of English and Comparative Literature at Columbia University and Dean of Columbia College. He has written the following books: *Freud and the Culture of Psychoanalysis: Studies in the Transition from Victorian Humanism to Modernity* (Norton, 1987); *Engels, Manchester and the Working Class* (Norton, 1985); *Representations: Essays on Literature and Society* (Random House, 1975); *The Other Victorians: A Study of Sexuality and Pornography in Mid-Nineteenth Century England* (Basic Books, 1966).

JEFFRIE G. MURPHY is professor of philosophy and law at Arizona State University. He has written *Retribution Reconsidered: More Essays in the Philosophy of Law* (Kluwer Academic Publishers, 1992); *Forgiveness and Mercy* (Cambridge University Press, 1988); *The Philosophy of Law: An Introduction to Jurisprudence* (Rowman and Allenhead, 1984); *Retribution, Justice and Therapy: Essays in the Philosophy of Law* (Reidel, 1979).

EDWARD PETERS is professor of history at the University of Pennsylvania. He is the author of *Inquisition* (Free Press/Macmillan, 1988); *Torture* (Basil Blackwell, 1985); *The Magician, the Witch and the Law* (University of Pennsylvania Press, 1982). He edited *Heresy and Authority in Medieval Europe* (University of Pennsylvania Press, 1980).

NIGEL WALKER is former Professor of Criminology and Fellow of King's College, Cambridge University. He has written *Why Punish?* (Oxford University Press, 1991); *Crime and Criminology: A Critical Introduction* (Oxford University Press, 1987); *Sentencing: Theory, Law and Practice* (Butterworth, 1985); *Punishment, Danger and Stigma: The Morality of Criminal Justice* (Basil Blackwll, 1980); *Crime and Insanity in England,* 2 volumes (Edinburgh University Press, 1868 and 1973); *Behavior and Misbehavior: Explanations and Non-Explanations* (Basic Books, 1977). He co-edited *Public Attitudes to Sentencing* (Gower, 1988).

BERNARD WEISS is associate professor in the Middle East Center of the University of Utah. He is the author of *The Search for God's Law: Islamic Jurisprudence in the Writings of Sayf al-Din al-Amidi* (University of Utah Press, 1992).

INDEX